THE TAXPAYERS OF
MEDIEVAL
GLOUCESTERSHIRE

THE TAXPAYERS OF
MEDIEVAL
GLOUCESTERSHIRE

*An Analysis of the 1327 Lay Subsidy Roll with a
New Edition of its Text*

PETER FRANKLIN

ALAN SUTTON

First published in the United Kingdom in 1993 by
Alan Sutton Publishing Ltd
Phoenix Mill · Far Thrupp · Stroud · Gloucestershire

First published in the United States of America in 1993 by
Alan Sutton Publishing Inc · 83 Washington Street · Dover NH 03820

British Library Cataloguing in Publication Data

Franklin, Peter, *1953–*
   The taxpayers of medieval Gloucestershire.
   I. Title
   336.23094241

   ISBN 0-86299-980-4

Library of Congress Cataloging-in-Publication Data applied for

Typeset in Times 10/12pt.
Typesetting and origination by
Alan Sutton Publishing Ltd.
Printed in Great Britain by
WBC, Bridgend, Mid Glam.

To Kathleen

'What Christ giveth, the Treasury taketh away'

Gerald of Wales

Contents

List of Tables

Preface and Acknowledgements

This book contains a new edition of the list of the taxpayers of medieval Gloucestershire which was drawn up for the first year of the reign of King Edward III. It is a record of the time when the kings of England had begun to impose frequent taxes on large numbers of their subjects, and when the Exchequer required that the name and assessment of every single taxpayer should be set down in great parchment rolls, each of which covered an entire county. The Lay Subsidy Roll printed here contains some 9,000 taxpayers' names, arranged in 500 local lists and forming a kind of gazetteer of the old county for the period when it still included the great port of Bristol. It is the only tax roll of this kind which has survived for Gloucestershire. This is not the first time that the list has appeared in print, for the antiquarian Sir Thomas Phillipps published an edition in the 1850s. Copies of his book are now extremely rare, and those which survive are awkward to use because he printed only the bare text of the document, without introduction or indexes. I have tried to make the new edition as useful as possible to the reader by providing an index of place-names, arranged by modern parishes, and an index of surnames, which gives us all the 4,500 distinct spellings of names which appear in the Roll.

Many tax rolls of this kind have been published for other counties, but this is the first to include a comparative study which follows up a sample of taxpayers in other documents. More than a hundred taxpayers from the Thornbury district can be traced in manorial records which are quite independent of the taxation system and which reveal a great deal about them and their families. With the aid of this source it has been possible to show just what kinds of people medieval taxpayers were, and to estimate in general terms how realistic their assessments were. The results provide further insights into the growing body of knowledge about the burdens born by ordinary men and women in the first Edwardian age.

I should like to express my thanks to Mark Riley and David Alan Gatley for their help with computer hardware and software, which was vital for a novice; to the Local Population Studies Research Fund for the grant which enabled me to work on the manuscript of the Tax Roll in the Public Record Office; to the staffs of the P.R.O. and the Staffordshire County Record Office, for their ready assistance; and to the staff of Gloucester Central Library, especially for making me a photocopy of one of the few surviving copies of Phillipps's book and for resolving an awkward query at a time when I could not travel.

The text of the Gloucestershire Lay Subsidy Roll of 1327 appears by permission of the Controller of H.M. Stationery Office.

Introduction

THE COUNTY OF GLOUCESTER AND THE KING'S TAXES

The County of Gloucester which existed in 1327 was larger and more important than the Gloucestershire of later times. At that date it still stretched all the way from the Warwickshire Avon to the Bristol Avon, and included within its boundaries the great port of Bristol, which vied for the title of the second largest city in England. It was a county dominated by its gentry. The earls of Gloucester had only a few large estates here. They were lords of Tewkesbury, where some lie buried, but their great power base of Bristol Castle had been lost in the reign of Henry II.[1] A hundred years later they were making legal attempts to recover it from the crown and were probably making long visits to their manor of Thornbury,[2] but most of their estates were spread out across southern England and Wales and they were not much involved in local affairs. Nor were the holdings of the church of very great importance, for all that Gloucestershire was home to as famous a house as Hailes Abbey, the goal of innumerable pilgrimages. Most political power rested in the hands of the gentry, a group whose landed possessions and influence varied to an enormous degree.[3] A few, such as John Giffard 'the Rich' of Brimpsfield or Maurice Berkeley III of Berkeley Castle, were major figures in the county or further afield because of their wealth and connections.[4] But most were people of far less importance, and some were very small gentlemen indeed, the lords of one or two tiny manors.

Most Gloucestershire people were the peasant tenants of these lords. Social differences within the peasantry were as great as those within the ruling class. Communities made up largely of serfs lay side-by-side with ones where most people were free. Many peasants still had enough land to be self-sufficient, but growing numbers had only a few acres or had managed to put together very large holdings. Nor were these divisions between rich, middling and poor identical with the division between freemen and serfs, for there were plenty of poor freemen and wealthy serfs. In the Vale, peasants' agriculture had much in common with the familiar picture of open fields with family holdings largely in the form of strips or selions of arable land, though many people had additional parcels which they had reclaimed from woodland or marsh.[5] Their major crops were wheat, barley, oats, beans and peas, but many also had small sheep flocks and orchards, and some Severnside peasants rented fisheries. Common rights in grazing and woodland enabled them to feed their livestock and collect timber for building and wood for fuel and other purposes. Larger-scale sheep farming had already been developed on the Cotswolds, where there were numbers of the wealthy graziers who are more familiar from the fifteenth century.[6] The sites of a few early fulling mills are known,[7] but most fleeces were bought up by the wool merchants for export. Across the Severn, the Forest of Dean had developed its own society and a distinctive economy marked by the production of timber, wood, iron and venison.[8]

But medieval Gloucestershire was also a place with many urban settlements. The great towns of Gloucester and Bristol were unique because of their size, their importance in regional and international trade, their great abbeys, royal castles and strong walls. They must have seemed strange and wonderful to local peasants – at least, until they saw the amount of urban poverty which institutions such as Gaunt's Hospital had been founded to relieve.[9] Most of the urban settlements were little country towns

with markets and, sometimes, fairs. Many had been given the status of boroughs by their lords in the thirteenth century, and by 1327 there were no fewer than twenty-six boroughs in the county: very few English counties had more, and only in Devon were they thicker on the ground.[10] In the long term they met with very different degrees of success: more than one eventually 'fell into the condition of a country village'.[11] But many were less than a hundred years old in 1327 and seem to have been coming through the difficulties of the times. They were often very small and had a rural air which was reinforced by many townsmen keeping a few animals. Townsmen often earned their livings through close involvement with the products of local agriculture – as traders, leather workers or textile workers. But their communities presented a complete contrast to the rural world which surrounded them, and were helping to change that world by encouraging nearby peasants to produce corn, livestock and craft products for sale, literally in the marketplace, rather than just for their own families' needs. Peasants also came to town to buy food and other goods – providing, of course, that they had money.

The English people had gone through great hardships in the reigns of Edward I and Edward II. The first reign had seen a ruinous period in the 1290s when many peasants died or were forced to give up their holdings. This has been interpreted in terms of a Malthusian crisis when the country's population had grown to such a size that many people lived on the very edge of subsistence.[12] The evidence leaves room for other interpretations, including one which would lay stress upon the large sums which peasants had to pay in taxes at that time.[13] Whatever the basic cause, there is little doubt that some parts of the country were experiencing grave difficulties even before the start of the Great Famine in 1315. The Great Famine was a disaster of European proportions which would have had grave consequences whether there was a Malthusian crisis or not.[14] Torrential rain destroyed most of the harvests of 1315 and 1316, leading to soaring prices and widespread hunger. The harvest of 1317 brought some relief, but the next year's failed, and the economic crisis was compounded by widespread outbreaks of disease both amongst people and amongst the livestock which were essential to the livelihoods of so many. The crisis dragged on into the early 1320s, but by 1327 there had been perhaps five years for recovery to take place.

TABLE 1. TAXES COLLECTED FROM GLOUCESTERSHIRE, 1290–1334[15]

Year	Tax yield		County ranking	Fractions paid in tax
	Total	(1327=100)		
1290	£4,018 15s 9½d	402	8	15th
1294	£2,447 7s 10½d	245	12	10th/6th
1295	£1,605 2s 2¾d	160	11	11th/7th
1296	£962 11s 10¼d	96	13	12th/8th
1297	£724 2s 6½d	72	17	9th
1301	£1,656 15s 8d	166	6	15th
1306	£1,135 15s 4½d	113	7	30th/20th
1307	£1,065 10s 11½d	106	10	20th/15th
1309	£863 9s 1d	86	12	25th
1313	£1,279 10s 10¼d	128	9	20th/15th
1315	£1,203 17s 2d	120	11	20th/15th
1316	£1,133 13s 8¾d	113	14	16th/15th
1319	£952 3s 8½d	95	14	18th/12th

1322	£1,528 11s 2¾d	153	10	10th/6th
1327	£1,000 17s 4¼d	100	7	20th
1332	£1,490 4s 2½d*	149	4	15th/10th
1334	£1,641 0s 6d	164	4	15th/10th

* exc. Bristol.

Graphic details of the famine were given by the chroniclers of the day,[16] but the detailed courses of these economic troubles have had to be painstakingly reconstructed from the best sets of local records which survive from different parts of England. Thus much of our knowledge of conditions in the 1290s comes from the Bishop of Winchester's manors in Hampshire, while there is excellent evidence for the course of the Great Famine in the records of the Yorkshire monastery of Bolton Priory.[17] The detailed Gloucestershire records which I shall use in the next chapter do not begin until the year 1327 itself, and it is unfortunate that we have little direct evidence for what local people had gone through during the forty years or so before that date. There is nothing to suggest that they had got off lightly. Table 1 shows that in 1290 they had had to pay the huge sum of £4,018 tax, and, whereas taxation had once been a rare event, they had had to pay in the four consecutive years from 1294 to 1297. They can hardly have escaped the Famine, which was reflected in high corn prices at Chepstow and in Oxfordshire.[18] Its impact must have been worsened by Edward II's demands for taxes in 1315 and 1316, and by his use of 'purveyance' – the seizure of people's livestock, corn and vehicles for the use of his army or household on the promise that payment would be made at some future date.

Nor had the county escaped the political troubles of Edward II's reign. Before the Famine many Bristol people were engaged in a violent quarrel with the constable of Bristol Castle, and refused to pay the tallage which the king demanded until the Earl of Pembroke arrived with an army and siege machines.[19] Though the death of the Earl of Gloucester at Bannockburn did not directly affect most Gloucestershire people, the division of his lands between three of the king's favourites began a crisis which was to involve many local lords in uprisings against the crown in 1321 and 1322. The first seemed to succeed, but in 1322 the king seized the initiative. He captured and destroyed John Giffard's castle at Brimpsfield and then marched northwards beside the Severn and forced many of the rebels to surrender near Shrewsbury. After defeating the northern branch of the uprising in Yorkshire, he returned to Gloucestershire to seize Berkeley Castle and other rebel strongholds. Few Gloucestershire lords are known to have died in the fighting, but many who had risen against the king now lost their lands and were imprisoned. Prison conditions were probably not good, for several leading rebels died there, including Maurice Berkeley III.[20] How much ordinary people had suffered at the hands of the royal and rebel armies, at a time when the countryside should have been recovering from the Famine, is impossible to say. When the king was finally overthrown (after abdicating at Bristol) and it was decided to move him from imprisonment in Kenilworth Castle, Berkeley Castle was a logical place to put him, where he would be guarded by people who had little cause to love him and in the midst of a population which had had its loyalty put to a severe test by the burdens of the past two reigns.

The 1327 Lay Subsidy was raised towards the end of an important period of change and development in the history of taxation and government finance. English country people had long been used to meeting the burdens placed upon them by lords of manors and by the church, but it was only in the reign of Edward I that the payment of taxes changed from being a special imposition to a frequent requirement, the great change coming about in order to finance the king's wars with the Scots and French.[21] Earlier taxation had been based upon holdings of land, and the taxation of personal property was an invention of Henry II's reign which was rarely used between 1166 and 1290.[22] The new taxes were levied on 'movables', which were so called literally because they could be moved from place to

place, and were assessed as fractions of their values. Thus if a man had oxen worth 100s, he would have to pay a fraction of that 100s to the government. This resembled the payment of tithes to the church, but there were basic differences: the taxes were assessed on property rather than on income, the fractions set varied between one-sixth and one-thirtieth, and they had to be paid in cash rather than in kind. The fractions often varied according to where the taxpayers' property was. When different rates were set, goods in 'taxation boroughs' and on ancient demesne land had to be paid for at a higher rate, but the 1327 tax was levied at the single rate of one-twentieth for property everywhere.[23] These fractions were often used as names for the taxes, so that people spoke of the 'twentieth of 1327' or the 'fifteenths and tenths' which became standard in 1334. The official name 'lay subsidy' reminds us that these taxes were paid by the laity. The clergy were taxed separately, but many had to make some contribution to lay subsidies because they had goods on land which had been acquired since the taxation of church property had been standardized in 1294.[24]

The change produced a major new record source for historians, because the thousands of new taxpayers were not allowed to remain anonymous. The Exchequer demanded the drawing up of tax rolls like the one printed in this book. They were produced for each of the sixteen taxes raised between 1290 and 1332, but many have been lost because it was not until 1323 that an official at Westminster was made responsible for their custody.[25] Only the 1327 roll survives for Gloucestershire. The system changed fundamentally in 1334, when the Exchequer decided to be content with taking fixed sums from each vill and there was no further need to record taxpayers' names or individual assessments. The less detailed records from that year have been published for the whole country by R.E. Glasscock.[26]

The 1327 tax was granted by the parliament which met at Lincoln in September that year. The reason for a tax was often not stated explicitly, but this one was clearly said to be for the defence of the country against the threat of a Scots invasion.[27] What had become an established mechanism of assessment and collection then swung into operation. The Exchequer appointed two local men to be the 'chief taxers' in each county. Official documents often call these men 'assessors and collectors' (*taxatores et collectores*), but I will use the word 'taxers' because it describes them so succinctly. The chief taxers appointed for Gloucestershire were Sir William Tracy and Robert de Aston. Tracy played a prominent part in local affairs as a knight of the shire and a commissioner of array. In 1327 he had completed his third year as Sheriff of Gloucester (he had also been Sheriff of Worcester), and in the next two decades he was to serve as a keeper of the peace and as a justice of oyer and terminer. He held four manors and some other properties, but enjoyed wider influence as a retainer of the Berkeleys.[28] Aston was less important, a small gentleman who was the lord of Dumbleton in the far north of the county and who had no clear links with the powerful. But he had surveyed rebels' estates which were forfeited to the crown in 1322 and worked as steward for Cirencester Abbey. Serving as chief taxer and as a knight of the shire for his county at the parliaments of February and April 1328 perhaps marked the high point of his career.[29] Official duties did not take up all of his time, for in 1327 and 1328 he was able to join other gentry in raiding some manors in the south of the county.[30] This was not an unusual activity for a medieval country gentleman at a time of political uncertainty. Scrupulous readers may question whether he was the right candidate for an official post, though others may feel he had the right qualifications for a tax collector.

The chief taxers chose men from each local area to be the 'subtaxers' (*subtaxatores*) who did most of the work. Tracy and Aston's instructions actually told them to appoint four or six subtaxers from each vill, or more if they thought it better.[31] This order would have required at least 1,800 appointments, and it got the treatment commonly reserved for such commands. They ignored it, and appointed just 240 men to cover the whole county. These were formed into forty-four groups, each comprising between two and ten men. Each group usually dealt with an entire hundred, but Gloucester was given its own group and Bristol no fewer than five. Vills which were parts of the ancient demesne got their own groups or shared them with other such vills. Chipping Campden and Tewkesbury were

given their own groups although they were neither taxation boroughs nor ancient demesne. The subtaxers were to value the taxable goods of all their neighbours who had had possessions worth at least 10s at Michaelmas 1327, the time when people would have most corn after the harvest had been gathered. They were required to swear on the gospels that they would tax the goods at their true values (*lour verroi valu*). They were to work out one-twentieth of each man's total and inform the chief taxers of the results, then return to collect the money (in two halves, as we shall see) and deliver it to the chief taxers.

The chief taxers were also to be busy. They were to go from hundred to hundred and from vill to vill to check that their subordinates' work was done properly and that no taxable goods were being concealed (*s'il troessent rien concele*). Anyone who did conceal goods was to reported to the Exchequer.[32] The chief taxers then had to value the subtaxers' goods and collect their taxes directly. The chief taxers' own goods were, in turn, to be valued by the Exchequer, and they were to add in their own payments before handing over the complete sums raised from their counties at Westminster.

The chief taxers' written instructions gave them little guidance as to what was taxable and what was not. They only stated that some of the prized possessions of the ruling class – armour, riding-horses, jewels, clothing, and gold, silver and brass vessels – were exempt, together with some of the property of townsfolk and of some communities of lepers. But chief taxers' instructions were usually of this kind and they did not mean that every other 'movable', every single piece of personal property, should have been valued and taxed.[33] The goods which actually were taxed can be found in the detailed local rolls which the subtaxers drew up to help them in their work. These documents provide lists of each person's taxable goods and their values. They form a fascinating local record, but also a rare one. The Exchequer did not normally require such detailed information, so it was unusual for them to be sent to Westminster or preserved elsewhere. Many thousands must have been made for the whole country, but only a few dozens are known to survive.[34] It is to be regretted that none of those which do survive cover part of Gloucestershire in 1327, but there is such a roll from Minety (which was then part of the county) for the tax of 1313.[35] The Minety roll, and others like it, show that most of the goods which were assessed were taxpayers' animals and corn. Whether all animals appear or not is another question, and so many country people had little or no corn among their listed goods that J.F. Willard argued persuasively that only corn which was for sale was taxed.[36] If this is true, then the taxers of 1327 and other years were following instructions which had only been issued officially in 1225 and 1283. But this is not difficult to accept: medieval people had long memories, and the old instructions may have become accepted practices when this kind of tax became frequent.[37] This would explain why household goods and agricultural implements were not usually taxed, although there are anomalies. Four Minety people, for example, were taxed on their cooking pots.

From the mass of data provided in the subtaxers' detailed local rolls, Tracy and Aston were to make two copies of a county roll listing every taxpayer and the sum which he or she was assessed to pay. They were to deliver one of these copies to the Exchequer the day after the feast of the Purification of the Blessed Virgin (3 February) 1328, but keep the other to use when collecting the tax. This was to be done in two parts, the first half being collected on the day after the Purification itself, and the second on the day after the feast of the Nativity of St John the Baptist (25 June) 1328.[38] Thus the tax was actually collected in 1328, but it is traditionally dated to 1327 because it was granted then and was based upon the value of people's possessions in that year.

The county roll which Tracy and Aston sent to the Exchequer is preserved in the Public Record Office, where I was able to examine it in September 1991.[39] Its text occupies twenty-eight parchment membranes which are sewn together at the head; a twenty-ninth membrane inscribed with the total amount of tax due was added at the Exchequer and forms an outer cover. These are between 25 and 34½ in. (63–88 cm.) long, and about 10 in. (25 cm.) wide. The text is divided into two parts: Part One, which covers taxation boroughs and the ancient demesne, and Part Two, which covers the rest of the

county. These are modern names given by myself, as in the original roll each part just bears the heading 'Gloucestershire' (*Glouc.*, *Gloucestr.*). The membranes have original numbers at their heads, sometimes obscured by the sewing, which follow the twofold division. Those containing Part One are numbered from 1 to 4, and those containing Part Two from 1 to 24. The added membrane has no number. To avoid confusion, I have referred to them as running in a single sequence from m.1 to m.29. Each of the first twenty-eight membranes has two columns of names and assessments on both the recto and the dorse, but the second column of the recto of m.4 and the dorse of that membrane have been left blank after the completion of Part One. Part Two begins on the recto of m.5. The second column of the recto of m.28 is also blank. The clerks' handwriting is neat and still legible, except for small areas of damage which are noted in the printed text below. There were originally about 9,094 taxpayers' names, but the damage has rendered about forty-one of these wholly unreadable and a further 123 partly so. The total excludes Tracy and Aston, whose assessments are not given in the roll.

The taxpayers' names are arranged in 516 local lists, of which 472 cover vills or the wards or quarters of Gloucester and Bristol, and forty-four cover groups of subtaxers. These local lists are grouped into thirty-three divisions. Part One begins with Gloucester and Bristol, the only ones of the county's twenty-six boroughs which the Exchequer counted as taxation boroughs in 1327, and these form divisions in themselves.[40] The vills which follow, which include Winchcombe and Minety, were ancient demesne but are not given a heading; nor is a total given for their tax assessments (as is done for every other division). I have given them the heading 'Miscellaneous Ancient Demesne Vills'. The two Bartons (*Berton juxta Bristoll* and *Berton juxta Glouc.*) follow, but are not called 'hundreds' in the Roll. In later times, the first became Barton Regis Hundred. The second became part of King's Barton and Dudstone Hundred, but Dudstone Hundred appeared separately in 1327. Part One ends with the division covering ancient demesne lands in Cheltenham Hundred, which is simply headed *Hundredum de Cheltenham*, though the rest of that hundred appears separately in Part Two.

The arrangement of Part Two is simpler: there are twenty-seven divisions, all of which are called hundreds except for the Liberty of St Briavels. Most of the hundreds are familiar from the great county histories of Sir Robert Atkyns and Samuel Rudder,[41] but readers should be warned that the arrangement is not exactly that of later times. The main changes may be rehearsed briefly here, but detailed ones affecting individual vills may be found by going through the text of the Roll. In the Tax Roll, Tibblestone and Deerhurst form a single hundred, whereas they were later counted as separate ones. Langley and Swineshead were separate in 1327 and were amalgamated in later times. As noted above, Dudstone and King's Barton were listed separately in 1327, perhaps because the latter part was ancient demesne. There are minor differences in names, such as Crowthorne and Minety Hundred appearing in the Roll simply as *Hundredum de Crouthorn*, and St Briavels and the two Bartons not being called hundreds. The little Duchy of Lancaster Hundred at the northern end of the Forest of Dean had not yet been carved out of the territory of Botloe and Westbury Hundreds. The only name which is unfamiliar to historians of later periods is that of Holford and Greston Hundred, the area around Winchcombe which later became the lower division of Kiftsgate Hundred.[42] The Tax Roll treats all hundreds as complete units, and does not split any into two or three divisions as modern sources do.

This is not the first time that the text of this Roll has appeared in print. Many Gloucestershire historians have used the edition which Sir Thomas Phillipps produced in about 1856, and I was glad of the opportunity to compare his text with the original document.[43] Phillipps was an obsessive collector of manuscripts and books who printed medieval records on his private press at Middle Hill, near Broadway, Worcestershire. Conditions there were far from ideal: one printer arrived to find that he was expected to live and work in rooms inside Broadway Tower, that monument being part of Sir Thomas's estate. The most respectable products of the Middle Hill Press (*Typis Medio-Montanis*) were the work of scholarly friends like Sir Henry Dryden, who produced his edition of William Twiti's *Art de Venerie* there.[44] Phillipps's own works are notorious for a wide variety of shortcomings – he used

cheap materials, produced no more than twenty-five copies of some titles, and avoided such luxuries as introductions, indices and dates of publication.

No one, however, seems to have made a detailed study of how accurate his texts were. His edition of the 1327 Tax Roll is a curious piece of work. I have made many detailed changes, including the correction of what are obviously printer's errors, but most of these are very minor. Bearing in mind the length of the document and the changes in conventions over the past 140 years, the quality of Phillipps's text is good. Only a dozen taxpayers' names have been completely misread and only two have been omitted.[45] This good work accords so badly with what we know of the man himself that it must be put down to some of the transcribers he is known to have employed.[46] Differences in the conventions used suggest that two transcribers worked on the roll. One strange feature is probably Phillipps's own doing. When names from a local list were left over at the foot of a column, the clerks continued that list at the head of the next column and usually began there with the heading *adhuc* ('also') followed by the name of the vill. In the first half of his book all these *adhuc* headings from the Roll have been ignored. In the second half, things get complicated: some are ignored, some are inserted in the wrong places, and some are printed which do not appear in the Roll. For example, from the dorse of m.22, Phillipps printed the heading 'Adhuc Yevynton' in the wrong place and inserted a heading 'Adhuc Wyghtfeld et App'leye' which is not in the manuscript because that list of names is not divided.[47] But (except for the two names omitted) the numbers and order of taxpayers' names within lists are always correct. These sins of omission and commission accord with what we are told of Phillipps's faulty methods and haste in rushing works into print. We can conclude that an angry contemporary's declaration that his works were 'all but worthless from their inaccuracies' is a gross exaggeration, yet breathe a sigh of relief that his ambition to be put in charge of printing the Public Records remained unfulfilled.[48]

My approach to editing the Roll owes much to the good advice in R.F. Hunnisett's books.[49] The brief passages in Latin at the start and end of the document have been translated. All the place-names used as headings have been given in their modern forms, for which I have consulted A.H. Smith's four volumes of Gloucestershire place-names,[50] but the original forms have been supplied in brackets as they may be of interest to readers. Subtaxers were identified in the Roll by their office being written alongside groups of their names or after individual names. This is clumsy to reproduce in print, so I have used 'Subtaxers' as a heading for each such group. The abbreviated word *De* ('from') which the clerks wrote before every taxpayer's name has been omitted in order to save the printers' ink and the reader's patience. The Tax Roll clerks moved between Medieval Latin, Anglo-French and Middle English even within the space of a single name, producing results such as *(de)* Ricardo le Taillur. I have translated forenames with the help of Trice Martin's list and E.G. Withycombe's *Dictionary*.[51] The Roll is peppered with the abbreviations beloved of medieval clerks, but the meanings of nearly all of these are clear and I have expanded them without comment. Those which could not be expanded safely have been indicated by an apostrophe or a full stop. Thus abbreviations which could stand for different genders or forms of a name have been left alone: Luc., for example, could be either Luke (*Luca*) or Lucy (*Lucia*).[52]

The few surnames given in Latin have also been translated, but the original forms have been supplied in brackets. Anglo-French surnames and elements within names, and Middle English spellings are retained throughout. Thus Ricardo le Taillur appears as 'Richard le Taillur', and Johanne Molendinario as 'John Miller (*Molendinario*)'. P.H. Reaney's *Dictionary* was used as an aid for grouping together different spellings of the same surnames for the index.[53] Readers who are interested in the meanings of surnames are recommended to his book. The clerks recorded sums of money in terms of pounds, shillings and pence, or (very rarely) in marks, and always used Roman numerals. I have retained the form of each sum given in the roll – for example, Richard le Taillur's assessment was 12d, not 1s – but have used Arabic numerals throughout. A very few names and assessments which

Phillipps's transcribers could read 140 years ago are now wholly or partly illegible, and I have accepted most of their readings because of the good overall standard of their work. The loss of all or part of a word or sum of money is indicated by three points. Any words which I have supplied are within square brackets. The local lists are not numbered in the Roll, but I have used entry numbers to distinguish them and have employed these in the Index of Place-Names and Index of Surnames.

Two final points may be mentioned here to save repetitious foot-notes. The word 'approved' (*probatur*), which is found beside the total sums of money after nearly every local list and division, is a later addition. What appears to be the same word has been written a second time after the totals in Tibblestone and Deerhurst Hundred: I have translated this as 'proved' to emphasize the point.[54] This may indicate double-checking, as the names of the original subtaxers for this hundred have been erased and replaced with new ones.

2

THE TAXPAYERS OF THORNBURY MANOR

The Tax Roll's information is fascinating in itself, presenting a series of cameo pictures of medieval communities in terms of which of their members had to pay tax. But many readers will want to know just what kinds of people the taxpayers were, and how realistic were their assessments. These are things which a lay subsidy roll will not tell us, but comparative studies undertaken over the past thirty years have started to reveal what lies behind the taxmen's lists of names and assessments, and I can now offer another such study which uses part of the Gloucestershire Tax Roll. Three principal studies have compared tax evidence with that of manorial records in order to determine how realistic were lords of manors' tax assessments or to find out which other members of the local community paid tax. These made use of all three kinds of manorial record – surveys, accounts and court records.[55] Surveys of different kinds describe the economic resources of the manor and the obligations of local peasants in their role as the lord's tenants. The quantity and quality of information given varies tremendously, but some surveys give peasants' names, holding sizes and obligations in detail, with lists of the lord's possessions. Accounts list the lord of the manor's receipts and outgoings in terms of money, corn, livestock and peasants' labour services. They say little about peasants' personal property, but much about the lord's. A.T. Gaydon and P.D.A. Harvey have used these sources to investigate the reality of tax assessments.[56]

Court records offer the greatest scope for finding out about ordinary taxpayers, because the medieval manor court had much wider functions than any modern court. It was both a criminal court and a civil court in an age when it was hard to carry on peasant agriculture for long without committing some minor offence, and when many people went to law in disputes with their neighbours. The court was the lord of the manor's property, but it also had something of the character of a popular assembly. Its functions were extremely wide, and hundreds of local people and outsiders might appear in its records as officials, offenders, litigants and sureties, and as people taking out licences, entering land and giving it up. The quality of such records varies tremendously. Some are clearly deficient and give a distorted picture of local society.[57] Others are much better and provide an impressive mass of detailed evidence. Court records are no more egalitarian than was medieval society itself. The local rich usually appear in them much more often than the poor, and male tenants much more often than their wives and children.[58] They have much to say about many ordinary members of the community, but rarely give lists of their possessions. But much more progress can be made towards reconstructing the lives of ordinary people from these records than from other kinds, and it is this source which E. Britton used to trace taxpayers in the last of the three comparative studies.[59] These works have established a picture of medieval taxpayers as coming from the better-off part of the rural community, a mixture of lords and wealthy peasants, and of the lords (at least) being substantially under-assessed by the taxmen. It is assumed, albeitly tacitly, that poorer peasants escaped until the advent of the poll taxes a generation

after the Black Death.[60] The present study of the Thornbury taxpayers aims to test, expand and refine this picture.

Thornbury Manor has been chosen because of the richness of its local records. Gloucestershire has good examples of all three kinds of manorial record, but the amount of evidence surviving from individual estates is usually very limited.[61] The Thornbury archive is by far the richest and the most extensive. Two surveys which are known to have been made for the lords of the manor have been lost, but a number which were made for the government have survived along with dozens of account rolls and literally hundreds of court rolls.[62] By chance, the surviving manorial records begin in the very year in which the 1327 tax was assessed and collected. Thornbury Manor lay beside the Severn estuary only a few miles south of Berkeley Castle.[63] Its land area covered more than 10,000 acres (or 17 square miles), including the great Oldbury Marsh which was subject to flooding from the river. The modern parishes of Oldbury upon Severn, Thornbury and Falfield make up its approximate extent, but the old manor also extended to the middle of the main channel of the river so that its lords could control fishing. It was one of the richest estates of a succession of very wealthy lords, including the Norman and Clare family earls of Gloucester. The last of the male line of the Clare family, Gilbert V, was killed at Bannockburn in 1314, and it was marriage to his sister Margaret which brought this manor and many others into the hands of King Edward II's favourite, Hugh Audley. Audley was himself created earl of Gloucester in the following reign, and the marriage of his daughter and heiress Margaret brought Thornbury into the hands of the Stafford family, later to be earls of Stafford and dukes of Buckingham. It remained the property of their successors, the Stafford Howards, until well into the twentieth century. By the start of the fourteenth century, these lords had reduced most of the local population to the status of serfs and exercised wide-ranging controls over their lives. The serfs had to supply them with unpaid labour to cultivate their demesne of about 500 acres, and to maintain the boundaries of the deer parks which had been created both for hunting and to restrict peasants' access to the local resources of timber, underwood and pasture. It is no surprise to learn that lord/peasant relations were bad, and the manor records reveal that a local peasant movement enjoyed widespread support in the 1330s and 1340s. The structure of the manor was complicated by the existence of little sub-manors within its boundaries, tiny estates whose lords acknowledged the lords of Thornbury as their overlords. It is unlikely that any of these covered more than 200 acres. The petty lords had demesnes, but their peasants owed very little unpaid labour and the legal position of most of them is unclear. These are characteristics typical of very small manors.[64]

Tremendous differences of wealth and status had developed within the local peasantry, which included many well-off people (both serfs and freemen) with large family holdings, and also many middling and poor folk. In order to explain what was happening to rural society in medieval England, we may borrow the idea of the 'process of the differentiation of the peasantry' which was developed to explain rural change in Tsarist Russia.[65] The basis of this idea is that peasant families had once produced just to satisfy their own needs and had possessed the resources in land and labour which they needed for this purpose. But as time went on this 'classical' peasantry began to break down, producing two offshoots – the 'rich peasant' and 'poor peasant' groups. Rich peasants, in this sense, were those who had acquired more land than was needed to support their own families. They used the extra to produce surplus corn and animals which they sold on a regular basis. In order to work the extra land, they employed other peasants and paid them wages, again on a regular basis. Poor peasants were those who had lost much of their land and did not have enough left to support their families. In order to get money to buy food they sold their labour by regularly working for wages. Both these groups had left the old peasant way of life, which was centred on producing for family needs, and were in regular contact with the world of buying and selling – with the markets for rural produce and for labour. It is important to stress that they did these things regularly. Any peasant might be involved in occasional transactions of these kinds, but they were essential features of the ways in which members of these two

groups lived. There still remained peasants who lived in the old-fashioned way without regular contacts with the market, and they are known as 'middle peasants'.

The market town of Thornbury at the centre of the estate is a good example of the country towns which helped to change peasants' economies by providing markets and fairs where surplus corn and animals could be sold, and where peasants could buy food, drink and many kinds of goods. The Clares had made it a borough in the thirteenth century, so that it was now legally separate from the surrounding manor, an island of urban society where people were free and had more control over their own affairs in a sea of rural life where most people were the lords' serfs. Some borough records survive, but they provide a much less detailed picture of a local community – partly because the lords had much less control over townsmen's lives.[66] For this reason my study of the Thornbury taxpayers has been restricted to the rural community of the manor, where firmer conclusions can be drawn.

The taxmen chose to cover this large rural community in eight local lists, with a ninth for the borough.[67] These lists divided up the local structures of large tithings, small sub-manors and scattered settlements in quite a complex way, but produced manageable groups of taxpayers. This treatment produced one anomaly – one list was supposed to include taxpayers from Oldland, down by the Bristol Avon, which was recognized as part of the manor in later times. But no Oldlanders were actually listed, so the eight lists do cover Thornbury Manor as a single unit.[68] The lists contain 122 names, but manor records show that three of the subtaxers for this hundred were Thornbury men[69] and it would be pedantic to exclude the lord of the manor just because he was listed under the borough. So the number of Thornbury taxpayers' names is not 122 but 126, and we will work with this figure.

TABLE 2. SUBDIVISIONS OF THORNBURY MANOR

Tithings	Corresponding local lists in 1327 Tax Roll	Taxpayers in 1327 Tax Roll
Oldbury Tithing	(Oldbury with the Marsh	26
	(Cowhill	8
Kington Tithing	(Kington	21
	(Sibland and Oldland*	8
Morton Tithing	(Morton	24
	(Woolford	3
	(Hope and Buckover	17
Falfield Tithing	Falfield	15
	Also subtaxers and lord of the manor listed elsewhere	4
		Total: 126

* Oldland lies outside the boundary of the manor

How many of these 126 names appear in the local records? In his study of the Abbot of Ramsey's manor of Broughton, on the edge of the Fens, E. Britton claimed to have found 90 per cent of local taxpayers' complete names, and 100 per cent of their surnames, in manorial records.[70] The reworking of his material by J.A. Raftis and M.P. Hogan suggests that these figures should read 82 per cent and 89 per cent,[71] but the problem with all these percentages is that they were produced by tracing the names of those

who paid tax in 1327 and 1332 in court rolls which cover a very long period of time: Raftis and Hogan used a period of seventy years, the length of Britton's period is not clear but was evidently substantial. How realistic is this? The John Smith who appears in a court roll the year after a tax is raised is obviously much more likely to be the taxpayer John Smith than a man of that name who only appears many years later, so I took careful note of the dates when Thornbury taxpayers' names appeared in local records. The Gloucestershire Tax Roll relates to Michaelmas (29 September) 1327. The manor account rolls begin on that very day, and the court rolls on 28 October 1328. Some early court rolls are missing and some peasants appeared in them less often than others, so I allowed several years for names to appear and took 1 January 1335 as the (albeit arbitrary) cut-off point.[72] I found that 109 of the 126 taxpayers' names occurred in the first seven years of surviving manor records (87 per cent), and that the surnames used by a further ten taxpayers occurred in that period, so that a total 119 names could be found (94 per cent).

In tracking down these names, I took a fairly liberal attitude to spellings because medieval clerks did not have fixed, 'correct', ways of spelling many English surnames, even if they were very familiar with them. (The exact spellings used in the Tax Roll have, of course, been reproduced in the edition of its text given below.) The Tax Roll clerks made a few errors with local names. A man called Robert Kyngewell appears in the Morton list immediately after Robert atte Welle. Kyngewell was not a local name, and it appears nowhere else in the Tax Roll. It is most likely that the clerk meant to write 'Robert Hyndewelle', the name of a local man who was certainly active at this time. Richard Cokkebury, also listed under Morton, also had a surname which does not appear in any local record, though it is found in other parts of the county.[73] Under Morton it is surely an error, but I cannot say what for. Two forenames are simple mistakes, for John Kyngeston and John Fortheye were women and the clerk should have written 'Joan'!

Of the 126 taxpayers' names, 109 can be found in the earliest local records but seventeen cannot, and it is worth looking briefly at the likely reasons why not. I noted above that in ten cases the surnames appear before 1 January 1335 but without the forenames found in the Roll. These people may have died or left the manor. Serfs' deaths should have been recorded, but loss of early court rolls may provide the answer. The remaining seven taxpayers used names which do not appear at all in Thornbury's records before the cut-off point, but the survey made for the government in 1322 shows that four were tenants in sub-manors. Two others may have been appearing under other surnames. Medieval people were often known by a number of surnames at the same time or in succession – names which might reflect their places of residence or origin, occupations or offices, personal characteristics or appearances. Not only women might change their names when they married.[74] This use of 'multiple surnames' has caused few problems, for the clerk has listed each person under a name by which he was commonly known: for example, the man who was known locally both as 'Edward Willes' and as 'Edward Beadle' appears as (*de*) Edwardo Wylles. In a few cases the clerk may have written down unusual names which I have failed to connect with those used more commonly by the same people. The last name which does not appear is the mysterious Richard Cokkebury.

No fewer that 109 of the Thornbury taxpayers' names can be found in the manor records, but what do these actually tell us about them? Far more can be found out about the lives of ordinary country people in the Middle Ages than most local or family historians realize, and this is largely because of the wide range of business dealt with in manor courts. All the information in the Thornbury records, and in other documents where Thornbury people appear, has been sorted under the personal names to which it relates, creating personal files for every name which appears. The amount of information in these varies enormously. One file may contain evidence on a single person, or on a number of people who used the same name. And, bearing in mind that both men and women might use two or more surnames during their lifetimes, one file may contain only part of the information relating to one person. A single file is printed here to show the quantity and detail of information available in various records on one of the names found in the Tax Roll. It is an example of better than average quality, but is by no means exceptionally good.

THE PERSONAL FILE OF JOHN ATTE PLEYSTUD, A POOR PEASANT FROM THORNBURY

The name John atte Pleystud appears in four kinds of document:

Local records:	1a)	Thornbury manor court rolls
	1b)	Thornbury manor account rolls
Government records:	2a)	Surveys
	2b)	Tax rolls

1a) Thornbury manor court rolls [each date is that of an individual court session]

8 Aug. 1329	Walter atte Field and J. agree in a plea of trespass. J. puts himself in mercy and is fined 6d. The beadle acts as J.'s pledge.
14 May 1330	J. is fined 3d for trespass by ten sheep in the lord's enclosure. His pledge is [ms damaged].
1 Oct. 1331	J. and twenty others were summoned to reap the lord's corn at harvest time. They did not come and are fined [J. pays 3d].
18 Feb. 1332	J. is fined 3d for trespass in Marlwood.
"	He is fined 2d for trespass in the lord's hedges.
9 Apr. 1332	He is fined 2s for 'contempt' to Robert Keten, the lord's bailiff.
21 May 1332	J. allowed his house to be ruined. He is fined 2s and ordered to repair it before the next court session.
13 Jul. 1332	He has not mended his house as ordered, and is fined 6d and again ordered to mend it.
"	J. and six others were summoned to weed the lord's corn and did not come. They are fined 6d each.
8 Sep. 1332	J. has not mended his house at Kington as he was ordered at the last court session, and is fined 6d, and ordered to mend it by the next court, under a penalty [no details].
"	J. and five others were summoned to reap the lord's corn and did not come. They are fined 3d each and pledge each other.
"	J. and seven others were summoned to reap the lord's corn and did not come. They are fined 3d each.
9 Feb. 1333	J. is fined 2d for trespass in Crawelefeld with one mare. William Newecomen is his pledge.
"	J. acts as pledge for Richard Fortheye.
18 May 1333	J. acts as pledge for Robert Cook.
9 Oct. 1333	J. and two others were summoned to thresh the lord's corn and did not come. They are fined 3d each.
"	J. was chosen to the office of Tithingman of Kington by all the tithing, and he swears the oath.
6 Nov. 1333	J. did not come to thresh the lord's corn, and he is fined 3d.
12 Feb. 1334	J. was summoned to work for the lord and did not come. He is fined 6d.
21 May 1334	J. did not come to harrow the lord's land, and he is fined 3d.
16 Dec. 1334	Distrain J., Roger Mautravers and William Hunt for entry to land in Badgeworth.
20 Feb. 1335	Ditto

18 Aug. 1335	J. and thirty-two others certified wrongly about the granting out of the lord's meadows, and they are fined. [J. pays 6d].
29 Sep. 1335	J. sat on the manor court jury with twenty-three other men.
"	John Champeneys is proceeding against J.a.P. and nine others in a plea of trespass [no details].
3 Nov. 1335	Champeneys' plea remains at the same stage.
29 Jun. 1336	J. broke the lord's pinfold twice, and took his own beasts out of it. He is fined 3d.
"	J. did not come to the last weeding of the lord's crops, and he is fined 3d.
"	J. is removed from the office of Tithingman, and Henry Puff is chosen to it.
20 Sep. 1336	J. was chosen to the office of Tithingman of [ms damaged] and swore the oath.
27 Nov. 1337	J. is the pledge of John Hook.
24 Jun. 1338	J. is the pledge of Julian atte Brook.
16 Apr. 1339	J. committed trespass with his horse in the lord's meadow, and is fined 2d.
"	J. puts himself in mercy for unjustly detaining 12d he owes to Walter Fishpool, and order him to pay it. He is fined 3d.
10 Jun. 1339	J. acts as essoin for William Poyshe.
1 Jul. 1339	J. acts as essoin for Thomas Penarth.
26 Jul. 1339	J. and five others did not come to work for the lord when the beadle summoned them, and they are fined 3d each.
"	J. did trespass to John Marlwood [no details given], and is fined 2d.
9 Feb. 1344	J. and Robert Wilkins reach agreement in a plea of trespass. J. puts himself in mercy and is fined 3d.
"	J. is fined 12d for trespass [no details].
"	J. is fined 6d for trespass [no details].
8 Mar. 1344	John Enefeld impleads J. in a plea of detaining two nets of his, worth 13s 4d. J. puts himself in mercy, and order him to give back the nets. He is in mercy for unjustly detaining them and is fined 3d.
15 Mar. 1345	J. is fined for trespass.
25 Apr. 1346	J. is Tithingman of Kington.
5 Jul. 1347	J. and fifteen others are chosen to enquire about the watchmen, and about the receiving of strangers outside the assize.
11 Oct. 1347	J. and 126 others are fined 3d each for not coming to work for the lord.
25 Jan. 1348	J. unjustly detained 2s 6d and one bushel of barley, worth 6d, belonging to John the son of Edith Lupeʒate. He is ordered to give it to him, and is fined 2d.
19 May 1348	J. is fined 2d for trespass [no details].
"	Thomas Sewy justly raised the hue and cry on J. in Kington tithing, and J. is fined 3d.
10 Aug. 1348	J. and nine others are fined 3d each because they did not come when the beadle summoned them to make the lord's hay.
24 Nov. 1348	J. held one messuage, six acres of 'work-land' and two acres of 'forland', and he has died. His heriot is a mare worth 2s, and Walter the son of William Kew gives 3s entry fine to have the holding.

1b) Thornbury manor account rolls [each roll covers one year beginning at Michaelmas, 29 September]

1327/28	J. holds 3½ acres 'at farm' in Momelewesfolde and Bykeleye, and pays 14d rent for them per year.
1329/30	Ditto
1330/31	Ditto
1331/32	Ditto
1336/37	£7 13s 3d was received from the sale of wood, by tally against J.
"	12d wages was paid to J., the lord's serf, for collecting money due from wood sold.
"	J. is quit of the rent of 6 acres of land, because he collected the money due from wood sold in Marlwood Park between Michaelmas (29 September) and the feast of St Thomas the Apostle (21 December).

2a) Surveys

1322	J. holds six acres of 'work-land' (*terra operabilis*) and three acres of Woolford holding, and pays 2s 2d money rent per year. He does two days' work each week of the year for the lord, and owes him one 'loveboon' at harvest time. [In total] he owes 2s 3d per year for money rent and Peter's Pence, and 6s 4d for labour services.

2b) Tax Rolls

1327	[Thornbury Hundred, Kington local list]
	J. assessed to pay 6¾d tax.

This file contains no fewer than sixty references to 'John atte Pleystud' – fifty-one in the manor court rolls, seven in the manor account rolls, one in a survey, and the one in the Tax Roll itself. It is likely that all but two of these relate to one person – the John atte Pleystud who lived at Kington in Thornbury Manor, paid tax in 1327, and died in 1348 when the Black Death swept through Gloucestershire. Someone of the same name was said to have entered land at Badgeworth in 1334, but this was more than 20 miles away and is unlikely to have been the same person.[75] Most of the court roll references show our John being prosecuted for minor offences or involved in private disputes with other local people. He admitted his guilt by 'putting himself in mercy' and paying a fine. Sometimes he had to have a pledge to ensure that the fine would be paid, and on occasion he acted as a pledge for others. He was involved with a wide range of Thornburians including some of the local *prominenti*, such as John Enefeld, who was the vicar, and Walter Fishpool who was the 'portreeve' (a later age would say mayor) of the Borough.

John's personal file builds up the picture of a serf who had to go along with his fellow serfs to do unpaid work for the lord of the manor. On several occasions he was prosecuted for refusing to do this. He broke open the lord's pinfold after the latter's men had seized some of his animals and impounded them there. He committed an offence against the bailiff, the officer in everyday charge of the estate. These acts of insubordination mark him out as an active member of the local peasant movement, and his removal from the post of Tithingman of Kington and success in regaining that post can be seen as parts of the movement's struggle. Such activities, together with the poor state into which his house had fallen, probably marked John out as a bad tenant in the eyes of the manor authorities. But this did not prevent them from giving him a part-time job collecting the money due from wood sold in the deer park near his home.

John held an official post, served as a juror and gave advice about local matters, but the file reveals that he was a poor peasant. The court rolls say nothing about how much land he held until his death in 1348, which makes the information from other sources particularly useful. Most of his land was the six acres of 'work-land' he had held at the time of the 1322 survey. The survey shows that it was aptly named, because as its tenant John owed a large amount of unpaid labour to the lord of the manor. The sources give varying accounts of his other land, and it may be that he held different parcels at different times. If the sizes given are accurate, then his total holding varied between 8 and 9½ acres in size. This puts him at the top of the range for poor peasants in this area, but there are good examples of poor peasant taxpayers from Thornbury with smaller holdings.[76] John's holding was too small to support a family, and, besides his money-collecting job for the lord, he must have done many labouring jobs for rich neighbours which have left no trace in the records.

The first use which we can make of the taxpayers' personal files is to show just who they were. Five were members of the ruling class. Hugh Audley, lord of Thornbury, heads the Borough list, and the four lords and ladies of sub-manors head the lists for the areas which covered their properties.[77] None of them, incidentally, was given any kind of title in the Tax Roll. The rest of the taxpayers were the heads of local peasant families, as we should expect. They were a mixture of serfs and freemen, and included many women (no fewer than 19 per cent, all or nearly all of them widows[78]). Some were Audley's tenants and some were tenants in the sub-manors. The total number of tenants in Thornbury was probably just under 200, so about 63 per cent of them paid tax.[79]

More importantly, the taxpayers included many from each of the three groups of rich, middle and poor peasants, which is not what Britton's work led us to expect. By no means all of the Thornbury taxpayers' family holdings are easy to trace in the manor records, and the sizes of many were not given until people died or gave up their land in the 1330s or 1340s. It is necessary to work backwards through the manor records and assess whether the sizes of holdings changed. The court rolls record some 650 land transfers in the twenty years before the Black Death, but such sources never provide a truly comprehensive record of land transactions and many may have been missed. There are always risks in estimating the size of a peasant's holding from what he (or his widow or heir) held ten or twenty years later. Some local families also had branches in different groups, so great care must be used when linking tenants in local records with taxpayers in the Tax Roll. But too much should not be made of these difficulties, for the court rolls suggest that only occasionally was enough land lost or gained to transfer tenants and their families between economic groups.

From the information in their files and in those of their families, I was able to recognize fifty-one of Thornbury's peasant taxpayers as rich peasants, nineteen as middle peasants, and twenty-six as poor peasants. The evidence for the remaining twenty-five was not good enough to enable them to be placed in groups: because of this we cannot say just what proportion of each group paid taxes, but it is clear that most rich peasants paid, and most middle and poor peasants did not. Half of the ninety-six who could be traced were rich, a fifth were members of the middle group, and more than a quarter were poor. In Thornbury taxes were not paid almost exclusively by the local rich, but by peasants from all sections of the community. Though parliament had set a minimum assessment below which 'the poor' should be let off paying, many local people whom we think of as 'poor peasants' were having to pay.

This is rather different from Britton's result, for he argued that no fewer than 86 per cent of Broughton taxpayers came from the 'better off' group and only 4 per cent from the poorest group.[80] The disparity may reflect problems of evidence and of method. Broughton court rolls said little about the sizes of holdings, so Britton divided families into three groups on the basis of how often they held offices and jury seats, and how long they stayed in the manor. He argued that those who held most offices and stayed longest were the 'better off' members of the community. This is probably true in many cases, but we know from other manors that many rich peasants never served as officials or jurors, so there may have been many more of these people in his other groups. He also assumed that

families stayed in Broughton for long periods because their names continued to appear in the court rolls, but those whose names appeared only for short periods may have been living locally but using different surnames or simply not appearing in the records. His three groups cannot be equated with the scientific division of the peasantry into rich, middle and poor groups, and this seriously weakens his findings. His conclusion that only 40 per cent of all heads of families paid is also suspect, because he was only able to estimate the numbers of families in the manor from the numbers of surnames in use. This may be misleading because of the use of multiple surnames.[81]

Not only were a substantial number of Thornbury poor peasants paying tax, but Table 3 shows that they were paying as much as the middle peasants and half as much as the local rich. The range of payments in each group was very wide. Each included at least one person assessed at only 6¼d and there was much overlapping between groups. I have tried to show this by means of the quartiles – the amounts between which the middle 50 per cent of the sums paid by the taxpayers in each group fell. For example, rich peasants' payments ranged all the way from 6¼d to 4s 9¼d, but the middle 50 per cent of their payments fell between the two quartiles of 12d and 27d. This is useful for making comparisons, and it emphasizes the similarity of the sums paid by poor and middle peasants.

TABLE 3. AMOUNTS PAID BY PEASANT TAXPAYERS AT THORNBURY, 1327

Group	No. of known taxpayers (d)	Highest payment (d)	Lowest payment (d)	Mean payment (d)	Upper quartile (d)	Lower quartile (d)	Total tax from groups (d)	%
Rich peasants	51	57¼	6¼	21.6	27	12	1,104	71
Middle peasants	19	21½	6¼	10.6	11¼	7	200½	13
Poor peasants	26	24	6¼	10	12	7	260¼	17

Many of the actual sums paid were small. Half of all Thornbury taxpayers paid less than 12d, indicating that they had goods worth less than 20s. Only twelve of them – including four members of the ruling class – paid 3s or more, indicating goods worth at least 60s. Under-assessment must have been rife, and two comparative studies suggest what had gone on behind the scenes. P.D.A. Harvey compared a list of Merton College's movables at Cuxham, Oxfordshire, (which was drawn up for a royal tallage rather than for a tax of this kind) with the record of the college's corn and livestock in the Cuxham manor account roll of the same year.[82] He found that the taxers' valuations were rather low, but that most under-assessment happened because some corn and animals were simply omitted from the list of goods to be taxed. A.T. Gaydon compared lists of lords' livestock and corn which had been taxed on six Bedfordshire manors with lists of their goods in surveys and account rolls, and concluded that the taxmen had under-recorded animals and large quantities of corn, though it is unfortunate that there were usually long intervals between the documents he used.[83] The Cuxham taxmen are known to have been bribed, and it would be easy just to say that the Exchequer was being cheated on a massive scale. But these low assessments were usually accepted by its officers, who can hardly have been ignorant of real values in the rural society which began only a mile from their doors. Those officers are, moreover, known to have set out a scale of conventional values of taxable goods and to have ordered young livestock to be ignored on at least one occasion, namely when the English tax system was extended to North Wales in 1292–3.[84] No such order to the taxers of an English county has been found, but surviving detailed local rolls suggest that these practices were common.[85] Underassessment through low valuations, conventional valuation and the ignoring of some goods may have been standard practices, and the Exchequer usually accepted the results. Perhaps this was considered to be a price worth paying in return for the speedy and peaceful collection of the tax.[86]

The detailed local roll of 1313 from Minety suggests that something similar was happening in Gloucestershire.[87] Valuations were not particularly low, but the taxmen used conventional valuation – every sheep was worth a 1s, every quarter of wheat 4s. There are no local records for comparison, but the lists of taxpayers' goods cannot be complete. Many Minety taxpayers had pairs of cows which could have bred enough oxen to keep full plough-teams up to strength, yet no one paid tax on a full plough-team, and few were taxed on any young bovines. The number who paid tax on some plough-beasts confirms that this was a corn-growing area, yet only two people had more than 10s worth of corn for sale![88] Thornbury's records do not provide lists of peasants' movables, but they give enough information to enable some estimates to be made. The local plough-team was made up of six oxen, and the court rolls have many references to rich peasants with four or six. The mean value of a rich man's ox was about 12s 4d,[89] so that the owner of four oxen should have paid 2s 5½d tax and the owner of a full team 3s 8½d (that is, one-twentieth of 49s 4d and 74s) on oxen alone.[90] But of the fifty-one taxpayers who can be recognized as rich peasants only twelve paid 2s 5½d or more, and only three paid 3s 8½d or more. Gilbert Dawe I of Oldbury[91] was one of a small group of local men who were developing interests in grazing before the Black Death. In the early 1330s he had at least sixteen bullocks and thirty pigs. These must have been worth more than £5, and he had plough oxen and the corn for sale from his large holding in addition, but the 'twentieth' he paid in 1327 was only 3s 3½d.

Many of the local rich must have been under-assessed to a considerable degree, and the same is true of the middle peasants. They would not normally have had corn to take to market, but trespass cases before the manor court suggest that it was usual for them to own two oxen. Middle peasants' oxen were worth an average 10s 11d each, so a pair would have been worth 21s 10d, and 13d tax should have been paid on them. Of the nineteen taxpayers who can be recognized as middle peasants, only three paid this much or more on all their taxable goods. It seems to have been common for poor peasants to own a mare for draught work and a limited number of smaller stock, like John atte Pleystud's mare and ten sheep. John's sheep should have been worth about 10s, and his mare anything between 3s 4d and 6s. (The one he owned when he died in the Black Death was valued at less because prices were falling then.) He should have paid between 8d and 9½d on these animals, and he actually paid 6¾d on all his taxable goods. He was probably paying the greater part of a true assessment, and it is easy to believe that the mass of poor peasant taxpayers in Thornbury – who paid between 6¼d and 12d each – were doing the same.

TABLE 4. HUGH AUDLEY'S TAXABLE GOODS, FROM THE 1327/28 THORNBURY MANOR ACCOUNT ROLL

Livestock Kind	Number	Value each animal*	Total value
Farm-horses**	4	5s 6d	22s
Foals	1	1s 8d	1s 8d
Oxen	33	12s 4d	£20 7s 0d
Cows	3	7s 10d	23s 6d
Heifers	2	?	?
Bullocks	14	?	?
Yearlings	3	?	?
Calves	3	?	?
Pigs	10	2s 6d	25s
Piglets	15	9d	11s 3d
Geese	6	?	?
			£24 10s 5d+

Corn for sale

Kind	Amount	Value per quarter***	Total value		
Wheat	55½qrs	59.3d, 56d	£13	11s	4d
Oats	52qrs	28.1d	£6	1s	7½d
			£19	12s	11½d
Total value livestock and corn for sale:			£44	3s	4½d+

* Based on values of rich peasants' heriots, when available.
** *Affri*.
*** Actual prices for which this corn was sold.

I have left the lord of the manor until last because his position was unique, but more can be said about his assessment. The oldest account roll lists the livestock he actually had at Michaelmas 1327 and reveals how much of his corn was sold during the following year. Not everything can be valued accurately. Nor is it clear what other goods might have been liable to tax. But his taxable goods can hardly have been worth less than £50. He should have paid at least 50s tax, but paid only 20s 2½d. No such lists can be made for the lords and ladies of sub-manors, but it is likely that they were also under-assessed to a large degree.

Nearly all the Thornbury taxpayers can be traced in the manorial records, and these show the very wide range of people who had been brought into the system. Taxpaying was not restricted largely to the 'better off' members of the community. It embraced many heads of middle peasant families, and, although parliament had set a minimum valuation below which 'the poor' should not pay, many people whom we would describe as 'poor peasants' also had to pay. A man like John atte Pleystud, who had so little land that he must have worked as a day labourer to make ends meet, was by no means an unusual figure among the taxpayers of medieval Gloucestershire. Such people did not have to wait until 1379 or later for the poll taxes to bring them into the tax system in large numbers. They were already paying.

The Exchequer had spread its net wide, but its system of assessment and collection was not marked by ruthless efficiency. Taxpayers were required to pay quickly, but got relief in other ways, for the chief taxers' duty to seek out untaxed goods and the subtaxers' oath to value their neighbours' goods at their true values were polite fictions. Without a detailed local roll we cannot fully appreciate how these men operated in Thornbury, but it is likely that they under-assessed local people by using low valuations, conventional valuation and by ignoring quantities of taxable goods, the methods which are known to have been used elsewhere. And the Barons of the Exchequer connived at this, at least to the extent that they accepted the results. The result was a system which could raise substantial sums of money quickly without putting rural communities under intolerable strain. But the Thornbury evidence suggests that it worked in a very inequitable manner. Those poor peasants who were assessed got little relief, and those who saved most were the lords and rich peasants whose social position was the strongest. Unfair taxation was no more an invention of the architects of the Poll Tax than was the taxation of the poor. By the start of the reign of Edward III, both were making a substantial contribution towards the royal finances.

NOTES

1. M. Altschul, *A Baronial Family in Medieval England: the Clares, 1217–1314* (Baltimore, Md., 1965).
2. P. Franklin, 'Thornbury woodlands and deer parks, part 1: the earls of Gloucester's deer parks', *Trans. Bristol & Glos. Arch. Soc.*, cvii (1989), pp. 149–69.

3. N. Saul, *Knights and Esquires: The Gloucestershire Gentry in the Fourteenth Century* (Oxford, 1981).

4. Maurice Berkeley III had married a half-sister of the Earl of Gloucester killed at Bannockburn, and his eldest son (by his first wife) had married the daughter of Roger Mortimer, Queen Isabel's lover. John Smyth, *The Berkeley Manuscripts. The Lives of the Berkeleys*, vol. i, ed. Sir J. Maclean (Gloucester, 1883); Saul, op. cit., *passim*; C. Given-Wilson, *The English Nobility in the Late Middle Ages: The Fourteenth-Century Political Community* (1987).

5. C.S. and C.S. Orwin, *The Open Fields* (Oxford, 1938).

6. E.E. Power, 'The Wool Trade in the Fifteenth Century', in E. Power and M.M. Postan, eds., *Studies in English Trade in the Fifteenth Century* (1933), pp. 39–90.

7. R.H. Hilton, *A Medieval Society. The West Midlands at the End of the Thirteenth Century* (1966), p. 208.

8. C.E. Hart, *Royal Forest. A History of Dean's Woods as Producers of Timber* (Oxford, 1966).

9. R. Graham, 'Religious Houses', in W. Page, ed., *V.C.H. Glos.*, ii, pp. 114–18; C.D. Ross, ed., *Cartulary of St Mark's Hospital, Bristol*, (Bristol Rec. Soc., xxi, 1959); S. Penn, 'The Origins of Bristol Migrants in the Early Fourteenth Century: the Surname Evidence', *Trans. Bristol & Glos. Arch. Soc.*, ci (1983), pp. 123–30.

10. M.W. Beresford and H.P.R. Finberg, *English Medieval Boroughs. A Hand-list* (Newton Abbot, 1973), pp. 49 Table 8, 111–17.

11. S. Rudder, *A New History of Gloucestershire* (Cirencester, 1779, new edn Gloucester, 1977), p. 604 (Prestbury).

12. M.M. Postan and J.Z. Titow, 'Heriots and Prices on Winchester Manors', *Econ. Hist. Rev.*, 2nd ser. xi (1959), pp. 392–417; M.M. Postan, *The Medieval Economy and Society. An Economic History of Britain in the Middle Ages* (1972); B.M.S. Campbell, ed., *Before the Black Death* (Manchester, 1991) offers an important reappraisal of the evidence.

13. M.C. Prestwich, 'Edward I's Monetary Policies and their Consequences', *Econ. Hist. Rev.*, 2nd ser., xxii (1969) pp. 406–16, has suggested that so much tax was collected in the 1290s that every English coin in existence passed through the Exchequer's hands once. But note that J.R. Maddicott, 'The English Peasantry and the Demands of the Crown 1294–1341' (*Past and Present Supplement I*, 1975), sees the 1330s as the period of heaviest taxation.

14. H.S. Lucas, 'The Great European Famine of 1315, 1316 and 1317', *Speculum*, v (1930), pp. 343–77; I. Kershaw, 'The Great Famine and Agrarian Crisis in England 1315–22', *Past and Present*, No. 59 (1973), pp. 3–50.

15. Sources: J.F. Willard, 'The Taxes upon Movables of the Reign of Edward I', *Eng. Hist. Rev.*, xxviii (1913), p. 519, and 'The Taxes upon Movables of the Reign of Edward II', *Eng. Hist. Rev.*, xxix (1914), pp. 319–21; Sir J.H. Ramsey, 'Statistics from Subsidy Rolls of Edward II', *Eng. Hist. Rev.*, xxiv (1909), p. 319; J.F. Willard, 'The Taxes upon Movables of the Reign of Edward III', *Eng. Hist. Rev.*, xxx (1915), pp. 72–3.

16. W. Stubbs, ed., *Chronicles of the Reigns of Edward I and Edward II* (2 vols., 1882–83), *passim*; *Vita Edwardi Secundi* (trans. N. Denholm-Young, 1957), *passim*.

17. Postan and Titow, op. cit.; I. Kershaw, *Bolton Priory. The Economy of a Northern Monastery 1286–1325* (Oxford, 1973).

18. H.R. Luard, ed., *Flores Historiarum* (1890), iii, p.340; E.M. Thompson, ed., *Chronicon Galfridi le Baker de Swynebroke* (Oxford, 1889), p. 9.

19. E.A. Fuller, 'The Tallage of 6 Edward II (Dec. 16, 1312) and the Bristol Rebellion', *Trans. Bristol & Glos. Arch. Soc.*, xix (1894-5), pp. 171–278.

20. E.A. Fry, ed., *Abstracts of Inquisitiones post mortem for Gloucestershire*. Part V. 30 Edw.I to 32 Edw.III 1302–1358 (1910), p. 219.

21. M. Prestwich, *War, Politics and Finance under Edward I* (1972).

22. Willard, *Parliamentary Taxes*, p. 3.

23. Taxation boroughs were often those sending members to parliament, but the two were by no means the same, and Willard concluded that this status was 'a riddle': J.F. Willard, 'Taxation Boroughs and Parliamentary Boroughs, 1294–1336', in J.G. Edwards, et al., eds., *Historical Essays in Honour of James Tait* (Manchester, 1933), pp. 417–35. The traditional definition of ancient demesne as land held by the crown when Edward the Confessor died was not always adhered to: M.A. Barg, 'The villeins of the "ancient demesne"', in L. de Rosa, ed., *Studi in Memoria di Federigo Melis* (Rome, 1978), i, pp. 213–37.

24. Willard, *Parliamentary Taxes*, pp. 102–9.

25. J.F. Willard, 'A Brief Guide to the Records dealing with the Taxes upon Movables 1290–1350', *Bull. Inst. Hist. Res.*, iii (1925), p. 32.

26. R.E. Glasscock, ed., *The Lay Subsidy of 1334* (1975).

27. Willard, *Parliamentary Taxes*, pp. 18–22; *Cal. Close. Rolls 1327–1330*, pp. 216–17; *Rot. Parl.*, ii, p. 425.

28. Saul, op. cit., pp. 72, 227 (Toddington, Doynton and a manor outside the county). Thornbury manor records show that he held two knight's fees of the earl of Gloucester, including the manors of Doynton and Gaunt's Earthcott (the latter granted out to Gaunt's Hospital), and property at Littleton-on-Severn and the Lee: Staffordshire County Record Office, D641/1/4C/1(i)-(ii) (court sessions 18 Aug. 1335, 12 Nov. 1338).

29. P.R.O. E142/24 is partly his work; Saul, op. cit., pp. 88, 153.

30. Yate, Frampton, Tormarton, Iron Acton and Elkstone, the properties of Sir John Wilington and Sir John de Acton: Saul, op. cit., pp. 182–3.

31. *Rot. Parl.*, ii, p. 426.

32. Ibid.

33. Ibid.; Willard, *Parliamentary Taxes*, pp. 77–9, 92–3.

34. J.F. Hadwin, 'The Medieval Lay Subsidies and Economic History', *Econ. Hist. Rev.*, 2nd ser., xxxvi (1983), p. 202.

35. P.R.O. E179/113/4 (Minety is m.13).

36. Willard, *Parliamentary Taxes*, pp. 81–5.

37. S.K. Mitchell, *Taxation in Medieval England* (ed. S. Painter; New Haven, Conn., 1951), pp. 139–55; *Cal. Pat. Rolls 1216–1225*, p. 560; E. Powell, *A Suffolk Hundred in the Year 1283* (Cambridge, 1910), pp. x–xi.

38. *Rot. Parl.*, ii, pp. 425–7.

39. P.R.O. E179/113/5.

40. Cirencester was sometimes counted as a taxation borough, Cheltenham, Minety, Newenham, Newent and Winchcombe occasionally so: Willard, 'Taxation Boroughs', p. 431.

41. Sir R. Atkyns, *The Ancient and Present State of Glostershire* (1712, 2nd edn, 1768); Rudder, op. cit.

42. C.S. Taylor, 'The Northern Boundary of Gloucestershire', *Trans. Bristol & Glos. Arch. Soc.*, xxxii (1909), pp. 109–39.

43. Sir T. Phillipps, *Gloucestershire Subsidy Roll, 1 Edward III. AD 1327* (Middle Hill Press, n.d.). The following account relies heavily upon A.N.L. Munby, *Phillipps Studies*, (Cambridge, 5 vols., 1952–6). The reference to an edition by Ralph Bigland in Glasscock, op. cit., p. 91, is erroneous.

44. Sir H. Dryden, ed., *Le Art de Venerie, par Guyllame Twici [sic]* (1840).

45. e.g. Bonvyle (list 65) should read 'Gonnyld'. Richard Baldwine and William le Eorl, both of Bishops Norton (list 317) were omitted.

46. Munby, op. cit., ii, pp. 25, 27, 59, 92, iv, pp. 74, 158.

47. Phillipps, op. cit., p. 40; lists 381, 390.

48. Munby, op. cit., ii, p. 100, iv, pp. 42–3, 109.

49. R.F. Hunnisett, *Editing Records for Publication* (1977) and *Indexing for Editors* (1972).

50. A.H. Smith, *The Place-Names of Gloucestershire* (Eng. Place-Names Soc., xxxviii–xli, Cambridge, 1964–5). Smith used the 1327 Tax Roll ms., but not Phillipps's edition.

51. C.T. Martin, *The Record Interpreter* (2nd edn, 1910), pp. 451–64; E.G. Withycombe, *The Oxford Dictionary of English Christian Names* (3rd edn, Oxford, 1977).

52. Albred. could be Albreda or Aubrey; Alex. Alexander or Alexandra; Cecil. or Seycel. Cecil or Cecily; Clar. Clare or Clarice; Clement. Clemence or Clement; Constanc. Constance or Constantine; Dionis. or Dyonis. Dennis or Denise; Felic. Felice or Felix; Is. Isaac or Isabel; Joh. or Johan. Joan or John; Marg. Margaret or Margery; Nich. Nicola or Nicholas; Ros. Rose or Rosamund.

53. P.H. Reaney, *A Dictionary of British Surnames* (1958).

54. The clerk has written pb. or pbat. instead of the usual prob.

55. Described in P.D.A. Harvey, *Manorial records* (1984).

56. A.T. Gaydon, *The Taxation of 1297*, Beds. Hist. Rec. Soc., xxxix (Streatley, 1959), pp. xviii–xx; P.D.A. Harvey, *A Medieval Oxfordshire Village* (Oxford, 1965), pp. 105–9.

57. L.R. Poos and R.M. Smith, '"Legal Windows Onto Historical Populations?" Recent Research on Demography and the Manor Court in Medieval England', *Law and Hist. Rev.*, ii (1984), pp. 128–52.

58. Z. Razi, *Life, Marriage and Death in a Medieval Parish* (Cambridge, 1980), *passim.*

59. E. Britton, *The Community of the Vill* (Toronto, 1977), pp. 70–6.

60. No minimum taxable amounts were set out when the tax system was remodelled in 1334, but it has been argued that they were still used in practice: R.E. Glasscock, ed. *The Lay Subsidy of 1334* (1975), p. xxii.

61. Many surveys have been printed in S.J. Madge, *Abstracts of Inquisitiones post mortem for Gloucestershire. Part IV. 20 Hen.III to 29 Edw.I. 1236–1300* (1903); E.A. Fry, ed., *Abstracts of Inquisitiones post mortem for Gloucestershire. Part V. 30 Edw.I to 32 Edw.III. 1302–1358* (1910); E. Stokes, ed., *Abstracts of Inquisitiones post mortem for Gloucestershire. Part VI. 33 Edw.III to 14 Hen.VI. 1359–1413* (1914). (Parts I–III cover reign of Charles I.) Few accounts or court rolls have been printed, but *vide* A.L. Browne, 'Wick Rissington Transcripts', *Trans. Bristol & Glos. Arch. Soc.*, lix (1937), pp. 211–19, and C. Swynnerton, 'Some Early Court Rolls of the Manors of Stonehouse, King's Stanley, Woodchester, and Achards', *Trans. Bristol & Glos. Arch. Soc.*, xlv (1923), pp. 203–52; Hawkesbury court rolls are used in R.F. Butler, 'Social and Economic History', in W. Page, ed., *V.C.H. Glos.*, ii (1907), pp. 127–73. None of the Thornbury manorial records have been printed.

62. The manorial records were kept at Thornbury Castle until the 1920s and then divided between Gloucestershire and Staffordshire County Record Offices. See Bibliography, below.

63. The following description is based upon my 'Thornbury woodlands and deer parks, part 1', *Trans. Bristol & Glos. Arch. Soc.*, cvii (1989), pp. 149–69, and 'Politics in Manorial Court Rolls', in R.M. Smith and Z. Razi, eds., *The Manor Court and English Medieval Society* (Oxford, forthcoming).

64. E.A. Kosminsky, *Studies in the Agrarian History of England in the Thirteenth Century* (ed. R.H. Hilton, trans. R.Kisch; Oxford, 1956), pp. 256–82.

65. The theory is most often associated with the names of V.I. Lenin and I. Hourwich, whose works are most readily available in English translations. Nearly all shades of Russian political opinion accepted this analysis, and it has since been applied to non-Russian peasantries. V.I. Lenin, *The Development of Capitalism in Russia* (2nd edn, Moscow, 1964), esp. Ch. 2; I.A. Hourwich, *The Economics of the Russian Village* (New York, 1892). For later criticism *vide* T. Shanin, *The Awkward Class* (Oxford, 1972).

66. R.H. Hilton, 'Lords, Burgesses and Hucksters', *Past and Present*, 97 (1983), pp. 3–15.

67. Lists 428 (borough), 429–36 (manor); The same arrangement was used in 1334, R.E. Glasscock, ed., *The Lay Subsidy of 1334* (1975), p. 101.

68. Oldland does not appear in Thornbury records before the Black Death. The missing taxpayers presumably appear in list 447 (Hanham Abbots and Oldland).

69. Beaubras, Masoun and Daau (list 444), rich free peasants who served on Thornbury's annual view of frankpledge jury.

70. Calc. from Britton, op. cit., p. 73.

71. Calc. from J.A. Raftis and M.P. Hogan, *Early Huntingdonshire Lay Subsidy Rolls* (Toronto, 1976), p. 23 Table III, 69–70, 93–4. They read some taxpayers' names differently and produced a total of sixty-five from the two tax rolls as against Britton's fifty-eight – readers may care to compare the respective lists. Raftis and Hogan, ibid., also undertook this exercise for five nearby manors, with similar results, but did not analyse the taxpayers.

72. Thirty-seven court rolls survive from this period; nine more are lost.

73. Lists 230, 265, 358, 363, including Sir Richard de Cokkebury at Postlip. Cockbury is a place-name in Cleeve Hundred, *vide* note to list 265.

74. Z. Razi, 'The Toronto School's Reconstitution of Medieval Peasant Society: A Critical View', *Past and Present*, 85 (1978), pp. 141–57.

75. Badgeworth, in Dudstone Hundred, sometimes appears in Thornbury records because it was another of Hugh Audley's estates. The Tax Roll records two Pleystudes in Shurdington (list 311), the next parish to Badgeworth, and a John atte Pleystude as a subtaxer for Dudstone Hundred (lists 315, 329). Roger Mautravers and William Hunt who were mentioned in the Badgeworth case were not Thornbury men, but John Mautravers and William le Hunte were listed as Shurdington taxpayers.

76. E.g. the Sibland taxpayer Gunilda Hodelond ('Hobelonde' in list 436) held only 6 acres and Thomas de Hope (list 429) only 4 acres. The local virgate contained about 36–8 acres.

77. Lists 429, 433–5. Elizabeth Chaumberleyn's husband Sir Simon had died in gaol after the 1322 uprising. This family (also called 'Hope') were gentry too small to appear in Saul, op. cit. Joan Kyngeston (listed as John) was the widow of Sir Nicholas, *vide* K.B. McFarlane, 'An Indenture of Agreement between two English Knights for Mutual Aid and Counsel in Peace and War', *Bull. Inst. Hist. Res.*, xxxviii (1965), pp. 200–10; cf. Saul, op. cit., passim. (Her name is given correctly in lists 241, 244, 250, 471 and 472.) John Chaumpeneys was a Berkeley retainer: Saul, op. cit., pp. 66–7. Isabel Clare was the half-sister of the last Clare earl of Gloucester and widow of Maurice Berkeley III: *vide* note 4.

78. After correcting clerk's errors with names; *vide* my 'Peasant Widows' "Liberation" and Remarriage before the Black Death', *Econ. Hist. Rev.*, 2nd ser., xxxix (1986), pp. 186–204.

79. I estimate about 140–5 serf and about twenty-three free tenants in the main body of the manor, and approximately twenty-seven tenants in the sub-manors, making a total of around 190–5 tenants. 121 of these peasant tenants paid the tax.

80. Britton, op. cit., p. 74, Table 17.

81. E.B. DeWindt's conclusion that 44 per cent of families on another Ramsey Abbey manor paid the 1327 tax must be subject to the same reservation: *Land and People in Holywell-cum-Needingworth* (Toronto, 1971), p. 198 fn. 104.

82. Harvey, *Oxfordshire Village*, pp. 107–9.

83. Gaydon, op. cit., pp. xviii–xx.

84. K. Williams-Jones, ed., *The Merioneth Lay Subsidy Roll 1292–3*, Board of Celtic Studs., Hist. and Law Ser. No. 29 (Cardiff, 1976), p. xiv.

85. e.g. W. Brown, ed., *Yorkshire Lay Subsidy being a Ninth collected in 25 Edward I (1297)*, Yorks. Arch. Soc. Rec. Ser., xvi (1894), esp. pp. xxiv–xxv (West Riding).

86. Little evidence has been found for popular opposition to these taxes in England, *vide* Willard, *Parliamentary Taxes*, pp. 170–2; Williams-Jones considers the part which such opposition played in the Welsh rising of 1294–5, op. cit., pp. xxix–xxxv.

87. P.R.O. E179/113/4.

88. Ibid., Adam Beauscyr, Adam Smalhobbe. Corn for sale made up only 3.5 per cent of Minety taxpayers' assessed wealth, and they were taxed on an average of only 3.8 bushels each – much less than Willard's figures for other areas: *Parliamentary Taxes*, pp. 81–2.

89. Livestock values are calculated from pre-Black Death heriots. So many beasts were taken after deaths in the plague that values plummeted then.

90. Dewindt uses the assessed values of Huntingdonshire taxpayers' goods in 1327 and 1332 to argue that many peasants were well above subsistence level, but neglects to discuss what items were taxed or what local livestock and corn were worth: op. cit., pp. 198–202.

91. Dalue (list 433).

The Gloucestershire Lay Subsidy Roll of 1327

P.R.O. E179/113/5

PART ONE

Gloucestershire

(*G L O U C .*)

The taxation of a twentieth from the [taxation] boroughs and the lord king's ancient demesne in the County of Gloucester, made by William Tracy and Robert de Aston, in the first year of the reign of King Edward, the Third after the Conquest.

GLOUCESTER
(*VILLA GLOUCESTR.*)

East Ward (*Warda Orientalis*)

1

Robert Pope	20s
Robert de Goldhulle	10s
Peter de la Hulle	13s 4d
Roger Heved	10s
John de Fladebury	6d
Steven le Carpenter	3s
John Canon	6d
Henry Elys	2s
Peter le Swyngare	2s
Robert de Stapelton	2s
John de la Hulle	6s
Henry Brid	6d
Henry le Draper	6s
John Craft	6d
Walter Slo	6d
William le Messeger	2s
John atte Strode	12d
Ralph atte Wode	12d
John le Welar	18d
William Averey	2s
Adam Gamage	10s
Thomas de Pendok	2s
Edward le Seler	12d
William Cryspe	6s 8d
William Pendok	4s
Walter le Chapman	4s
Nicholas Dyke, baker (*pistore*)	6d
Philip Crok	5s
John Tendefuyr	2s
Hugh le Veltare	6d
Robert de Cromhale	12d
Joan la Knyt	12d
William de Boxwelle	12d
Thomas Craft	12d
Thomas de Cheltenham	6d

Total of the said ward, £6 4s 6d

West Ward (*Warda Occidentalis*)

2

Adam Hunsom	3s
Robert de Elmor	2s
Roge le Hopere	6d
Simon Dun	6d
William le Peyntur	12d
Walter atte Were	6d
William Montayn	12d
Richard Pode	2s
Thomas Glaswryght	6d
Adam Pode	3s
Richard Sevare	12d
Lawrence Sevare	4s
John Straunge	6d
Adam Wardessip	2s
Richard de la Bote	8s
William de Lyndeseye	10s
Robert le Webbe	6d
Roger de Wygemor	12d
John le Dyeare	10s
John le Webbe	6d
Richard de Rodmarleye	6s
Henry de Bulemulle	3s
Peter de London	12d
Nicholas le Duc	6d
Philip le Droys	8d
Roger le Knyt	12d
John le King	12d
William atte Home	6d
William le Teylar	18d
John de Foxcote	12d
Nicholas Stoyl	2s
John de Lynham	6d
John de la Pole	18d
Henry le Peyntur	12d
John le Tannare	2s
John Reod	6d
Alex. Honsom	6d
William de Leden	2s
William de Haukescombe	6d
Margery Hebelot	6d
Agnes Cumpere	2s
Edward de Leye	10s
John Hasfeld	12d
Richard Blowelot	12d
Nicholas le Mulleward	2s
William de Tettebury	2s
Walter de Bekkeforde	6d
Agnes la Chaungeour	6d
Richard atte Wode	6d
William le Tannare	18d
William West	2s
William Pouke	12d
John de Masud. . .	6d
Walter le Roo. . .	2s
Richard de Oxen. . .	12d
Richard le Chaun. . .	6d
Walter de Pa. . .	12d
John de . . .	. . .s
William de W. . .	. . .
Thomas de B. . .	. . .
Warren le Ke. . .	. . .
Alice, widow of Robert . . .	. . .
John de Cy. . .	. . .d
Richard le Ha. . .	6d
William atte . . .	6d
William de . . .mor	4s
Thomas le Goldsmyth	6s 8d
Matilda la Goldsmyth	12d

Also West Ward

Nicholas le Tannar	6d
Richard Poterne	2s
Richard le Carpenter	6d
William de Wyght	2s
Adam le Keyberare	5s
Richard Austyn	12d
William de Pleyleye	6d
William, son of Henry le Draper	5s

Approved. Total of the said West Ward, £7 6s 4d

North Ward (*Warda Borialis*)

3

Henry Patrik	5s
John de Lamput	2s
John Wenge	4s
John de Boyfeld	7s
Thomas de Neuwent	2s
William de Mathiue	12d
William le Goldsmith	12d
William de Podemor	2s
Ralph Wardeyn	6d
Roger de Hynham	12d
John Botte	6d
Thomas le Mariner	6d
John de Prestebury	3s
Walter Silvestr	3s 4d
Richard de Fydinton	12d
Reginald de Derherste	4s
William de Ryouns	12d
Robert Peit	18d
Richard Shot	10s
Thomas de Foxcote	2s
Henry Emmesone	12d
Thomas le Bole	6d
William le Spicer	4s
Steven Broun	6s 8d
Thomas Maryman	16d
John de Lylton	2s
Reginald de Hokelot	2s

Steven de Faluwe	12d
Ralph le Sherare	6d
John de Paunteleye	12d
Johne de Combe	12d
Thomas le Hopere	2s
John de Lemenstr	5s
Nicholas Beorsy	4s
Robert de Lydeneye	5s
Ralph le Teylare	2s
Henry de Lydeneye	5s
Emma de Hertforde	12d
Richard Scot, barber (*barbour*)	3s
Julian de Matteshale	2s
William Chychely	6d
Hugh le Loksmyth	12d
Hugh de Prestebury	3s
John Compayn	3s
Robert Pynoun	6d
Nicholas de Honiton	4s
Richard le Pottare	6d
Henry Pigaz	12d
William le Mareschal	6d
John de Northwich	6s 8d
John Moraunt	4s
Walter le Aumblare	12d
William le Harpour	6d
Isabel Wynebold	2s
Richard le Taillur	12d
William Leulyn	12d
Philip Wyteby	12d
Richard le Skinnar	6d
John de Dursleye	2s
John le Teylare	2s
Margery Hodeknasshe	2s
Nicholas de Tame	4s
Isabel de la Stowe	2s
John de Hathleye	6d
Alexander Sojornaunt	12d
John de Baysham	3s
Walter le Whelare	3s
Walter Blakeneye	4s
Richard Keys	6d
Adam le Whelare	6d
Nicholas de Berton	12d
Edmund de Bauerton	2s
John de Kydemunstr	2s
Margery la Webbe	6d
William le Hopere	20d
William de Overe	6d
John le Smyth	6d
Adam atte Brewarne	6d
Roger de Clyfford	2s
Robert Holchip	6d

Alice Maynard	3s
Richard Someter	6d
Thomas de Clyve	6d
Simon le Porter	6d
Adam de Compton	6d
Henry de Wy. . .eston	6d
John de Munstreworth	5s
Ellis le Knyt	2s
John de Muggeleye	2s
Hugh Megre	2s
John de Wyndesore	6d
William Peleynamer	2s
William de la Berton	3s
Richard de la Wateringstude	5s 4d

[Membrane 1 dorse]

Also North Ward

Richard de Ettefeld	6d
Martin le Carpenter	6d
Roger Haukyn	2s 8d
John Brid	12d
Lawrence de Marcle	6d
William Broun	5s

Approved. Total of the said North Ward, £10 7s 2d

South Ward (*Warda Australis*)

4

Philip le Calewe	3s
Isabel la Politer	3s
Richard de Thornbury	4s
Walter le Garlekmongere	4s
Robert de Berkeleye	18d
Henry Heved	8d
Richard Lardeyn	6d
Andrew de Pendok	2s
Robert de Eldesfeld	6d
Henry le Mareschal	6d
Thomas Hunsom	2s
Geoffrey le Hirdeman	20¼d
Matilda de Cumpton	2s
William Bullok	6d
Agnes de Stanforde	12d
John de Holteleye	2s
John de Catewyke	12d
John de Froucestr	3s
Gilbert de Mathiue	3s

Martha de Godeleye	12d
Philip Waleys	12d
John le Tannar	2s
Robert le Longestoyl	12d
John de Bradenebirr	6d
Richard le Parkere	18d
John de Marcle	6s 8d
Nicholas de Edythstoke	2s
Steven de Grenden	18d
John de Ocle	18d
Roger le Mercer	12d
Richard Bullok	2s
Alex. de Elmor	6d
Hugh de Graunden	3s
William de Longeneye	2s
Hugh de Dymmok	8d
Reginald de Mathiue	12d
Thomas de Cherlton	2s
William de Hawe	3s
Nicholas Bernard	6d
William de Dene	6d
Thomas Soty	6d
William Bayleben	3s
John de Aston	2s
John de Dousewelle	18d
Richard de Aston	6d
Richard de Bromshulph	6d

Approved. Total of the said South Ward, 78s 8¼d

Overall total of the twentieth of the vill of Gloucester, £27 16s 8¼d

Subtaxers (*Subtaxatores*)

5

John de Cheddeworth	12d
Ewen de Wyndesore	12d
Ranulph le Wheolare	12d
Walter le Southerne	12d
Adam atte Hulle	12d
Ellis de Longeneye	12d
Thomas atte Grove	12d
Ranulph de Bekkeforde	12d

Total, 8s

Approved overall total of the vill of Gloucester with the subtaxers' taxes, £28 4s 8¼d

BRISTOL
(*VILLA BRISTOLL*)

Redcliffe Quarter (*Quarterium de la Radeclyve*)

6

William Hayl	12s
Roger Stapelton	3s
Robert Westb'	8s
Robert Stapelton	5s
William Thornbury	5s
Robert Geryng	12d
Thomas atte Hulle	8s
John Kerdyf	3s
Adam Welyshote	4s
Everard Fraunceys	20s
John North	8s
William de London	3s
John de Keynesham	43s
Roger Teslare	16s
William Edward	2s
Agnes Curteys	8s
William Bruges	2s
John Wermenstr	2s
Christine Mauduyt	4s
John Wycombe	6s
John Marsfeld	7s
Roger Bonde	5s
William le Veltare	3s
William atte Forde	12s
Robert Hayl	12d
John de Okynton	4s
John de Veltare	10s
John Bonde	2s

[Membrane 1 dorse r-h col.]

Also Redcliffe Quarter

Geoffrey le Veltare	3s
Philip le Webbe	4s
John le Botiller	4s
Robert Cameleye	4s
Robert Wyldemerssh	3s
Robert le Taillur	4s
Roger Stanes	12d
John Mynty	2s
Edward atte Dogh	12d
Robert le Mareschal	12d
John Broun	12d
Thomas Uppehulle	6s
John Dykare	2s
Mereyo de Welles	½ mark
John Frye	12d
Thomas le Veltare	2s

Roger Pebbelewe	8s
Nicholas de Pridie	4s
Richard Plomer	3s
Richard de Stoke	4s
Robert Fenel	2s
John Welysshote	4s
Richard Heyne	4s
Walter Malleden	12d
Margaret Rondulph	4s
John atte Merssh	3s
Hugh le Tylar	12d
Richard Leyr	8s
Richeman de Welles	40s
John Hugges	4s
John Methelan	7s
Robert Muleward	4s
Philip Standissh	8s
William Wasshema	2s
Simon Webbe	4s
Walter de Welles	14s
Henry de Welles	3s
Thomas Hendy	5s
Robert le Heyward	2s
Richard Bel	6s
Walter Scir	4s
Adam Irissh	2s
William de Handlesettare	2s
Henry le Shipman	20s
John Cok	6s
Walter Prentiz	14s
John Milton	4s
William Brid	3s
John atte Pole	5s
Robert Wryngton	6s
Roger Cok	3s
William Eweyn	4s
Robert Page	6s
Gilbert Pekerel	3s
Walter atte Rigg	12d
Robert Spakston	3s
John de Coumbhaweye	10s
William Fort	12d

Approved. Total of the twentieth of the said Redcliffe Quarter, £24 14s 8d

Subtaxers (*Subtaxatores*)

7

William de Cumpton	8s
Thomas Dygel	8s

John le Preyour	8s
William Warman	6s
John de Dene	2s
Hugh le Proute	10s

Total, 42s

Approved. Total of the twentieth of the said Redcliffe Quarter with the subtaxers' taxes, £26 16s 8d

All Saints' Quarter (*Quarterium Omniorum Sanctorum dicte Ville Bristoll*)

8

Henry le Taillur	2s
Robert Cocus	12d
Richard Bryan	18d
John de Stoke	18d
Thomas le Sullar	5s
Roger le Gurdlar	12d
Margaret de Stapelton	20d
John le Hunte	3s
William Reynald	5s
Reginald Lek	3s
Thomas Laminer	6s
Stephen le Spycer	13s
Walter Cornek	4s
Thomas de Romeseye	3s
John Cory	6s
William de Wyght	12d
Robert de Horhust	12s
William Cornwaleys	. . .d
Thomas de London	. . .s
John Porsere	. . .s
William Gurdlar	. . .s
Richard Gurdlar	. . .s
John Draper	. . .s
Thomas Wath. . .	. . .s
Nicholas le Dr. . .	. . .s
Hugh . . .	. . .
Edward . . .	. . .
Henry Teuc . . . sur	. . .
John Horncastel	15. . .
William le Sullar	6. . .
Richard de Stanedissh	12s
John le Crokkare	3s

[Membrane 2]

Also All Saints' Quarter

Robert atte Tour	12d
Richard de Panes	5s
Walter Writh, ironmonger (*irmongere*)	12d
Thomas Pouchard	5s
John Pecok	12d
John le Sullar	3s
Robert Snow	5s
William le Taillor	2s
Robert Longeford	5s
John atte Fisshwere	18d
John Peutrer	8s
Simon le Taillor	2s
John Colpek	2s
Philip le Wodeward	5s
Lucy de Chesebergh	15s
Roger de Wodhulle	7s
Thomas Russel	5s
Thomas de Chyselbergh	10s
Richard Writhe	25s
Matilda Russel	15s
John Hopere	2s
Robert Frelond	3s
John Fichet	2s
John de Derby	5s
Richard Blanket	7s
Geoffrey Methelan	?s
John Donnyng	2s
William Babey	12d
Walter Taillor	4s
Roger Breware	18d
Robert Passour	10s
Philip de Camull	12d
Robert Taillor	5s
Richard Taillour	12d
William Ropere	12d
William de Wyrcestr	9d
Richard atte Shoppe	2s
Richard de Wodhull	7s
Adam le Ropere	12d
Adam Carpenter	3s
Edith Sanekyn	9d
Richard Ropere	3s
William de Derby	4s
Robert Wrythe	5s
Hugh Payn	2s
Richard Soutar	12d
Alexander de Berdewyk	12d
Joan de Hanyngfeld	12d
Sybil de Purye	12d
Alice atte Ok	12d

Approved. Total of the twentieth of the said All Saints' Quarter, £16 19s 8d

Subtaxers (*Subtaxatores*)

9

Roger Pluph	2s
Richard de Apperleye	4s
Simon de Ely	5s

Total, 11s

Total of the twentieth of the said All Saints' Quarter with the subtaxers' taxes, £17 10s 8d

St Ewen's Quarter (*Quarterium Sancti Audoeni dicte Ville Bristoll*)

10

Richard Langebergh	12d
Isabel Skynnar	2s
Margery de Wallok	12d
Agnes Bonewall	12d
William Bonde	3s
Margaret de Romeneye	4s
Thomas de la Grave	12d
Thomas Pennard	14s
Robert Gyan	25s
John Godman	2s
Nicholas de Roubergh	2s
John Mathon	4s
John Wysman	10s
Gervase de Cary	12s
Roger Beauflour	5s
William de Clyf	6s
John Reymond	12s
. . . Turtle	2s
. . . Loksmyth	12d
. . .he de Oxon	12d
John Ropere	4s
R. . . atte Walle	5s
William Celram	12d
Peter Riche	12d
. . . de Axebrugge	4s
. . . atte Walle	25s
. . . . . .eleche	10s
. . . Pygon	12d
. . . Turtle	5s
. . . Fraunceys	2s
. . . Walssh	12d
. . . . . .mbrel	5s
. . . Fraunceys	8s
. . . Methilan	10s
. . . . . .pas	10s
. . . . . .year	2s
. . . . . .shale	3s
. . .ne Mariner	12s
. . . . . .devill	2s
. . . Plomer	12d
. . . . . . the elder	10s
. . . . . .	2s
. . . . . .hur	3s
. . . . . .	12d
. . . . . .	18d

. . . . . .	10s
. . . . . .	25s
. . . . . .	20s
. . . . . .	2s
. . . . . .	12d
. . . . . .	12d
. . . . . .	3s

[Total of the twentieth of the said St] Ewen's [Quarter],[1] £14 10s 6d

Subtaxers (. . .)

11

. . . . . .	20s
. . . . . .	15s
. . . . . .	12s
. . . . . .	4s

[total, 51s]

Approved. [Total of the twentieth of the said St Ewen's Quarter with the subtaxers' taxes, £17 1s 6d][2]

Virgin Mary's Quarter (. . .)

c. four names illegible[3]

[Membrane 2 r-h col.]

Also Virgin Mary's Quarter

12

Simon Varstal	13s 4d
Thomas Fourbor	12d
Roger Chaundeler	12d
Richard Sheftebury	2s
Thomas de Haukesbury	2s
Thomas de Bristeltone	12d
Walter Goby	4s
William de Kyngeston	12d
William Medewell	12d
David de Haleweye	12d
William de Stapelton	12d
John le Porter	4s
Robert Wybynden	12d
Ellen de Camme	2s
Nicholas Donstere	12d
William Newmayster	20s
Thomas Lymages	12d
Roger Ondeslowe	3s
John Chedderne	6s
Robert Boddebur	12d
Thomas Trillyk	12d
Thomas Broun	12d
Thomas Abraham	4s

Thomas de Roubergh	4s
John Jolyf	12d
John Chaloner	12d
John Wylmyg	18d
Nicholas Modewell	5s
John Valet	18d
William Stevene	12d
William Whyte	4s
Stephen Pridie	12d
William Reygnald	12d
Roger Peutrer	2s
Robert Cottler	10s
William de Wynchestr	13s 4d
Henry de Frompton	20s
Roger de Frompton	2s
John Hunte	3s
Walter Colemor	12d
Adam Gurdlar	12d
William Randulph	3s
Richard Multon	2s
John Forthrugg	12d
Walter Latham	12d
Thomas Trepyn	6s
Roger Westram	12d
John Vyssher	12d
John Curteys	12d
John Douse	6s 8d
Walter Barbour	12d
John Turtle	3s
William Depinge	12d
Hugh de Langebrugg	6s 8d
William Baker	6s
Henry Chaloner	18d
John Romeseye	6s 8d

Approved. Total of the said Virgin Mary's Quarter, £10 2d

Subtaxers (*Subtaxatores*)

13

John Regnald	4s

Robert Halewy	4s
Roger de Apperleye	5s

Total, 13s

Approved. Total of the twentieth of the said Virgin Mary's Quarter with the subtaxers' taxes, £10 13s 2d

Holy Trinity Quarter (*Quarterium Sancte Trinitate dicte ville Bristoll*)

14

Philip Gurdlar	5s
John Legh	4s
Ellis Averey	8s
Robert Bremel	5s
Thomas de Salop	15s
Miles Dosy	3s
Alice Clere	5s
Peter Mountestevene	6s
Margery Masoun	2s
John Pigaz	5s
John de Axebrugg	2s
William le Taverner	2s
Adam atte Bour	2s
Henry de Berkele	12d
Edith atte Markete	3s
Thomas Tybaud	5s
David Tymbresbergh	4s
Walter de Purie	6s
Robert Gurdlar	12d
Thomas Shepherde	12d
Richard Passour	12d
Walter Cote	5s
Richard Devenyssh	2s
Roger Dowell	7s
Thomas Rosselyn	2s
Walter de Tokynton	2s
Richard Beauflour	3s
Robert Leof	3s

Michael Whyttawyar	4s
John Bat	3s
John de Boyfeld	2s
John Delrobe	12d
Simon de Stoke	2s
Edith la Hunte	2s
John Hendybody	12d
Richard atte Heyhome	2s
Thomas Fynet	2s
Thomas Swetyng	2s
Robert le Mareschal	2s
Florence de Stoke	12d
Robert Heybone	5s
Richard Cartere	10s
Robert Tylar	2s
Adam Sawyar	2s
John Leche	12d
Simon de Apperlegh	12d

Total of the twentieth of the said Holy Trinity Quarter, £7 15s

Subtaxers (*Subtaxatores*)

15

Robert Tumbrel	4s
John Morcok	4s
John de Wydyhull	5s
Walter Hervy	3s

Total, 16s

Total of the twentieth of the said Holy Trinity Quarter with the subtaxers' taxes, £8 11s

Approved. Total of the twentieth of the whole vill of Bristol with the subtaxers' taxes, £80 12s

[MISCELLANEOUS ANCIENT DEMESNE VILLS][4]

Cirencester (*Villa Cyrencestre*)

16

John de . . .	8d
. . . . . .	6¼d
. . . . . .	4s 4d
Walter Wyly	6d

[Membrane 2 dorse]

Also Cirencester

Agnes Crouse	2s 6½d
Philip Roger	9d
Henry de Arderne	7¼d
Richard de Haile	6½d
John de Bristoll	11d
Nicholas Coyfestare	5s 4d
John Goterest	20s 3½d
William Swelle	15¼d
William de Dodecote	7d
Walter Panelman	9d
Martin Sely	16d
John de Crekkelade	5s
John de Matteshale	7d
William de Frome	9½d
Ralph de Matteshale	6½d
Thomas Payn	16½d
John Estcot	18s 2¼d
John Scot	5s 2¼d
Ralph de Yevele	12d
William de Yevele	6d
Geoffrey de Mersshton	20s 3½d
William Whythed	6d
Walter Gorest	2s
Nicholas Dyear	2s 4d
William Knotte	6¼d
John de Penynton	3s 2½d
John Cartere	18d
Thomas But	7½d
William Cotyler	7d
Philip Corviser	11½d
Adam Evesham	12½d
Peter de Derham	20s 3¼d
Henry Ryngwode	15½d
John Smyth	9d
Thomas de Tettebury	8½d
Henry Dillyng	7d
John Wygeput	7½d
John Playn	9d
John Couleye	2s
Richard Vole	6½d
Thomas Bollewell	6¼d
John Holte	7d
John Northerne	7½d
Joan Waleys	9d
Walter Northerne	17s
Walter Moryn	5s
John Moryn	3s 4d
William Waleys	2s 0½d
John Lucesone	12d
Reginald Goldsmyth	12d
William Agodeshalf	6¼d
Edward Purs	18d
William Wymond	2s
Abraham de Haile	10¼d
William Sharpe	4s
Richard Smyth	9d
Nich. de Bristoll	6½d
Stephen Lannal	15s
Andrew de Wynston	15d
Nicholas Kernar	11d
John Robus	9d
John Page	8d
William Taillur	6¾d
Elizabeth Carpenter	12¼d
William Rothewell	7¼d
John de Weston	6¼d
Alban Baker	6½d
Walter Ferbras	2s
Luc. Chapman	3s 1d
Macer. Peuter	7½d
John Ceynestar	21s 1½d
William Kene	21s
Nicholas Wyggewold	9d
Nicholas Muleward	13d
William Walkere	9d
Thomas Guyssh	12½d
Warden of St John	13d
Ralph Hopere	6¼d
Warden of St Lawrence's House	7d
Robert de Avebury	17d
William Walkere	2s 3½d

Approved. Total of the twentieth of Cirencester, £12 17s 2¾d

Subtaxers (*Subtaxatores*)

17

Richard Skarnynge	12d
John Eycote	12d
Richard Shayl	12d
Richard Hereward	12d
Henry de Foxcote	12d
Richard Moryn	12d
Richard Dyear	12d

Total, 7s

Approved. Total of the twentieth of the vill of Cirencester with the subtaxers' taxes, £13 4s 2¾d

Winchcombe (*Villa Wynchecomb*)

18

John de Aldrinton	3s
Richard Frend	2s
Robert le Webbe	18d
Robert le Smyth	12d
Ralph Palefrayman	18d
John Thorstayn	14d
John Cheltenham	12d
John Braundon	18d
John Parchementer	20d
Thomas Taman	12d
Richard Shirebourn	8d
Henry Hopere	2s
William Sklattare	6d
Richard G. . .yng	2s
William Hod. . .	12d
Ralph Nanchard	12d
John Taillur	12d
John S. . .y	2s
Thomas atte Hulle	16d
A.	8d
Margaret . . .	9d
. . . atte Frome	8d

[*c.* ten names illegible[5]]

[Membrane 2 dorse r-h col.]

Also Winchcombe

Richard Malemo	4s
William Kembar	6d
John de Teynton	2s
William Jolyf	12d
Walter Stowe	2s
William Momelard	3s
Henry Addy	2s
John Miller (*Molendinario*)	6d
Robert Petyt	2s
Henry Jabel	12d
John Parfay	2s

John Croy	2s
Peter Wyshaud	12d
Walter Jelemay	13d
Walter Saltere	12d
William Pysleye	2s
Walter Reyner	12d
Ralph Turnour	2s
Walter Scott	12d
Thomas Coleman	12d
Robert Frend	10d
Ralph de Gretton	8d
John Leggare	6d
Henry Keys	2s 6d
Agnes Winter	6d
John Benne	12d
Anketil (*Anketild*) [*sic*]	12d
Edith Sturdy	12d
Richard Blebury	8d

Total of the twentieth of Winchcombe, £4 10s

Subtaxers (*Subtaxatores*)

19

Henry atte Celer	12d
John Maltman	12d
Thomas Carpenter	12d

Total, 3s

Approved. Total of the twentieth of Winchcombe with the subtaxers' taxes, £4 13s

Minety (*Villata de Mynty*)

20

John Sewyne	3s 7d
Philip Hamound	18d
John Inthehale	4s 1½d
Richard Asser	18½d
Is. Beusire	3s 8½d
Henry Gilbert	18½d
Thomas Smalhebbe	2s 2d
Adam Fraunceys	3s 8d
Adam Bruthre	3s 9d
John le Smyth	14d
John Palmer	13¾d
Robert Knyt	2s 9d
Adam Hering	17½d
Walter Hurde	2s 2d
William Inthehale	2s 2¾d
John Gurnay	17d
John Russel	18d
Roger Cele	23d
John atte Steorte	2s 4d
Julian Myle	17d
Henry Hurde	18d
Thomas Machen	13¼d
Matilda Daunteseye	16¾d

Adam Gilbert	11¼d
John Asser	15¼d

Total of the twentieth of Minety, 51s 3½d

Subtaxers (*Subtaxatores*)

21

John Bisshop	12d
Simon Sterte	12d
Thomas Neuman	12d
John Shyrwold	12d

Total, 4s

Approved. Total of the twentieth of Minety with the subtaxers' taxes, 55s 3½d

Rodley (*Villata de Rodleye*)

22

Richard, son of Richard de Heydon	10s
Simon Mey	2s
Roger Holte	2s
John Tuyles	6d
Richard Storye	12d
Benedict Vounar	6d
Isabel Mody	12d
Ellen Holkeleye	10s
Adam Gnat	6d
John Abbehale	12d
William Vyel	2s
Alice Fylote	12d
Adam Bert'e	6d
Roger Hirdeman	2s
Richard Berde	8d
Robert de Chaxhulle	6d
Henry ʒonge	12. . .
Thomas Blount	. . .
Henry Holkeleye	12d
Thomas Bonde	6d
John Heydon	. . .
William Beneg	. . .
William atte Pirie	. . .
Henry de Rodleye	. . .
John de Polton	. . .
Henry Whinikel	. . .
Robert Kege	. . .
Richard de la . . .	. . .
Hugh Danyell	. . .
Thomas Hok	. . .
Nicholas Shephurde	. . .
Walter de Cly. . .	. . .
Petronilla Cole	. . .
John atte Grene	. . .
Alexander Basse	12. . .
Maurice Martyn	6d
Richard de Wyke	. . .
Ellen atte . . .	. . .

John Kyng	. . .
Cecil C. . .	. . .
Ellen B. . .	. . .
Thomas W. . .	7d
Henry . . .	. . .
Richard . . .	. . .

[Membrane 3]

Also Rodley

John de Wyke	2s
John atte Grene	12d
Richard Billyng	11s
William, son of the Smith (*Fabro*)	7s 11¾d

Approved. Total of the twentieth of Rodley, 100s 3¼d

Newnham (*Newenham*)

23

John de Sully	2s
John le Deyare	2s
Andrew le White	6d
Richard de Rodleye	12d
John de Nethlonge	2s
Robert le Smith	6d
Richard de Munstreworth	2s
Agnes la Longe	6d
John atte Home	12d
William Peit	6d
Andrew Peit	12d
William de Gloucestr	6d
John de Overelonge	12d
Ralph de Mewode	18d
John Culvard	6d
William atte Walle	9d
Adam Peit	6d
William de Hokkeleye	2s
Joseph Peit	6d

Approved. Total, 20s 3d

Minsterworth (*Munstreworth*)

24

John le Barber	9s
Roger de Munstreworth	5s
Geoffrey de Mersshton	5s
William de Dene	12d
John Ernald	8s
William Everard	12d
Thomas Noble	14s
Henry Constable	2s
Henry Patrik	2s
John Peytevin	6s
William Houwe	12d
Henry Astmare	12d
John le Knyth	6s
William Inthefelde	12d

Gilbert Morice	12d
William le Peintur	2s
Roger Kenelok	3s
John de Mattesdon	12d
Petronilla Perys	6d
Walter Inthefelde	2s
William Shepherde	2s
John de la Felde	12d
Richard Newemon	2s
Alice de Morcote	2s
Amice Aylmound	2s

Approved. Total £4 6d

Subtaxers (*Subtaxatores*)

25

John le Mareschal	12d
John de Boyfelde	12d

Total, 2s

Approved. Total of the aforesaid [three] vills with the subtaxers' taxes, £10 3s 0¼d

Dymock (*Villata de Dymmok*)

26

William de Penebrugge	8s
John Deverois	3s 4d
Richard Chaundois	2s 6d
Alice Habbegod	10s 6d
Thomas de Hewe	12d
Isabel Woole	8s 6d
William Elene	6d
Joan Algar	3s
Henry atte Mulle	18d
Sybil Hunfrey	13d
Edmund de Boys	3s 0½d
Henry Spileman	10½d
John Baldewyne	18d
William de la Hulle	2s 6¼d
Robert de Craswalle	18½d
Walter atte Burstude	. . .
Jordan atte Walle	18d
William Coteeverard	2s
Richard atte Rok	8d
Margery Glof	16d
Henry Netherton	17d
Henry le Duyr	15d
Roger Notherton	16d
Roger Spileman	18d
Richard Stinte	12d
Robert Parcar	6d
Walter atte Brugg	12d
William le Blake	17d
Matilda Wodenot	14d
Adam le Riche	12d
John Carpenter	8d
John Crouwe	2s
Robert Byke	21d
Henry . . .h. . .ulle	16d
. . . Wyngate	15d
. . . . . .	2s 6d
. . . . . .	15d
. . . . . .	10d
. . . . . .	2s
. . . . . .	12d
. . . . . .	21½d
. . . . . .	6s 2d
. . . . . .	15½d
. . . Wymond	22½d
. . . . . . yn . . .	. . .
. . . atte . . .	12d
. . . . . .el	21½d
. . . Not	16d
John . . . Mare	2s
Richard Dryu	9½d

[Membrane 3 r-h col.]

Also Dymock

Agnes Klynton	2s 1d
Robert Huntele	2s
John de la Putte	12d
William Palmer	9d
John de la Lynde	14¼d
Walter atte Snede	12d
Walter Agar	15d
Isabel Serich	3s
Henry Haket	7s
Walter atte Brodeyate	6s
Walter Smith (*Fabro*)	7s 1d

Total, £6 13s 8½d

Subtaxers (*Subtaxatores*)

27

John de Wylyton	12d
William Marmioun	12d

[Total, 2s[6]]

Approved. Total of the aforesaid vill with the subtaxers' taxes, £6 15s 8½d

St Briavels and Hewelsfield (*Villata de Sancto Briavello et Huwaldesfeld*)

28

William Hathewy	3s
Osbert Malemort	3s 7¾d
John Malemort	2s 11¼d
Thomas, widow of Richard Malemort	18½d
William, son of Ralph Hathewy	2s 1½d
Gilbert Botte	12½d
Walter Whitheud	3s 0½d
Walter Aleyn	20d
John Phelip	18d
William Frenssh	12½d
John Whyte	12d
Adam Whyte	12d
John Thanar	18d
Philip Ivor	21d
William Bol	19¼d
Walter Dangervill	18d
John Aleyn	2s
Llewelyn (*Leulino*) Hombrid	16d
John atte Lude	18d
Philip Selewode	2s
Robert Muleward	2s
William Locar	2s

Approved. Total, 40s 8¾d

Newland (*Hamelett de Nova Terra*)

29

Philip Joce	3s 0¼d
John de Wysham	6s 6½d
Hywel (*Howelo*) ap Howel	2s
William Brut	13¾d
Roger Ely	18d
Walter Gay	2s 9¼d
Richard Axtel	18d
John Yawan	10d
Richard Robard	12d
Robert Michel	9d
Walter, son of Hugh	18d
William Barrich	2s 6d
John Rolf	2s 7¼d
Payn de Norton	2s
Nigel Hathewy	12d

Total, 30s 8d

Subtaxers (*Subtaxatores*)

30

Geoffrey Shater	12d
John Draylaȝ	12d
John Coluerham	12d

[Total, 3s][7]

Approved. Total of the whole aforesaid vills with the subtaxers' taxes, 74s 4¾d

BARTON BY BRISTOL
(*BERTON JUXTA BRISTOLL*)

Mangotsfield (*Villata de Mangotesfeld*)

31

Robert Batyns	3s 4d
John atte Forde	18d
Thomas Dasshel	10d
Robert Dasshel	10½d
John atte Walles	10d
Roger atte Clyve	14d
John in la More	2s
John atte Staple	6½d
Roger Bromleye	9½d
Stephen Wiring	11½d
John atte Forde	12d
Thomas atte Lupeet	8d
John Morette	20d
William atte Staple	7d
John atte Staple	6½d
. . . . . .	10d
William P. . .	6d
William Hey	21¾d
Walter atte Welle	20d
William atte Brok	18d
Roger atte Halle	6½d
John Othelam	3s 0½d
Roger Beselyn	6½d
Philip Selman	2s
Richard atte Welle	14d
Roger atte Mulle	3s
Robert atte Clyve	11d
Henry atte Berwe	6½d
Robert Jordan	16½d
Robert Asselin	13d
John Underhulle	2s
John Iryssh	7d
Alice la Blount	3s 4d
Thomas in the More	2s 6d

Approved. Total, 46s 2¾d

Stapleton (*Villata de Stapelton*)

32

William Staunsted	. . ½d
Peter le Rede	10d
John de De. . .	6½d
Philip . . . Beche	. . .
Philip Duraunt	. . .
John B. . .	. . .
Richard Rede	3s 0¼d
John Bo. . .	3s
Thomas A. . .	. . .
Walter Sr. . .	6d
Robert Heved	13½d

[Membrane 3 dorse]

Also Stapleton

William Colur	12½d
John Clerk	12d
Henry Peres	2s
Roger Mous	6½d
Gilbert Wilde	18d
Adam Goshelin	12½d
Henry Seymor	6½d
John Sleye	12½d
Benedict Burton	18d
John Huwet	6½d
Stephen Lange	6½d
William Coppedethorn	13d
Master of St Bartholomew's House	3s 4d
William Stevenes	12d
Julian Gore	10d

Approved. Total, 32s 3½d

Easton (*Villata de Eston*)

33

Peter Jeyard	13d
Adam Wyring	14½d
John Gos	6¾d
John Estmust	6½d
Robert Frinch	6½d
Robert Cauer	6½d
Roger Pouke	7d
Clement Chaunflour	13d
Robert Hamond	13d
Thomas atte Nasshe	13½d
William Palefray	8d
Robert Brid	7d
Roger Donnyng	10d
Richard North	7d
Stephen Crisp	16d
Thomas Fynch	6½d

Geoffrey Cory	23d
William Dodde	6½d
Alan North	2s
Robert Poo	2s
Robert Rogers	20d
Robert atte Ston	12d
Peter Mey	6½d
William Laurence	13d
John Wyring	2s
John Dru	3s 2½d
John Turtle	2s
Richard Tilly	6s
Master of St Lawrence's House	5s

Approved. Total, 41s 10¼d

Clifton (*Villata de Clyfton*)

34

John de St Lo	10s
Nicholas Passour	6½d
Reginald Hayward (*Messer*)	8d
Stephen Shepherde	6½d
John Underhull	9d
Nicholas Ken	20½d
William atte Clyve	6½d
William Honypyn	5s

Approved. Total, 19s 9d

Total of the whole aforesaid Barton, £7 1½d

Subtaxers (*Subtaxatores*)

35

John de Oldebury	12d
Ellis de Oldebury	12d

[Total, 2s][8]

Approved. Total of the whole aforesaid Barton with the subtaxers' taxes, £7 2s 1½d

BARTON BY GLOUCESTER
(*BERTON JUXTA GLOUC.*)

Barton Street (*Bertonestret*)

36

Cecily Mayel	2s 8d
William Baumot	6d
John Riueray	8d

Approved. Total, 3s 10d

Harescombe[9] (*Harsecoumbe*)

37

William atte Hulle	13d
John Organ	13¼d
Agnes de Munstreworth	6d
Robert Rendulph	10d

Approved. Total, 3s 6¼d

Twigworth (*Twyggeworth*)

38

William Letherhose	7d
John atte Elme	7d
William Jones	12½d
William Thedolph	6d

Approved. Total, 3s 2½d

Kingsholm (*Kyngeshome*)

39

John Daubeneye	6s 6½d
Hugh Megre	12d
John atte Wynyard	6d

Approved. Total, 8s 0½d

Upton St Leonards[10] (*Upton*)

40

Thomas de Berkeleye	4s 0¼d
Gilbert le Ruys	2s
William Eweny	14½d
John Wych	18d
Walter Pope	12d
William Swyngar	13¼d
Nicholas Organ	6d

Robert . . .	17d
John . . .	9d

Approved. Total 13s 6d

Pitchcombe (*Pychsecombe*)

41

Robert Maundeville	6s 0¼d
William Dru	18d
Robert Lord	6d
Agnes Hamond	6d

Approved. Total, 8s 6¼d

[Membrane 3 dorse r-h col.]

Wotton[11] (*Wottone*)

42

Nicholas Peticlerk	21¼d
Alice Peris	6d
Walter le Welar	2s

Approved. Total, 4s 3¼d

Matson (*Mattesden*)

43

Isabel de Mattesden	6d
William Dikkeleye	2s
Ralph Whitbred	21d

Approved. Total, 4s 3d

Longford[12] (*Longeford*)

44

Walter Engel	12½d
John Bonde	6¾d

Approved. Total, 19¼d

Sandhurst[13] (*Sandhurst*)

45

Walter Kek	2s 0¼d
Henry atte Cherche	2s 2½d

John de Ruyssheleye	7¼d
Richard de Apperlegh	2s 5¾d
Thomas atte Chirche	8d
Henry Hore	6d
Thomas atten Elme	15d

Approved. Total, 9s 8¾d

Up Hatherley (*Uphatherleye*)

46

Robert de Prestebury	4s
Thomas de Hatherleye	12¼d
Henry Ermyte	6d

Approved. Total, 5s 6¼d

Woolstrop (*Wolvesthrop*)

47

William Walssh	5s 8½d
Richard Heghnes	13d

Approved. Total, 6s 9½d

Bruern (*Brewarne*)

48

John le Botiller	2s

Approved. Total, 2s

Total of the whole aforesaid Barton, 74s 9½d

Subtaxers (*Subtaxatores*)

49

Walter le Clerk de Church	12d
William Pope	12d

[Total, 2s][14]

Approved. Total of the whole aforesaid Barton with the subtaxers' taxes, 76s 9½d

ANCIENT DEMESNE IN CHELTENHAM HUNDRED
(*HUNDREDUM DE CHELTENHAM*)

Cheltenham (*Villata de Cheltenham*)

50

John de Whitewell	2s
Henry Lilie	14¾d
Thomas Cockes	2s 10d
John de Stoke	9d
Ralph Dyeare	3s 5¾d
Walter Selawe	15d
Hubert le Mareschal	6d
Richard le Dyeare (*Wheelar*[15])	18d
Walter de Elebrugge	6d
Joan de Neweton	12d
Nicholas le Mulleward	12d
Thomas Roluepe	12¾d
William le Newe	2s
Simon Baude	18d
John Wery	2s
Walter Dyear	20¾d
Walter Peres	3s
William Gamull	12d
William Shalewere	2s
Walter Wemely	3s 1¼d
Margery Cockes	15d
John Stub	12d
William Pouwer	4s 1¼d
John Olive	2s 6d
Nicholas Goldewyne	2s
William le Newe	12d
Margery de Upton	2s 6¼d
Thomas Hendeman	18d
Matilda Heringmongere	2s 0½d
Christine atte Grene	2s
Simon Serle	2s 6¼d
John Gode	6d
J. . . . . .e	6d
Simon Gille	2s
John Lone	5s 6d
Thomas Hawethorn	6d
Thomas Maiel	12d
Thomas Kempe	6d
William Maiel	2s 0¼d
John Dunskin	3s

Approved. Total, 71s[16] 4¾d

Westal (*Westhale*)

51

William de Graundon	5s
Richard le Yonge	3s
John Withie	12d
Walter le Hale	3s 3d
Thomas atte Mull	3s
John Stoute	2s
Henry Levyar	12d
Robert de Bradestok	2s 7¼d
Walter Crisp	18d
John Coppinger	. . . 6d
Thomas le Boste	. . .
Hugh Chaplain (*Capellano*)	. . .
Thomas Gedma	. . .
John Colverhous	. . .

Approved. Total, 42s 0¼d

Arle (*Alre*)

52

Thomas . . .un	. . .
John, son of Robert . . .	. . .
Robert Heort	. . .
John Dore	. . .
Reginald B. . .he	. . .
Thomas Heort	. . .
Reginald B. . .l. . .r. . .	. . .
. . . Monek	3s
. . . . . .dulph	9d
Thomas Pruke	2s . . .

Approved. Total, 24s 1¼d

[Membrane 4]

Alstone (*Alveston*)

53

John le Hunte	2s 6d
Richard de Nasse	3s 2d
John Stuk	2s
John de Aure	18d
John Ball'	3s
Joan de Northeye	5s 1¼d
John Dawe	3s
Richard Persoun	6d
Thomas atte Stile	6d
John le Wydewe [sic]	5s 0¼d
John le Ray	2s
Thomas Hard	3s 7d
William de Barkeston	12d
John Dyeare	12d

Approved. Total, 33s 10½d

Charlton Kings with Ham and Northfield (*Cherleton cum Home & Northfeld*)

54

John Houwes	2s 6d
William Bele	2s
John de Fortheye	5s 9d
Thomas Baret	2s
Matilda atte Mulle	18d
Hugh Inthehale	3s
Robert atte Oke	2s 7¼d
Julian Marten	12d
Walter Alisaundr	2s
Thomas atte Well	6d
Margery Thopas	2s 3d
Richard de Northfelde	3s 0¾d
John Gater	2s
William Colverhous	2s 6d
John le Rok	12d
Joan de Netfeld	8s 9d
Walter Bravel	2s 8d
John Bele	2s
John Whithorne	2s 3d
John le More	3s 6d
John Rose	18d
Thomas le Yonge	6d
John le White	5s 4¼d
Hugh Reynalde	12d
William Hawthorn	21d
John Haiel	4s 3¾d
Thomas Mussegros	2s 6d
John Calebus	3s 2d
Isabel Hawethorn	2s
Reginald Knyt	6d
William Bullok	12d
William Fraunceys	3s 0¼d
Thomas Wateman	16d
Walter Thedulph	12d
Robert de Goldewell	6d
Hugh Hathewy	2s 2d
Thomas de Northfeld	21d
Lucy atte Nouerhouse	2s 7d
Richard Blockehun	18d
John Hathewy	6d
Edith Godrich	3s 6d
Thomas Coppinger	2s
John Hathemere	2s
Hugh le Hore	9d

[Total, £4 19s 0¼d][17]

Total of ancient demesne in the whole hundred [blank]

Subtaxers (*Subtaxatores*)

55

John de Alre	12d
Walter Sturmy	12d
Simon le Forester	2s

[Total, 4s][18]

Total of all the ancient demesne vills in Cheltenham Hundred, £13 15s 5d

Overall total of the twentieth granted to the lord king of all the [taxation] boroughs and ancient demesne in the County of Gloucester, £174 16s 8d. Proved (*pb*).

[Membrane 4 r-h col. and dorse blank]

[PART TWO]

Gloucestershire

(*GLOUCESTR.*)

The taxation of a twentieth granted to the lord king from the laity in the County of Gloucester, except from the [taxation] boroughs and the lord king's ancient demesne, made by William Tracy and Robert de Aston in the first year of the reign of King Edward, the Third after the Conquest.

[Membrane 5]

CROWTHORNE HUNDRED
(*HUNDREDUM DE CROUTHORN*)

Wiggold (*Wyggewold Hamelett*)

56

Roger Normaund	4s 7d
Richard atte Churcheye	4s 9d
Walter Wyssh	16d
William Intheden	2s 6d
Alice Gibbes	23d
Emma Gerald	20d
William Bole	14d

Approved. Total, 17s 11d

Baunton (*Vill. de Baudynton*)

57

Reginald Broun	2s 7d
Ralph Whyteye	11½d
Richard le Chapman	2s
John de Weston	2s 1d
Thomas Shirwold	8½d
John Bayn	13d
Alice Burgeys	3s 4d
Matilda Broun	10d
Adam le Shepherde	2s 2d

Approved. Total, 15s 9d

Ampney Crucis (*Upameneye Vill.*)

58

Henry Picher	21d
Walter Damalde	2s 4d
Alice la Bailif	12½d
Walter Broun	11d
Alex. Smyth	16d
William Ryndecombes	12d
Simon Camel	13d
Nicholas Porter (*Infra Portam*)	12d
John Onwyne	23d
Walter le Knyt	19d
Henry Palmere	13d
John Mullare	6s 0¾d
Ralph Bovetoun	2s 1d
Simon Taillor	22d
William Damalde	9s 4d
Henry le May	2s
Agnes Graunger	10d
Richard Coliare	3s 2d
Thomas Bodyn	4s 10d
William le May	21d
William Godkane	7s 6½d
Adam Stoby	6s 6½d
Christine Aunger	16d
Thomas Dodecote	12d
Geoffrey Mullar	4s 9d
Walter Smart	10d
Richard Taillour	10¼d
William Aunger	9½d
John Waltres	7d
William Brentemersh	10d
Nicholas Huldecote	12d
Simon de Honibourn	22d
Thomas Cole	16d
Philip de Weston	6s 8¼d
Thomas atte Fortheie	13d
William Stoby	13d
Robert Coppynger	13d
Richard le Rouge	13d
Alice Rogers	9d
Geoffrey atte Style	11s 9¼d
Richard Wydie	3s 8d
John de Clifton	2s
Thomas le Valk	12½d
John Avebury	10d
William Bovetoun	10d
William George	2s 4d
John Lovekyn	11d
Henry le Smyth	7d
Geoffrey Cockel	3s 2d
John Rycheman	10¼d
William Bedyn	12d
Adam Rouge	16½d
Simon Ymston	11½d
Walter Childeyene	14s 10d
William atte More	11d
William Damargary	12d
Robert le Palmere	20d
John Cavel	10d
Margaret atte Hall	2s 3¼d
Simon Pyk	6s 8d

Approved. Total, £7 7s 6d

Down Ampney with The Wick (*Vill. de Dounameneye cum Wyk membr.*)

59

Francis de Ameneye	16d
William Heved	3s
Agnes Brice	2s

[Membrane 5 r-h col.]

Alice de Joydon	12½d
William Nony	2s 1½d
Walter Norrey	11d
John Deope	4s 4d
Adam Bray	6s 5d
Alice Serjaunt	3s 2¼d
John Hughe	2s 3d
Isabel de Shirebourn	23d
John le Walshe	3s 7d
Richard Fraunkeleyn	12d
Adam Jones	21d
Henry de Ameneye	6s 7d
Matilda Richoun	3s 3d
Christine Mottyng	12d
Walter le Bonde	16d
Simon Paradys	17d
Christine Rogers	9½d
Richard Hughe	13d
William Paradys	18d
William Show	4s 3d
Robert Catuline	4s 9d
Ralph atte Wyke	4s 10¾d
Margaret de Valers	15s 3¼d
William Rouge	16d
William Fouke	13d

Approved. Total, £4 3s 4¾d

Meysey Hampton (*Villata de Hampton Meysy*)

60

John le Wylde	22d
Henry Burgeis	6s 2d
Roger Stobhorn	16d
John Reybald	12d
William Wilde	18d
Everard Durable	3s 4d
John Deyville	19d
Joan de la Rede	9d
William le Knyt	6s 10d
John le Freman	2s 5d
John Crompe	19d
Robert Fraunkelein	16d
Henry Sevare	7d
Adam le Masoun	13d
Nicholas Hickes	8d
Nicholas Palude	19d
Hugh Travayl	19d

Thomas de St Maur (*Sancto Mauro*)	8s 2d
Hildebrand de London	10s 10d

Approved. Total, 54s 2d

South Cerney with Cerney Wick (*Villata de Southcerneye cum Wyk membr.*)

61

John Korm	2s 4d
Simon Watyn	9d
Simon Rolves	22d
John Chobbe	13d
Walter Walkare	10d
Henry Simond	2s
Miles Pope	2s 3d
Walter Belefraunk	15d
Henry le Couherde	13½d
Richard Mulleward	10d
William Kynny	21½d
Miles Corm	18d
John Straunge	2s 3d
Nicholas atte Mulle	13d
Simon Clement	18d
Simon le Bonekare	9d
Alice la Knyt	2s 10¼d
Simon Brawe	3s 9d
Felice Haleweston	2s 1d
John le Yonge	3s
Jordan Chapeleyn	3s
John Seward	2s 9d
Agnes Spake	20d
John de Sloughtr	4s 1½d
Robert Rangail	12½d
Nicholas de Stourton	2s 7d
William de Wokham	16d
John atte Pole	12d
William Lovekyn	12d
Richard Bruce	9d
Richard le Neweman	3s 1d
Richard le Bohun	3s
Ralph Godenere	11d
Thomas Shaveryl	10¼d
John Bacoun	15d
Matilda la Palmere	3s 2d
William Leche	14d
John Walkare	17¼d
Thomas Randulph	12d
Simon Heved	13d
Simon White	4s 1d

[Membrane 5 dorse]

Also South Cerney with Cerney Wick

Thomas Croppelon	3s 5d
Edmund Herteshorn	18½d
Agnes Lorkyn	9d
Richard Thedrich	10d
Henry Hikedys	3s 1d
John Haleweston	13d
John de St Amand (*Sancto Amando*)	11s 8d
William Bithewatere	6s 9½d
Richard Nitherhard	5s 4¼d
Simon Almrich	3s 1d
Thomas Spake	16d
Richard Inthehale	12d
John atte Weole	12d
Robert Pyk	3s
Simon le Frere	12d

Approved. Total, £6 1d

Driffield with Harnhill (*Villata de Driffeld cum Harnhull Hamelet*)

62

Alice Fereis	12d
John Asselon	17d
William Wattes	7s 2¾d
John Pleiare	4s 1d
Thomas Wattes	16d
Richard Taloun	12½d
William Bonde	14d
Robert Brayn	2s 2d
Robert Lode	2s 2d
Robert Pynchoun	15d
John Lomb	3s 5d
Thomas Colkote	4s 6d
Walter Reynald	14d
Henry Drip	5s
Nicholas Duyk	2s 3d
Richard atte Hide	20d
Richard Guyting	12d
John Brayn	16d
John Kent	2s 2d
John Bon	2s 3d
Walter Croppelone	3s 2d
John Sawiare	14d
Robert Spakeman	16d
Agnes Lassh	15d
Henry de Harnhull	8s 0¾d
William le Cok	5s

Approved. Total, 67s 7d

Preston with Norcott (*Villata de Preston cum Northcot membr.*)

63

William Allod	12d
Walter Gagy	11d
Alice Nith	9d
Adam Ywayn	18d
Henry Aylward	12d
Walter Serjaunt	10d
Richard de Wygeput	20d
Thomas Ywayn	20d
Walter Pauncefot	2s
Walter Jurdan	18d
John Taillour	13d
Richard le Wyle	12d
Richard le Bray	2s 6d
Thomas Abbod	20d
Thomas Asselon	9½d
Thomas Mayde	12d
John le Kaa	15d
Cecily Mullare	4s 10d
John Bagely	15d
Roger le Mortimer	15d
Margery atte Grove	4s 5d
Richard le Valk	7s 4d

Approved. Total, 41s 2½d

Siddington with Chesterton (*Villata de Sothinton cum Chesterton membr.*)

64

Robert de Arderne	12½d
John Chamberleyn	15s 1d
Simon Inthemore	3s 4d
Robert atte Mulle	20d
Agnes Shepherde	10d
Nicholas Henries	3s 6d
William le Yonge	10s 11d
Stephen atte Well	2s 6d
John le Vorn	3s 6¼d
Lawrence Cerles	12d
Robert le Leche	16d
Alice Cok	11d
Alice Shirwold	2s 7d
Nicholas Skynnare	3s 10d
John Skarlet	6s 0¼d
Peter Taillour	6s 6d
John Duncecake	2s
Henry Miles	4s 6d
Robert Beldame	2s 6d
Robert Godulph	10d
William Bagge	9d
Robert de Levesham	12¼d
Henry Assmond	15½d
Joan Bicote	11d
Henry West	9d
Roger Rolves	5s 3d
Robert atte Putte	9d
Adam de Kemele	2s
John Rogers	9d
Robert atte Yate	14d
Earl of Kent (*Cantium*)	3s 4d

[Membrane 5 dorse r-h col.]

Also Siddington

Adam Gagy	19d
Ellis de Langeleye	3s 9d
Adam le Yonge	5s 7½d
Joan atte More	5s 7d
Robert Longe	9d
William Davy	5s

John Davy	19d
Roger de Ledecote	3s 5d

Approved. Total, 119s 7¼d

Coates and Tarlton, Trewsbury House and Hullasey House (*Villata de Cotes et Torlton, Trussebury et Hulaicide membr.*)

65

Walter Wilkynes	19¾d
Matilda de Lullebrok	8s 1½d
John Cokerel	4s 4d
John de Wysham	17d
Philip de Cotes	18d
Walter de Cirencestr	2s 1d
Thomas atte Yate	4s 8d
William de Trosbury	12d
John Reod	13d
Alice Doun	2s
Alice Walshe	14d
Walter Gonnyld	12d
Matilda Elemore	3s 9d
John Aldreman	12d
John Kaym	14d
Christine de Hunlaicyd	7s
John de Munden	6s
John de Colkerton	3s 1d
Richard Lacy	2s 1d
John Bovetoun	20d
Richard Kaym	18d
Alice Dykes	7s 6d
Nicholas de Haylegh	12d
Richard le Whight	16d
Walter Averay	18d
Simon Spekke	4s 4d
Julian la Wight	23d

Approved. Total, 74s 10¼d

Duntisbourne Rouse with Pinbury Park (*Villata [de] Dountesbourn Rous cum Pendebury membr.*)

66

John de Rous	2s 6d
Stephen Umfray	22d
John Springald	3s
Agnes Cole	12d
William Rede	14d
John Flemyng	18d
Richard Payn	17d
Richard Oldebury	15½d
William Shepherde	17d
Roger Pedwardyn	9s 6d
William de Oldebury	21d

Richard de Foxcote	3s 3½d
William Yver	18d
William de Cornwell	3s 4d
Reginald atte Besthrop	14d
Robert Webbe	10d
William atte Bury	19d
Reginald de Westbury	2s 3d
John Wodeward	11d
William Kebbel	17d
John atte Putte	12d
Thomas le Mulleward	2s 3½d
Edith Kyng	13d
Henry le Kyng	12d

Approved. Total, 48s 0½d

Bagendon (*Villata de Bagyndon*)

67

Richard de Baginden	3s 9d
Lucy de Bagynden	10s 5d
John Sprengeheose	21d
Walter Gybbes	15d
Adam Holle	16d
Simon atte More	19d
John Lollay	2s 2d

Approved. Total, 22s 3d

Stratton with Daglingworth (*Villata de Stratton cum Dagelyngworth membr.*)

68

Richard de Hompton	8s
Thomas Edmond	2s 8d
Robert atte Hall	10d
Richard atte Hall	4s 7d
John Ridare	2s 1d
Walter de Stratton	17d
John Marton	7s 10d
William atte Well	22½d
John de Celecombe	2s 9d
William de Mynty	18¼d
Christine Sprengheose	2s 1¼d
William de Cridwell	2s 2d
William Rogers	13d
Reginald Renheued	3s 8d

[Membrane 6]

Also Stratton etc. [*sic*]

William Warden (*Custos*)	14d
John atte Halle	15d
William de Pulham	18d

Thomas de Cotes	14d
Ralph Bluet	2s 4d
Adam Kynny	2s 4¼d
William Archebaud	4s 2d
Roger Somer	9s 4d
John Robyn	16d
Roger Kyry	12d
John Bonde	2s 7¾d
Godfrey Brugeman	11d
Robert de Hakebourn	9s 4d

Approved. Total, £4 13d

Duntisbourne Abbots (*Dontesbourn Abbatis*)

69

John Uppetoun	15d
Simon Chaplain (*Capellano*)	2s 4d
John Aylrich	22d
Walter Prat	8d
Julian Dauwes	8d
Thomas Rogers	10d
Robert Dauwes	13d

Total, 8s 8d

Total of the whole hundred, £45 2s 1¼d

Subtaxers (*Subtaxatores*)

70

Robert Barbast	12d
Walter de Campeden	12d
William de Campeden	12d
Simon le Fraunkeleyn	12d
Walter Bolefeu	12d
Geoffrey Aylwyne	12d
William de Netherton	12d
John Fraunkeleyn	12d

Total, 8s

Approved. Total of the whole hundred with subtaxers' taxes, £45 10s 1¼d

RAPSGATE HUNDRED
(*HUNDREDUM DE RESPEGATE*)

Chedworth (*Cheddeworth*)

71

William Beye	7s 8¾d
Alice Kynges	6s 0¾d
Thomas atte Style	4s 3¾d
Nicholas Lilie	22d
Thomas Edward	3s 3d
Richard atte Chambre	18¼d
Ralph le Large	7s
Robert le Northerne	2s 2¼d
Walter Mabbe	3s 7d
Robert Peornele	10¾d
Walter le Smyth	15¾d
Nicholas atte Hegge	14d
John Norreys	2s 6¼d
Geoffrey Perys	11¼d
William Cotecrofte	3s 3¼d
Henry Norreys	3s 9¼d
William atte Style	16¾d
John de Horsleye	4s 6¾d
Adam Peornele	23d
John Warde	18¾d
John atte Broke	19d
Walter Styward	10d
Nicholas Aleyn[19]	15¾d
Henry atte Broke	22d
Roger de Hodokenassh	2s 6½d
Thomas de Gochurche	17d
Richard atte Wode	3s 2¾d
Nor' de Boys	10d
Robert de Boys	2s 6¾d
Stephen Lendeby	2s 2d
John atte Forde	13d

Approved. Total, £4 2¼d

Rendcomb with members (*Ryndecombe cum membr.*)

72

Hugh Cole	2s 9d
Nor' Fickes	4s 1¼d
Henry Cole	15d
John Wymond	22¾d
William Symound	18d

[Membrane 6 r-h col.]

[Also][20] Rendcomb with members

Walter Sende	21d
Matilda de Wodemancot	5s
William Colines	2s 0¼d
John de la Mare	9s 8d
Robert Underhulle	2s 2¾d
Julian la Walkar	22d

Approved. Total, 34s

Woodmancote (*Wodemancot Hamelet*)

73

Julian Godman	6s 4d
Richard Page	2s
Henry de Hauleye	11¾d
Walter Yvor	2s 1d
John le Bonde	4s 11d
Adam le Bonde	2s 4d
William Hugin	10¾d
Thomas atte Hulle	2s 0¾d

Approved. Total, 21s 7¼d

Calmsden (*Calemundesden*)

74

Thomas Ragelan	2s 3¼d
Roger Mering	3s 6d
Thomas atte Welle	2s 3¼d
John atte Welle	10¾d
Walter Aunger	10¾d
Robert le Bonde	14d
Roger de Berleye	4s 6¾d
Henry Bovetoune	10¾d
William Graundoun	17¾d

Approved. Total, 17s 11¼d

North Cerney (*Northcerneye*)

75

John Adam	5s 1d
John Brounyng	2s 3¼d
Peter Godman	3s 3¼d
Henry Wattes	15¾d
Geoffrey Beel	13d
William le Gynnour	11d
Richard Ragelan	12¼d
Agnes Hubard	21¼d
John Herry	8d
Adam atte Watere	16d

Approved. Total, 18s 8¾d

Duntisbourne Leer (*Duntesbournelyre*)

76

John Shorweye	4s 6¾d
William de Irlaund	3s 2d
Henry Jones	14d
Walter Clarice	19d
Thomas Susanne	10d
Adam le Mareschal	2s 9d
Walter Emelot	15¾d
Philip atte Notebeme	3s 0¼d

Approved. Total, 18s 4¾d

Coberley (*Cobberleye*)

77

Thomas Jannes	2s 6¾d
Robert Jannes	4s 4¾d
William Jannes	16d
Thomas de Eldeffelde [*sic*]	4s 7¾d
Thomas Jones	21d
John Phelippes	9¼d
Richard Jones	17d
John Colynes	2s 0¾d
Thomas Muryval	19d
Sir Thomas de Berkeleye	10s 1d
Nicholas de Blockesham	19¾d
Robert Mody	9¾d

Approved. Total, 33s 0¾d

Cowley (*Couleye*)

78

Richard de Couleye	2s 4d
Robert le Couhirde	11¾d

Approved. Total, 3s 3¾d

Stockwell (*Stokwell*)

79

Matilda la Ȝongerobines	9¼d
Richard le Clerk	21d
Richard de Syde	2s 2d
William de Cocleforde	2s 10¼d

John Botevylein	8¾d
Robert Lyne	2s 9½d
John de Pegelesworth	19¾d
John Wishunger	8¾d

Approved. Total, 13s 5¼d

Elkstone (*Elkeston*)

80

John de Colne	2s 9d
Richard Warde	16¾d

[Membrane 6 dorse]

Also Elkstone

William Alayn	3s 9¼d
William Coppe	19¾d
Matilda Colines	11¼d
John Davy	21d
Sir John de Actone	6s 3¼d
John Joye	3s 5¾d
Sybil Persay	22¾d
John Weldwyne	2s 8d
William le Rede	18d
John Bernard	12¾d
William Alsy	2s 1d
Adam de Oldebury	13¾d

Approved. Total, 32s 4¼d

Syde (*Syde*)

81

Margaret Giffard	3s 4d
William atte Churcheye	12¼d
Henry atte Oke	18½d
John Jones	9¾d
Richard Waltres	2s 2¼d

Approved. Total, 8s 10¾d

Colesborne (*Collesbourne*)

82

John Beye	5s 10¼d
Philip Fraunkelein	2s 10¾d
John Torald	10¾d
John de Cobberleye	4s 3¼d
Thomas atte Combe	12¾d
William le Ȝonge	6s 9d
Matilda atte Coumbe	9¼d
Christine (*Cristene*) de Solers	15d
Simon Wyring	17d
Simon Wyring the elder	16¾d
Gilbert le Hore	22d
John le Boucher	22½d
Henry Sutor	16¾d

Approved. Total, 31s 8d

Brimpsfield (*Brymesfeld*)

83

Julian de Ruggeweye	3s
Reginald atte Hulle	2s 5¼d
Richard atte Castle	18d
Thomas de Caldewelle	19d
Walter Pope	13¼d
Thomas Holewow	2s
William le Bercare	6s

Approved. Total, 17s 7½d

Cranham (*Cranham*)

84

William Mallesone	9d
Orable [*sic*] le Hayward	13d
Henry Toly	8¼d
Ralph Batecok	11¼d
Thomas Batecok	19d
Henry de Stokwelle	13¾d
John atte Hasele	18¾d
Alice Perys	22½d
Henry atte Hulle	5s 6d
Nicholas Braderugge	3s 4d
Walter atte Crofte	2s 1d
Philip atte Crofte	12¾d
William Gosselyn	2s 0¾d
Walter atte Mulle	2s 7¼d

Approved. Total, 26s 4¼d

Total of the whole Hundred of Rapsgate, £17 17s 6¾d

Subtaxers (*Subtaxatores*)

85

John le Lohont	12d
William Solers	12d
Richard le Smith de Cranham	12d
John le Voy de Syde	12d
Thomas atte Orchard	12d
Robert Sopare	12d
Walter de Chalyngworth	12d

Total, 7s

Total of the whole hundred aforesaid with the subtaxers' taxes, £18 4s 6¾d

[Membrane 6 dorse r-h col.]

BRADLEY HUNDRED
(*HUNDREDUM DE BRADELEYE*)

Northleach Parish outside Borough[21] (*Northlecch Forinseca*)

86

William le Proute	11¼d
Henry de Wall	12s 0¼d
John Bouwan	17½d
Ralph atte Nelme	3s 10d
Agatha de Paunteleye	12¼d
Dyonis. de Wall	23¾d
Stephen de Gale	11¼d
William de Wall	13¾d
Richard Sprot	3s 10¾d
John de Borynton	2s
Robert de Rysindon	2s 6d
John de Lammar	3s 3d
Walter Coring	2s 6¼d
Julian Reynald	2s 3d
William le Reve	17d
Ralph Adam	12¾d
William le Rede	4s 8¼d
Henry le Swon	14d
Dennis atte Welle	11¾d
Henry Golding	5s
John de Culn	15¼d
Thomas Saundres	17¼d
Robert Upethehulle	3s 0½d
Adam le Graunger	13¾d
Richard Mayde	3s 10½d
Walter atte Nelme	21d

Approved. Total, 66s 7d

Northleach Borough[22] (*Norlecch*)

87

John le Tannare	3s 6d
William Blysse	18½d
Adam de Turbed	15d
John le Meneman	9½d
Richard Smith (*Fabro*)	12d
Henry le Webbe	2s 6¾d
Henry Staunedissh	12¼d
Robert de Brokthrop	14¼d
Adam Burnel	13d
William Lovering	6¾d
Robert Burnel	2s 11½d
John Alpays	4s 5¾d
Nicholas de Anneforde	11d
Henry Bovetoun	3s 1¾d
Thomas Baker (*Pistore*)	2s 10d
William Alpays	2s 9d
Richard le Porter	8½d
Ralph Drinkewater	12½d
Walter Lyune	7¼d
Reginald le Meneman	12d
William de Astone	15d
Richard Broun	3s 3¼d
John le Ponyter	22d

Approved. Total, 41s 3½d

Brockhampton with Sevenhampton (*Brohampton cum Seveshampton*)

88

Robert de Solers	3s 6d
John le Eyr	9¼d
John atte Welle	4s 1d
Henry le Palmere	14¾d
Robert Coplond	2s 7¼d
Geoffrey Colynes	13½d
Thomas Brid	2s 4d
Richard Lyplof	18½d
Robert de Hales	12¼d
Geoffrey de Wytwelle	20¼d
John Henryes	22d
Nicholas Fraunceys	21¾d
Agnes atte Welle	20d
Alice atte Shawe	11d
Robert le Hattare	8½d
Richard Davy	6½d
Robert Brid	15½d
William de Seveshampton	11½d
John Justice	7½d
Henry Reyner	7½d
John Reed	9s 4d

Approved. Total, 40s 2½d

Winson (*Wyneston*)

89

Alan Brounyng	3s 8½d
Richard Robynes	12¼d
John Houwes	18d
Henry le Seman	2s 3¾d
Edith atte Grove	17¾d
Walter Rolves	18½d
Robert Hamound	14½d
Roger de Solers	4s 2d
Henry Perys	23d
John Bernard	2s 6¼d
Roger le Gas	20½d

[Membrane 7]

Also Winson

Walter Wyllam	3s 3¾d
John le Kyng	2s 8½d
Henry Inthehurne	2s 11½d
John atte Grene	2s 2¼d
Isabel Prattes	10d
Felice de ʒaneworth	2s 5d

Approved. Total, 37s 6d

Coln Rogers (*Culn Rogerr*)

90

John Horsman	11½d
Richard atte Water	2s
Walter atte Nasshe	11¼d
John le Neuman	13¼d
Walter le Neuman	19¼d
Felic. Inthehale	23d
Matilda la Stompar	6½d
Julian Edward	16¼d
Robert Upthehulle	11d
Richard Upthehulle	2s 6d
William Golding	12½d
Thomas Athelone	12s 0¾d
Henry atte ʒate	2s 1½d
Walter atte ʒate	2s 1¾d[23]
Richard atte Mulle	2s 0½d
Thomas Chiliene	6½d

Approved. Total, 33s 9½d

Whittington (*Whytinton*)

91

William de Stanleye	6½d
John Copping	8½d
William Cutel	6d
Hugh Thomas	9¾d
Geoffrey Body	13½d
Richard Inthehale	11d
Henry atte Grene	13d
William le Chapman	18¾d
Adam Henries	9¼d
Dyonis. Inthehale	11d
John Cutel	12d
John Hugges	14¾d
Richard de Croupes	4s 2¼d

Approved. Total, 15s 5¼d

Yanworth (*Ʒaneworth*)

92

Matilda Cosines	2s 5d
Robert atte Mulle	16¾d
John Faukes	2s 7¼d
John Inthelon	2s 1½d
John Willames	21½d
Richard Robyles	22¼d
Walter le Chapman	2s 5d
John Steresiod	3s 6d
Thomas West	3s 8¼d
Adam le Reve	2s 8¼d
John Launeman	2s 10¼d
William atte Nassh	3s 7½d
John atte Style	2s 2¾d
Marg. atte Dene	2s 1¼d

Approved. Total, 35s 3¾d

Hazleton (*Haselton*)

93

John Mabely	17½d
Agnes Thommes	23¼d
Clement. atte Halle	22¾d
Henry le Neuman	12½d
Roger Brattram	15¼d
Henry le ʒonge	18¾d
William Harding	14¼d
Agnes atte Croyce	2s 1d
William Pecke	9¼d
Robert le Treuman	14d
Walter Inthelane	2s 2¼d
John Inthelane	16¼d

Approved. Total, 17s 11¼d

Withington (*Wydindon*)

94

John le Whyte	2s 6d
Henry de Chaddresleye	14¼d
John Osbarn	2s
John Capel	12½d
John le Neuman	6s 10¾d
Walter le Mulleward	16d
William Upthehulle	17½d
Stephen Inthehale	2s 5d
Richard Upthehulle	6½d
John le Neuman the younger	2s 4d
William Morbel	19¾d
Walter Ivor	2s 4d
Henry le Holdar	16d
John Beʒondethetoun	14½d
John Russel	4s 8¾d
John atte Stable	10½d

Approved. Total, 33s 9d

Owdeswell (*Oldswell*)

95

Prior de Stodleye	5s 9d
William de Culne	19d

[Membrane 7 r-h col.]

Also Owdeswell

Walter atte Brugg	8½d
John de la Mare	6s 0¼d
Silvester de Huldicote	15¾d
John le Bercare	15¾d
Thomas Cole	3s 4¼d
Thomas de Foxcote	3s 11¾d
Sybil Gerard	4s 3d
John atte Welle	13½d
John Crossum	6s 6½d
William de Thornden	17d
Gunilda de Thornden	19½d
Christine de Upcote	3s 0¼d

Approved. Total, 42s

Dowdeswell (*Doudeswell*)

96

Henry de Cheddeworth	20d[24]
Thomas de Doudeswell	4s 2¾d
Ralph Lambard	3s 4¼d
Matilda de Doudeswelle	3s 0½d
Richard le Wodeward	6½d
Henry le Swon	14¼d
John le Persones	12d
Thomas Chaplain (*Capellano*)	20d
Robert Underhulle	20½d
Alice Lambart	6d
Thomas de Aumondesham	4s 0½d
John Heved	2s 5d
Richard le Bercare	22¾d
Richard de Annesforde	18d
Nicholas de Annesforde	10d
Robert Dreu	21¾d
William de Nategrave	2s 2¼d
John Cogge	11½d
Thomas Cedde	13½d
Hugh Dreu	20½d
William de Rosteleie	5s 3¼d

Approved. Total, 42s 7¾d

Shipton with Hampen (*Shipton cum Hannepenne*)

97

Henry le Lucy	3s 7d
Richard Bilech	3s 3¾d
Henry atte Mede	3s 11d
Luc. Upthehulle	5s 7¼d
Henry Waryn	14d
Robert atte Watere	4s 11d
Roger le Bercare	4s 11d
John de Shipton	2s 3¾d
Henry Heved	13¼d
Geoffrey le Kniʒt	9½d
Robert de Solers	5s 6¼d

Approved. Total, 37s 1¾d

Aston Blank (*Aston*)

98

Henry le Reve	3s 4d
John Hachet	2s 0¾d
Alice Hachet	4s 3d
William Abraham	18¼d
John Upthehulle	3s 9d
Nicholas Jannes	14d
Robert Passe	6d
John Dauwes	18¼d
Ralph le Hauekare	16d
John Denwy	2s
Adam le Reve	2s 2d
Walter Dauwes	7d
Robert Hasard	12d
Robert le Husschet	12s 0½d
William Denwy	3s 4½d
Sybil Wattes	2s 0¾d
Walter Clerk (*Clerico*)	10d
John Chyriel	12¾d

Approved. Total, 44s 6¾d

Notgrove (*Nategrave*)

99

John de Annesforde	2s 10¾d
Henry Colyn	12d
Alice Gerard	3s 0¼d
Thomas Bocke	8½d
John Alice	2s 0½d
Ralph le Reve	4s 6d
Adam le Hauekare	17d
William le Hauekare	2s 0¼d
Richard Roger	2s 0¾d
Henry Mayew	16¼d
Robert de Solers	2s 4d
Richard Wydeʒate	15½d
William Saundres	12¼d
Ellis de Hickumbe	3s 1d
Walter de Wydecote	2s 2½d
Alice Traves	2s
John Jannes	4s 0½d
Walter de [*sic*] Hauekare	8¼d
William atte Welle	19¼d
Joan de Rodberwe	4s 0¼d

Approved. Total, 43s 3¾d

Turkdean[25] (*Thorkeden Superior*)

100

William Tosseley	4s 6d
John de Palton	4s 10d

[Membrane 7 dorse]

Also Turkdean

Luc. in [the] Corner (*Angulo*)	2s 3¼d
William le Palmere	8¾d
Agnes atte Benche	3s 7½d
William Brounyg	20½d
William le Hunge	4s
Richard le Cartere	3s 1¼d
Thomas Belon	21½d
Nicholas Brounyg	2s
Robert Davy	2s
John atte Welle	5s
Richard de Foxcote	4s 3¾d
Roger de Palton	3s
William Upthehulle	3s 0¾d
Roger de Dene	15½d
Roger le Fader	20d

Approved. Total, 48s 10¾d

Salperton (*Salperton*)

101

William Andreu	3s 4½d
Stephen Benet	2s 4¾d
William Malle	3s
Stephen de Salperton	5s 0¾d
Alice Jannes	2s 8½d
Walter Dammarie	8d
William Beleye	3s 10d
Henry Benet	2s 2d
Henry de Well (*Fonte*)	2s 2d
William le Bercar	2s 3d

Approved. Total, 27s 7½d

Turkdean[26] (*Thurkeden Inferior*)

102

Adam atte Clive	4s
Thomas atte Clive	4s 6d
Henry Jones	4s 0¼d
Thomas Damalisaundr	7s 1d
William Payn	2s
Joan Brounyg[27]	21d
John le Cok	3s 6¾d

Approved. Total, 26s 11d

Hampnett (*Hamptonet*)

103

Christine de Hamptonet	5s
Henry Clerebaud	6s 0¼d
John Foreward	3s
John le Mulleward	3s 5d
Robert atte Halle	19d
John Woderove	12½d
John atte Hulle	12½d
John atte Watere	7d
William atte Fortheye	7d
John atte Hasele	13¾d

Approved. Total, 23s 5d

Compton Abdale (*Magna Compton*)

104

Sybil Roberdes	2s
John le Cartere	2s 3¾d
Richard Mabely	3s 0¾d
Ralph Mabely	3s 1¾d
William le Whyte	3s 3¼d
Richard Pecke	15d
Geoffrey le Sclattar	14d
John Pole	20d
Henry Roger	16½d
John Partrich	2s 0½d
Geoffrey Adam	17¾d
John Jakeman	10½d
John Geffreys	23d
Nicholas Hod	2s 3¼d
William Sare	2s 0½d

Approved. Total, 29s 10d

Upper Coberley (*Parva Cobberleye*)

105

Philip le Heyward	20d
Henry atte Slade	2s 0¾d
John Abraham	6½d
Roger le Sedare	12½d

Approved. Total, 5s 3¼d

Farmington (*Thermarton*)

106

Thomas Anetheward	15¾d
John Aylwy	15½d
John Godman	12d
William Selewy	15d
Thomas Robad	9d
Geoffrey Levering	17d
Richard le Whyte	21½d
William de Peynton	7d[28]
Thomas Robat	16½d
John Pachet	5s
John de St Philibert (*Sancto Philiberto*)	5s 3¾d
John le Cok	12d
Julian Henr	18d
Walter de Paunteleye	18d

[Membrane 7 dorse r-h col.]

Also Farmington

Thomas le Botyler	14d
Thomas Wattes	8¼d
William Janykenes	16d
Simon Janykenes	12½d
Alice Gregori	2s 1¾d
Henry le Botyler	13d
William le Roo	11½d
Thomas Balle	11½d
Walter le Roo	13¼d
William Damenie	7½d
Constance la Mareschal	13½d
John Hobekines	14d
William atte Nelme	22d
Ralph Lovering	17d
Richard le Bercare	20d
Richard le Hayward (*Messer*)	23¾d

Approved. Total, 45s 5½d

Stowell (*Stouwell*)

107

William le Eyr	10¼d
Simon Willames	23½d
Alice la Fox	15½d
Robert le Bercare	15¼d
John de Stonwell	10s
John le Stagges	19½d
William atte Ʒate	8½d

Approved. Total, 17s 8½d

Total of the whole hundred aforesaid, £37 16s 7¾d

Subtaxers (*Subtaxatores*)

108

Robert de Upcote	12d
John de Paunteleye	12d
John de Fyffide	12d
John de Bannebury	6d
Richard atte Halle de Haselton	12d
John de Walleye	6d
Nicholas de Compton	6d
Philip de Gothurste	6d
Roger le Reve de Compton	12d
Robert Ondeby	6d

Total, 7s 6d

Total of the whole hundred aforesaid with the subtaxers' taxes, £38 4s 1¾d

BRIGHTWELLS BARROW HUNDRED
(*HUNDREDUM DE BRICHTWOLDESBERWE*)

Lechlade (*Lecchelade*)

109

Sir Edmund, earl of Kent (*Vant.[sic]*)	10s 6d
Henry Smith (*Fabro*)	2s 1½d
William le Hebbare	2s 0½d
Alflus Hernon	2s 11d
Thomas Fouk	2s 0½d
John Norman	2s 0½d
John Wynteshir	20d
Ralph Pure	2s 1d
John Westman	4s 6d
William Hernon	12d
Thomas Abbot	2s 1d
Ellis Hernon	6d
Robert de Kelmescote	2s 10½d
John le Hebbare	14d
William Wranne	10d
Thomas le Hebbar	2s 4¾d
Robert Aunger	2s 1½d
Robert Nony	2s 3½d
Peter de Hocwelle	2s 5d
Robert de Mill (*Molendino*)	9s 7d
Robert Edward	3s 4d
John Inthehurne	2s 10½d
William Dammesoyle	21½d
William Tilling	18½d
John Abbot	18½d
John Phelip	8d
Thomas le Taillur	12d
John Cocus	12d
John Lutelkene	12d
Richard Cocus	18d
Robert de Everlegh	23d
John Depham	20d
John de Salesbury	13¼d
William le Tannar	18d
Durling Godchild	6d
Alice la Tannars	2s 5½d
Thomas le Fissher	9d
Henry le Jogelour	2s 4d
Geoffrey Pomyas	6d
Thomas Lucas	12d
Henry Lauwes	2s 6½d
William Miller (*Molendinario*)	16d

[Membrane 8]

Also Lechlade

Gilbert Tailor (*Cissore*)	6d
Adam atte Fenne	3s 1½d
Matilda Chicches	6d
John le Botyler	2s 2d
Alice Neles	3s 6d
William Brekebat	2s 10d
Edith Jackes	12d
William atte Forde	4s 7d
John Wastel	12d
Robert le Westman	4s 1d
Robert Damedith	2s 5½d
Avice atte Doune	2s 8½d
William atte Forde	3s 2d
Edith Cahs	9d
Simon Pirk'	2s 10d
Edith la Vatte	2s 10d
Robert le ȝonge	2s 3d

Approved. Total, £6 11s 3¾d

Fairford (*Fayreforde*)

110

Henry Broun	4s 7d
Robert le Hendy	6d
John atte Nelme	14¼d
Simon de Havering	18d
John Dolby	2s 1½d
Simon Sire	6d
Isabel Reynald	6d
Matilda de London	6d
John de Penynton	12d
Robert de Redinge	19d
James (*Jacobo*) Mannyng	2s 6d
John le Skimer	6d
Edith de London	2s
James Baker (*Jacobo Pistore*)	21d
John Baker (*Pistore*)	6d
Isabel Kynny	6d
John Hoggeshale	6d
William le Fitz [*sic*]	6d
John Tropenel	15d
Richard Rocleye	12d
William le Vlips	6d
Isabel Boures	12d
John Martin	12d
Adam le Murie	6d
Adam le Graunger	2s
Henry Smith (*Fabro*)	14d
Richard le Chapman	6d
Thomas Gunyld	3s 2½d
John de Mulford	15d
Nicholas Rogers	21d
Peter le Wolmonger	9d
William Spark	9s 4d
William le Bour	2s 3d
Robert Hikeman	9s 3d
John Reeve (*Preposito*)	18¼d
William Pirk'	2s 5¼d
Richard Joye	12d
Thomas Garyn	12d
William Pirk'	17d
William Hathewy	17d
John Bisshop	5s 0½d
William Pye	23¼d
William Abbot	2s 7d
John Gille	12d
Alice Horcote	12d
Robert Pirk'	4s
Richard Baret	19d
Matilda la Longe	12d
Nicholas Durling	23¾d
John atte Nassh	2s 9d
Agnes Gerald	6d
Agatha de Clifford	6d
William Clement	6d
William le Knyf	3s 2d
Thomas atte Fenne	12d
John Dod	6d
Thomas Hauekin	18d
William atte Hide	16d
William Kynni	23d
John atte Hoke	4s 4d
John atte Fortheye	18d
Robert Aynolf	12d
William le Reve	3s 1d
Walter le Hayward	19d
John atte Welle	3s 11d
John Hereward	2s 8d
Andrew Pirk'	3s 4d
William Hamound	12d
John Pye	9d
Agnes le Longe	23d
John Burgeys	2s 11½d
Agnes Maynes	12d
Robert le Neuwe	14d
William Hathewy	15d
William Sywet	4s 9½d
John Colly	4s 0½d
William le Longe	3s 4d

[Membrane 8 r-h col.]

Also Fairford

Alice atte Trouwe	6d
John Wyn	3s 2½d
Agnes Jopes	3s 0¾d
Lady Alice (*Alesia*), countess of Arundel (*Arundell*)	5s 6d

Approved. Total, £7 17s 11¾d

Kempsford (*Kynmaresforde*)

111

Sir Henry, earl of Lancaster (*Lancastr*)	12s 1¼d
Seleman [*sic*]	2s 8d
Matilda Baret	23¾d
Matilda la Budeles	17d
Thomas Cok	17¼d
John atte Oclonde	23d
Henry atte Oclonde	21½d
Adam Nicholes	22d
John Sefoul	21¼d
James (*Jacobo*) Asshard	6d
Sir John Patrek	8d
Geoffrey le Swein	9¾d
Robert Cobald	18½d
John Nicholes	6d
Henry Sefoul	2s 5½d
Agnes le Longe	3s 2d
Richard Simon	6d
Walter Garyn	12d
Walter le Ferrour	3s 0½d
John David	9d
William Geffreis	20d
John le Portreve	15½d
William de Teinton	9d
William le Cok	18½d
Alice Champions	7d
Walter Kitte	11d
Walter Patryk	19½d
Robert Hickes	19d
Patrick Wattes	4s 2d
William Jones	12d
John Oclonde	6d
John le Wariner	4s 1d
Geoffrey le 3onge	2s 2d
William Muryele	15d
William Reybald	4s 2d
John Reybald	2s
Gilbert Hikedon	21½d
Nicholas Sare	23¾d
Agnes Aylwy	2s 1½d
Nicholas Page	4s 2d
John Bolde	15½d
Matilda Spikes	6d
John Selewine	5s²⁹ 1d
John le Gaiour	15½d
Isabel Beles	16d
Henry Maline	12d
John Geffreis	18½d
Henry le Palmere	6d
Walter le Budel	13d
Amice de Mill (*Molendino*)	3s 5d
Robert atte Berue	15d
John Malicorn	6d
John le Bedel	20d
Alice la Goldar	21½d
Alice Neles	15d
Alice Jones	3s 2d
Hugh Monk (*Monacho*)	12½d
Thomas Jones	12d
Thomas Fisher (*Piscatore*)	2s 9d
Alice Brounes	13d

Richard Richeman	13d
John Malicorn	14d
William le Muchele	21½d
Agnes Wilmotes	9d
Henry Hobbes	6d
Richard West	6d
Matthew Garin	6d
Robert atte Mulle	23d
William Swyft	12d
John Thomes	2s 11d
John le Bercar	21d
John Fisher (*Piscatore*)	2s 6½d
John Bisshop	2s 9d
Patrick Savage	2s 0¼d

Approved. Total, £6 15s 0½d

Coln St Aldwyn (*Culn Sancti Aylwyn*)

112

William Burgeis	19¾d
Walter Osbarn	16d
Simon atte Nelme	21¼d
Robert le Palmere	9½d
William le Reve	2s 9d
Ralph Alfrich	17¼d
Walter Priest (*Sacerdote*)	9d
Thomas atte 3ate	16d
William Smith (*Fabro*)	3s 8d

[Membrane 8 dorse]

Also Coln St Aldwyn

William Lifholy	21d
John Friday	3s 6½d
Henry Don	6s 1¼d
Alice Stanward	9½d
Reginald atte Nassh	9¾d
Cecil Forneis	9d
John de Cross (*Cruce*)	4s 9d
John de Haule	2s 4¾d
John Vicar (*Vicario*) de Coln	9d

Approved. Total, 37s 2d

Hatherop (*Hatherop*)

113

Julian Portreve	18d
Ellis le Heort	6d
Alexander Bovetoun	12d
Henry Portreve	19d
Gwenllian (*Wentliana*) atte Water	6d
Robert le Sherreve	15d
Richard Wattes	14¾d
Richard Hobbes	18½d
Sir Reginald Priest (*Presbitero*)	9¾d³⁰
Edith atte Fenne	2s 5½d
Ellis de Cheddeworth	2s 8d
John Broun	6d

Philip atte Grene	9d
William Hobbes	19¾d
William³¹ Welikembd	21d
Agnes Reynald	15¾d
Alice Lovekin	6d
Thomas le Moldar	15d
Thomas Edrich	6d
Ralph le Reve	3s 7d
John Wilkines	6d
William de Cattelove	15d
Alice Swindones	14d
Robert Miller (*Molendinario*)	23d
Richard Craky	13d
Ralph Bauer	14¼d
John Benet	12d
Robert Broun	6d
Christine West	2s 9d
Thomas le Eyr	21d

Approved. Total, 39s 11½d

Eastleach Turville and Williamstrip Park (*Lechtorville cum Willamesthrop*)

114

John Leython	6d
Thomas le Botiler	9d
Henry Fraunceis	3s 2½d
Walter atte Stile	6d
John Brandeslegh	2s 0½d
John Barry	2s 7d
Walter de Stanford	6d
Thomas le Breware	6d
Agnes Deverous	9d
John Bussh	16d
Felic. Lok	6d
Thomas Hayde	6d
John le Draper	6d
William de Lideforde	12d
William le Breware	15d
William Chaplain (*Capellano*)	15d
Hugh le Persones	21d
Nicholas Miller (*Molendinario*)	9d
John le Quarreour	6d
John de Haule	3s 7d
Simon atte Felde	6d
John Asselyn	18d
John Cokerel	11d
Sybil le Freynsh	6d
Richard By the Way (*juxta Viam*)	6d
Gilbert Halvacre	12d
Nicholas Cotes	6d
John Miller (*Molendinario*)	3s 2½d

[No total, see below]

Williamstrip Park (*Willamesthrop*)

115

Thomas le Meysy	2s 7d
Agnes Broun	15d
Henry Rolves	9d

Thomas Thorkeden	15d
Richard le Meysy	10d
Robert Felice	10½d
William Jones	2s 5d
Thomas Chaunceis	3s
Margery Jackes	3s 6d
Robert atte Walle	2s 2d

Approved. Total, 51s 6d [114 and 115]

Eastleach Martin with Fyfield (*Estlecch cum Fifide*)

116

John de Cotes	21d
Dowsabel (*Dulc.*) de Cotes	6d
William de Stanforde	2s 3d
Isabel (*Tybot.*) atte Cote	18d
John Alissaundr	9d
William atte Brugge	18d
Henry Halvacr	2s[32]

[Membrane 8 dorse r-h col.]

William Bovetoun	21d
Peter Godgrom	19d
William Canoun	18½d
John Canoun	22d
William le Palmere	18½d
Robert Maynard	5s 2d
Robert Walewain	19d
John atte Nelme	8s 9d
John de Pauntelegh	13½d
John de Fishide	2s 1¼d

Approved. Total, 37s 2¾d

Southrop (*Suthrop*)

117

Peter de Cocus	3s 0½d
Roger Abovetoun	2s
John le Tresshare	9d
Richard le Kinge	15d
Philip Richarde	3s 3d
Robert atte Lauende	2s 4d
John atte Plodde	3s 4½d
William Janekines	2s 4d
Matilda le Webbe	12d
Henry Hobbes	14d
Peter le Mareis	6d
John Reeve (*Preposito*)	3s
Nicholas Miller (*Molendinario*)	2s 9½d
Sir John de St Philibert (*Sancto Philiberto*)	6s 7d
Robert de Mill (*Molendino*)	5s 6d
John Ȝateman	3s 6½d
John Stilman	15½d
Robert le Eyr	15d
Stephen de Halveslegh	20d
William le Nyng	12d
John de Coln	2s 6d
Joan Widow (*Relicta*)	12d

Approved. Total, 51s 1½d

Quenington (*Quenynton*)

118

Preceptor[33] de Quenynton	17s 3½d
Thomas Robert	13¼d
John Inle Dene	22½d
Walter de Hall (*Aula*)	7d
John atte Tounesende	20d
Robert Benger	16½d
Walter Torald	23½d
William Aunger	8½d
Thomas Faukes	16¼d
Walter Edde	10d
Robert Athelard	8¼d
John Benge	16d[34]
Andrew le Neuman	9¼d
John Brice	2s 3d
John Benge	16½d
Peter Halling	18¼d

Approved. Total, 36s 8¾d

Barnsley (*Barndeslegh*)

119

Sir Edmund, earl of Kent (*Cans'[sic]*)	5s 3d
Margery Wilkokes	15d
Henry le Kniȝt	4s 1d
Walter Colles	15d
Thomas le Wyse	21d
Nicholas Purie	3s 8½d
Reginald Payn	15d
William Scot	23d
Alice la Finch	8s 6½d
John le Nevours	18½d
Alice atte Watere	15½d
Roger Coppe	15½d
Thomas Scot	15½d
Alice Hickes	6d
John Willames	18½d
Alice la Bonde	21d
Walter Pain	20d
Ralph le Large	12d
Alexander atte Welle	18d
Thomas Shirwold	18d
Matilda Eves	10d
Henry Deuebald	6d
Eva Baynel	18d
Walter le Finch	3s 10d
William le Sley	6d
William Walters	12d
Wade[35] Scot	18d
John Reynald	6d

Approved. Total, 54s 0½d

Eycotfield (*Eycote*)

120

Sir John de Acton	20d
Richard le Walkare	12½d
Richard Geffrey	12d
Richard Cave	13d
Simon Dauwe	18d

[Membrane 9]

Also Eycotfield

Agnes Drois	18½d
Richard Page	5s 8½d
Richard Dygon	6d

Approved. Total, 14s 4½d

Bibury (*Bybury*)

121

Alice Digon	9d
Christine Bodyn	18½d
Robert de Garsintone	2s 11d
Robert Crups	3s 5d
John Messeger	9d
Henry Gratton	9½d
William le Factour	2s 3d
William le Messeger	4s 3d
Robert le Swein	17d
Robert le Chapman	2s 9d
Matilda Collies	10½d
Richard le Heyward	2s
Thomas de Cestre	3s 7d
Hogh le Ray	6d
Simon atte Hurne	12d
William le Ray	2s 1d
John le Cartere	14d
Richard le Swein	15d
William Durable	2s
Geoffrey le Factour	3s 8d

Approved. Total, 38s 11½d

Ablington (*Ablynton*)

122

Benedict (*Benet*) atte Mulle	16½d
Edith le Picchere	19d
William Golding	10d
Thomas le Mareis	2s 3d
Walter de Caumpeden	18d
Adam le Pointer	15d
William Wiring	2s 9d
John atte Watere	5s 11d
Sir John de Wylington	5s 1d
William Manning	18d
Richard atte Dene	6d
Geoffrey atte Dene	6d
Walter Stevene	3s

Simon Robin	6d
John Golding	12d
John de Ledere	14d
John Haliday	6d
John le Hert	2s 2½d
Robert Brounyg	3s 8d
Adam le Mareschal	13d
Nicholas le Nethere	18d
William Grymstede	20d
Gilbert atte Rest	18d

Approved. Total, 42s 10d

Aldsworth (*Aldesworth*)

123

John Rogers	2s 8d
William Yuyll	5s 3d
John Colies	2s 8d
Richard Eliot	18d
Richard atte Walle	6d
John Don	12d
William Godynow	6d
Agnes Reynaldes	6d
Matilda la Straunge	9d
Thomas atte Brugge	6d
John atte Watere	2s 8d
Robert Sherich	2s 8d
Walter Hatherop	13d
John Greg	11d
Henry atte Grene	3s 4d
John le Murie	14d
Nicholas Godiniwh	2s 1d
Matilda Robines	19½d
Walter Richard	6d
John Palmares	2s 9½d
John atte Brugge	2s 3d
Adam atte Hyde	12d

John Umfray	15d
Adam de Ameneye	12d
William Golding	3s 4d
William de Caldecote	9d
John atte Hide	20d

Approved. Total, 45s 11d

Arlington (*Alfrinton*)

124

Benedict le Graunt	20d
Richard Walteres	2s 6d
John Frary	19½d
William le Hert	19d
Matilda Gibbes	15d
Hugh le Bercare	4s 8½d
John Peion	16d
Walter Frary	11d
William Elote	15d
Walter Lovekin	21½d
Walter le Kni3t	15d
Geoffrey Giffard	15d
Robert Symon	4s 10d
Walter Nichol	2s 3d
Walter Prat	2s 1½d
William Boton	15d
William Prest	6d
John Lovekin	22½d

[Membrane 9 r-h col.]

Also Arlington

Simon le Walkare	6d
John le Bercare	21d
Sir John de Penybrugge	4s 10½d

William Shupp	6d
Roger Norman	8s 4d

Approved. Total, 49s 11d

Total of the whole hundred, £46 4s 1d

Subtaxers (*Subtaxatores*)

125

Thomas Don	12d
John le Masoun	12d
Warren le Grys	12d
Richard de Staneforde	12d
John Faukes	12d
Geoffrey Mareschal	12d
Richard de Bristoll	12d
William Barbast	12d

Total, 8s

Approved. Total of the whole hundred with the subtaxers' taxes, £46 12s 1d[36]

LONGTREE HUNDRED
(*HUNDREDUM DE LANGETRE*)

Tetbury (*Tettebury*)

126

Walter le Cook	8s 1¼d
Margery Cope	3s 4½d
John Morice	3s 6½d
John le Webbe	3s 0¼d
William de Caldebourne	3s 4d
William Prior (*Priore*)	12d
Roger de Stonhous	6d
John Monek	2s
William de Mottesfoute	18¾d
John Wyldefuir	6d
Ralph le Cornmongere	2s
John le Garlekmongere	3s
William le Bere	3s 4d
Richard le Corvyser	2s 0¾d
Geoffrey Bruselaunce	6d
John atte Mulle	18d
John de Weston	5s
John Bonion	20½d
Alice Morice	2s
William Jones	18d
Walter le Palmere	2s 6¼d
Julian Sweting	6d
Richard le Fox	21d
Christine la Smyth	2s
John le Palmere	18d
John Phippes	21d
Thomas le Bakere	2s 6½d
Stephen le Maunch	21d
William Partrich	2s 3d
Walter Twynilepypin	2s
Roger Burdun	6d
Walter le Tour	12d
Walter le Taillur	18d
Luc. de Boneville	2s 6d
William le Sone	3s 0½d
William le Mulleward	12d
Geoffrey Ryson	5s 11¾d
John Snow	18d
John de Rodemerton	18d
Walter Bruselaunce	6d
Roger le Cook	4s 0¼d
Margery Chese	6d
Nicholas Kenewrek	12d
Robert le Skinner	3s 0¼d
John de Stokwelle	2s 2¼d
John Bonhome	12d
Nicholas le Webbe	2s
Walter le Fissher	18d
Nicholas atte Cornere	12d
John Hickes	18d
Henry atte Grene	21d
William Godman	6d
Walter le Forest	12d
Ralph Paternoster	6d
John le Coltherde	12d
Henry le Flexman	18d
Agnes Breuouse	7s 0¼d
Walter Boneville	6d
John Livere	6d

Approved. Total, 119s 1½d

Charlton House (*Cherlton*[37])

127

John Bisshop	3s 6¼d
Robert Pracy	15d
Edith Morice	2s 6¼d
Walter le Knyf	15d
Walter le Cartere	12d
Joan Thomas	12d
John Hereward	2s
Nicholas Pynnok	12d
Simon le Cartere	2s

[Membrane 9 dorse]

Also Tetbury [*sic*]

John Everard	2s 7½d
Thomas le Cartere	2s 0¼d
John de Wyke	2s 0¼d
Walter Mahutild	21d
Stephen le Fissher	2s
Thomas de Lutlecote	6d

Approved. Total, 26s 5¾d

Doughton (*Doughton*)

128

Walter Morice	2s
Walter le Monek	2s 6½d
Richard le Freke	18d
John Inthehethe	2s 4¼d
Julian Bonhome	2s 6d
Walter Perys	3s 2¼d
John Inthelane	2s
Simon atte Pride	3s 2d
Roger le Hopere	2s 8¾d
Eva Bonhome	3s 2¼d
Richard Bonhome	18d
John le Monek	3s 4d
John Inthehethe	2s
Julian Fraunceis	2s
Thomas Cave	12d
Henry le Skinner	6d

Approved. Total, 35s 7d

Elmestree (*Almundestr*)

129

John Tropinel	2s 3½d
Robert Est	2s 6¼d
Robert Gilbert	2s 7d
Lady Mary [*sic*]	6s 8d
Richard le Sherman	12d
Felice Sherman	2s 0¼d
William le Mulleward	18d
John atte Boure	6d
William le Spir	2s 6d

Approved. Total, 21s 7d

Tetbury Upton (*Uptone*)

130

Robert Hathewy	2s 7d
John Wylkines	2s 6¼d
Adam Chavenedissh	18d
Roger Pycot	9d
William North	18d
Alice Wylikin	2s 1¼d
John Burdon	6d
William le Heort	21d
Richard atte Pile	2s
William le Herde	18d
Margery Waryn	2s 6d
John Stevenes	6d
John atte Pyle	21d
Isabel la Skay	18d

Approved. Total, 22s 11½d

[No heading]

131

Boniface de Peruch	37s 1½d

Approved. Total, 37s 1½d[38]

Horsley (*Horslegh*)

132

Richard Mundy	3s 0½d
John le Bowyare	3s 6¾d
Henry le Glaswriȝt	2s 0¼d
Geoffrey le Cook	15d
Thomas le Graunt	10¼d
Roger de Touneswelle	2s 2¼d
Thomas Toffyn	11d
Walter Damayde	6d
Richard Inthehale	17d
John Pynnok	6d
Nicholas le Cartere	6d
William Crips	2s 0¼d
Robert King	15d
Matilda de Chaddeseie	6d
Geoffrey de Holeweye	2s 2d
Nicholas Upehulle	11d
Joan Upehull	16d
William Underwode	12d
Peter de Hackeburn	14d
Richard Tikemor	18d
William Inthehale	6d
Thomas Adam	16d
Thomas le Taillur	12d
Thomas Willes	11d
John Gateherde	6d
John Caperoun	13¼d
Richard Inthehale	19d
Richard atte Bertonende	2s 3d
Adam Torac	12d
Ralph Jolif	18d
Richard Maundeville	18d
Richard de Briddeleye	16d
Ralph Bonechurche	17d
Geoffrey Sampson	6d
Nicholas Inthecumbe	8d
William Toret	11d
Thomas de Naillesworth	8d
Henry le Rook	3s

Approved. Total, 50s 3½d

Lowsmoor Farm (*Loddesmor*)

133

Ralph de Lodesmor	2s 8d
Ralph Fouke	2s 4¼d
Alexander de Havenyng	3s 6½d
William de Rugwode	12d
William Maundeville	18d
. . . . . .ode	4s

[Membrane 9 dorse r-h col.]

Also Lowsmoor Farm

Richard Pynnok	12d
Peter Martin	12d
Adam de Chavenedissh	6d

William Pynnok	2s 2d
Richard le Heyward	18d

Approved. Total, 21s 2¾d

Woodchester (*Wodecestre*)

134

Geoffrey le Stedeman	2s
Robert Adam	6d
Richard Jones	9d
Nicholas Clot	9d
William le Shephurde	13d
Robert Braunche	12d
Henry Caperon	18d
Roger le Steor	6d
Alexander West	11d
Richard Thomas	16d
Robert Bronegare	12d
Hugh Wymond	2s
John Adam	8d
John le Huware	10d
Sir John Mautravers	5s
Edith Cokes	2s 9½d

Approved. Total, 22s 7½d

Culkerton (*Culkerton*)

135

William le Duk	4s 9¾d
Thomas le Freman	15d
William le Geg	20d
Alice Perys	12d
Agnes Launsing	12d
William West	8d
Walter atte Mere	20d
John Bernard	6d
Thomas Neel	10d
Roger Perys	3s 10d
Thomas Flemmyng	10d
Alexander South	10d
Matilda Custaunce	7¾d
John West	6d
Walter le Reve	2s 5d
James (*Jacobo*) Waldwrith	2s 6d
Walter Broun	8d
Hugh le Lanȝfole	8d

Approved. Total, 26s 3½d

Rodmarton (*Rodmerton*)

136

Thomas Bovetoune	22d
Richard Inthelane	10d
Reginald de Lanȝfole	11d
Alice la Hopere	20d
Thomas le Hopere	12d
Robert Bovetoun	15d

William Burdon	10d
Robert le Reve	21d
Walter Curteis	9d
Robert le Wetherherde	6d
John Burdon	16d
William le Welssh	6d
Thomas le Prest	12d
Nicholas Inthelane	13d
Stephen de Clenchcham	2s

Approved. Total, 17s 3½d

Hazelton Manor Farm (*Haselden*)

137

Boniface de Peruch	46s 0½d

Total, 46s 0½d[39]

Cherington (*Chyrinton*)

138

Adam Neel	7s 6¼d
John Amyard	6d
Alice la Bonde	15d
Nicholas Inthehale	20d
John Westhrop	2s
John Pynnok	20d
William atte Erbere	2s 2d
Walter le Fraunkelein	2s
Johan. Howel	16d
Walter atte Combe	10d
William Crisp	18d
Adam atte Grene	6d
Gilbert atte Mulle	15d
William atte Clive	8d
Geoffrey Bygod	2s 6d
William de Lavynton	6d
Alice Inthehale	6d
Robert Burdon	21½d
Walter Alein	6d
John de Annesleye	2s
Walter atte Clive	8d
Matilda Symondes	8d
Geoffrey Godman	2s

Approved. Total, 35s 11¾d

Shipton Moyne (*Shiptone Moygne*)

139

William de Aldrintonc	3s 0¼d
William Plassat	9d
Robert le Smith	10d
William le Botyler	14d
Hugh de Colesburn	6d
John le Harr	17d
John atte Mulle	6d
Walter Fynian	2s 3d

Reginald le Smith	13d
John Lovecok	12d
Alice de Hydebury	13d
Walter de Fordewelle	13d
John Aylrich	14d
Walter Cleregise	13d
Marg. Bernard	20d

[Membrane 10]

[Also] Shipton Moyne

John Justice	15d
William West	15d
Robert Donnyng	6d
William Knap	18d
Matilda Bernard	16d
John de Northcot	3s 0¾d
Robert Selyman	6s
Adam le Longe	15d
Ralph Fynian	14d
William atte Style	12d
Reginald Knap	16d
Reginald de Northcote	18d
Alice la Harre	2s
John Beauboys	3s
William Bisshop	18d
Margaret de Estcourt	18d
William Mile	2s 6½d
Ralph atte Mulle	2s
Robert Maynard	12d

Approved. Total, 53s 3¾d

Weston Birt (*Westone Bruyt*)

140
William Scot	3s 6½d
Richard Sevare	12d
Thomas Sevare	14d
Robert de Monekynton	12d
William le Skay	15d
John Snyte	12d
Jolc' de Lamburne	15d
Adam le Cook	2s
Richard le Clerikes	12d
Agnes Hughes	18d
Thomas Jones	6d
Adam Thomas	18d
William Godrich	6d
John de Wylington	4s 9d

Approved. Total, 21s 11½d

Lasborough (*Lassebergh*)

141
Robert de Goldhulle	8s 8¾d
John Bovetoun	6d
William Bovetoun	12d
Richard Somerfoul	12d

John atte Porche	15d

Approved. Total, 12s 5¾d

Minchinhampton (*Hampton*)

142
Richard le Cook	2s 6d
William Gregori	2s 11d
John Jordan	9d
William atte Grenehulle	20d
William Fager	20d
Richard Huwelot	12d
Thomas de Chalkforde	2s 2d
Alice de Beuleie	12d
Agnes atte Hyde	14d
William de Colecumbe	12d
Thomas Hamewelle	2s 6d
John Gille	18d
William Jolyf	2s 10d
Ralph le White	20d
Richard de Bremescombe	14d
William Averay	6d
Robert atte Tochale	2s
John le Hopere	18d
John le Reve	2s
Henry Mile	14d
Matilda la Swon	19d
William le Mulleward	10d
Robert de Brideleye	2s 2d
Hugh Cole	12d
John Swele	13d
Roger de Alsleye	8d
Henry de Rome	10d
Henry de Bampton	15d
Richard de Langeforde	2s 6d
Richard atte Hulle	2s 7d
Geoffrey le Masoun	6d
Hugh le Bakere	6d
Richard le Taillur	6d
John le Masoun	6d
Mabel de Langeforde	10d
Geoffrey Coterich	12d
Henry le Smyth	12d
Henry le Whyte	6d
John de Alsleye	6d
Robert le Smyth	6d
Ellis le Heyward	7s 0¼d
John atte Mapele	6d
Richard Busshel	8d
William atte Hyde	6d
Richard Dauwe	2s 6¼d
Richard Hardewine	16d
Hugh de Beuleye	8d
Richard Myblaunk	6d

Approved. Total, 67s 2½d

Rodborough (*Rodbergh*)

143
John Spilman	4s 0¼d

Philip Jonet	8d
John Elevaunt	15d
Thomas atte Horstone	2s

[Membrane 10 r-h col.]

Also Rodborough

Walter[40] atte Horstone	14d
Thomas atte Berue	15d
Robert Coterich	15d
Ralph le Walkar	10d
Thomas de Rodbergh	2s 6d
Joan de Rodbergh	14d
Walter le Taillur	16d
Adam Saundres	19d
Ralph de Grenehulle	3s 6d
Henry de Brechcumbe	6d
William de Alsleye	14d
Robert de Alsleye	18d
John le But	6d
Walter le But	18d
Benedict Huwelot	2s 6d
Robert le But	12d
Adam Larke	8d

Approved. Total, 31s 10¼d

Avening (*Avenynge*)

144
Henry Acke	2s
Walter Baroun	12d
John le Fraunkelein	15d
Matilda Wych	12d
John Osebarn	10d
Henry le Smyth	12d
John Wylikin	16d
Walter Coterel	10d
Robert de Wyke	10d
John Aylwine	12d
John le Reve	15d
John Upehulle	18d
William Sparwe	6d
John Straungebowe	8d
Roger atte Putte	8d
Richard Scot	8d
Robert Upehulle	6d
John Pollard	6d
Thomas atte Wode	2s 0¼d
Richard West	8d
John Hamound	8d
John Busshel	7d
John Rye	10d
Benedict Holdewold	10d
Henry Benet	12d
Alice Doddebrok	6d
Adam Axbed	18d
John de Horsleye	8s

Approved. Total, 33s 11¼d

Aston Farm (*Astone*)

145

William atte Halle	5s 0¼d
Walter Upehulle	14d
William le Palmere	20d
Adam Burdoun	14d
Henry Straungebwe	8d
Alice la Sopere	8d
Walter de Redwine	20d
John Scot	14d
Henry Bithewine	12d
Geoffrey Bridleie	16d
Ellis Harding	2s 0¼d

Approved. Total, 17s 6½d

Approved. Total of the whole hundred, £36 10¾d

Subtaxers (*Subtaxatores*)

146

William de Boxwell	10s
Richer de Cherlton	12d
Walter le Warenner	12d
John de Avenynge	12d
William de Forwode	12d
Robert Passelewe	12d
Adam le Hayward	12d

Total, 16s

Approved. Total of the whole hundred with the subtaxers' taxes, £36 16s 10¾d

SLAUGHTER HUNDRED
(*HUNDREDUM DE SLOUGHTRE*)

Great Barrington (*Bernynton Magna*)

147

Adam Pain	12d
Henry le Scalewarde	12d
John atte Hulham	3s 3d
Walter Balle	21d
John Wylikin	2s 1¼d
Thomas de Dene	4s 3¼d
Richard Upehulle	2s 8d

[Membrane 10 dorse]

Also Great Barrington

Henry atte Lepeȝate	18d
Joan la Walkere	21d
John Silvestr	21¼d
Thomas Lambard	16d
John Gundevyle	2s 0¼d
John le Bonde	2s 9d
John le Eem	12d
William Machen	2s 0¼d
William le Weluyne	16¼d
Thomas Donnyng	9d
Simon le Eem	2s 1d
William Pope	14½d
Adam atte Fortheye	11½d
Edmund le Bercare	7s

Approved. Total, 43s 6½d

Little Barrington (*Bernynton Parva*)

148

Alice Cunstaunce	2s
Agnes de Wynchestr	14d
John Crosson	3s 1d
Robert Crosson	3s
Nicholas Bythebrok	2s 4d

Approved. Total, 11s 7d

Clapton on the Hill (*Clopton*)

149

Robert le Bercare	2s
John Aluyne	19d
Nicholas Willames	2s 6d
William Alayn	2s 4d
William Bythestrete	14d
Richard Hobekin	2s
John Symound	2s
John de Crouwell	12d
William atte Welle	16d
Julian Clerekes	12½d
Joan Laurence	15d

Approved. Total, 18s 2½d

Bourton on the Water (*Borouton*)

150

Robert de Nethercote	8s
Robert Wattes	21½d
John de Nethercote	12d
Walter le Welshe	3s 9d
Adam Inthediche	6d
William Ballard	20d
John Huwes	18d
Walter Reygnald	12½d
Richard Reygnald	3s 11d
Agnes Reygnald	9d
Mariot Pateman	8½d
Matilda Reynald	2s 8d
John Persoun	12d
John Hynlon	20½d
Richard Martin	4s 1¼d
Alan Burimon	18½d
Robert Aluyne	15d
John Henries	2s 6d

Approved. Total, 39s 4¾d

Little Rissington (*Rysyndon Parva*)

151

John Appelheved, shepherd (*bercare*)	8s
Richard Roger	16d
John David	14d
Henry le Treumon	15d
Ralph West	9d
Thomas Hickeman	12d
Henry Cok	3s
John Josep	2s
William Josep	14d
Florence le Mulleward	12d
John Godgrom	12½d
Robert Miller (*Molendinario*)	16d
William Lovekin	6d
Valentine Hicheman	14d
Nicholas de Bamptone	12d
William Gunne	2s 2d
Hugh le Tornour	15d
Joan de Henor	12d
John Trillowe	3s 4d
Aline Burnel	5s

Approved. Total, 38s 5½d

Wyck Rissington (*Wyke*)

152

Roger le Hayward	2s
Hugh le Spenser	18d
William de Chaddeswelle	12d
William de Dorne	13d
William Medecroft	18d
Christine Richard	6d
Thomas de Saltforde	3s 2d
Abbot of Evesham	11s 8d

Approved. Total, 22s 5d

Widford (*Wydeforde*)

153

John Colly	12d
Matilda Colly	16d
Richard le Walkare	2s 2d
John Devote	12d

Approved. Total, 5s 6d

[Membrane 10 dorse r-h col.]

Sherborne (*Shirebourne*)

154

Julian Godeline	9d
Agnes atte Bewe	20d
John Loverich	12d
Henry Godewinn	3s
Thomas atte Fortheye	18d
John Dauwe	11½d
Matilda la Coroner	6d
Christine Brithwy	19d
Agnes de Selton	15d
Richard Belamy	18¼d
Richard Michel	18d
Adam Michel	12d
Gilbert Heynes	12d

Richard Jannes	2s
Thomas Capy	12d
Thomas le Playdur	12d
Henry Arnald	18½d
Adam Bartor	14d
John Heynes	9d
Alice Lovekin	6d
Henry le Veysyn	18½d
Robert atte Welle	12¼d
Richard le Broun	18d
Richard le Veysyn	10d
Richard Thurstein	21d
John Huwes	12d
Robert atte Barre	18d
Henry Thursteyn	23d
Christine la Coroner	16d
William le Hunte	12d
William Reynald	2s
Ellis le Coroner	12d
William le Walkere	6d
Richard Symond	12d
Alan Upehulle	12d
Henry Todeforde	2s
John Umfray	6d
John Scag, mercer (*mercatore*)	10s

Approved. Total, 56s 7d

Bledington (*Bladynton*)

155

John Kenteys	2s 2d
Ralph Jordan	12d
Thomas atte Berwe	18d
William Houwes	22d
William Ibote	14¼d
Walter Dameysabele	20d
Agnes Herman	18d
John Colin	12d
John le Whyte	18d
John Mallun	12¼d
William Skeil	2s 4d
Robert Broun	18d
Thomas Skeil	14d
Walter atte Stretende	16¾d
Joan Damemme	2s 6d
William de Lynham	12d
Ralph Robyn	13d
Robert le War	13d

Approved. Total, 26s 5¼d

Icomb (*Iccumbe*)

156

Richard Aperel	18¾d
Robert Chaplain (*Capellano*)	6d
Ellis Eliaunt	2s
John de Hamwelle	2s 0½d
John Statherne	5s

Approved. Total, 11s 0¾d

Great Rissington (*Rysindon Magna*)

157

Alice Vilein	10s
John Pestel	12d
John le Cartere	6d
William de Caldicote	12d
Robert Veyse	12d
William Gase	12d
Hugh Benchmaler	15d
Hugh Shakelok	14d
William Cut	18d
Emma Gurgan	18d
Philip Shakelok	11d
Gunnora Bartram	21d
William le Hopere	15½d
Alice Gurgan	13d
John Hegun	9d
Walter Herebard	9d
John le Tornor	2s 0¼d
Isabel Chaddewelle	21d
John de Chaddewelle	2s 3½d
John Kyng	14d
Philip Holder (*Tenatore*)	4s 6½d
John atte Gotere	18¾d
Henry le Heose	12s
John Bette	5s 3d

Approved. Total, 57s 0½d

Westcote (*Combe Westcot*)

158

Simon de Strode	13d
Robert Richard	12½d

[Membrane 11]

Also Westcote

William Budde	9d
William Hulles	14½d
Thomas de Iccumbe	5s
John and William de Iccumbe [*sic*]	5s
Roger Gurgan	18d
William Jarmeyn	9d
Ralph de Wylton	15d
Robert Inthehurne	13¼d
William Geffes	3s 6¾d
Ralph Robyn	14d
John atte Welle	9d
William Skyl	12½d
Agnes Wylles	12d
John atte Welle	2s 3½d
Agnes, who was the wife of Nicholas Hugges	12d
Henry Hugyn	15d
Robert Geffes	2s 1d
Hugh Hulles	20d
John Stephen	14d
Robert Smert	6d
John le Coupere	12d

Luc. de Westhalle	9d
William Upclive	9d
Adamar Pauncefot	5s 6d

Approved. Total, 44s 2d

Windrush (*Wenrich*)

159

John le Veysyn	12d
Robert Bone	14d
William in [the] Corner (*Angulo*)	20d
John atte Oke	18½d
John Abraham	6d
William Lammare	16d
Adam Mille	3s 6d
Geoffrey Saundres	9d
Agnes Kun	3s 7d
John Bone	18d
Robert le Mareys	18d
John Elys	2s

Approved. Total, 20s 0½d

Naunton (*Newenton*)

160

Emma de Shipton	10s
John Abovechirche	18d
John le Sclatter	4s 0½d
Robert Thomas	23¼d
Thomas atte Welle	6d
John Cok the younger	9¼d
Thomas Dauwes	20¾d
William Cok	15d
John Cok the elder	9d
Walter le Walker	12d

Approved. Total, 23s 5¾d

Harford (*Hertforde*)

161

Master Richard de Clare	4s 2¼d
Roger le Rede	18d

Approved. Total, 5s 8¼d

Aylworth (*Eylesworth*)

162

William de Eylesworth	18d
Richard de Cerneye	9d
William Gibbe	12d

Approved. Total, 3s 3d

Eyford (*Eyforde*)

163

Geoffrey de Aston	6s 4½d

Approved. Total, 6s 4½d

Lower Slaughter (*Sloughtr Inferior*)

164

Robert Miller (*Molendinario*)	16d
William le Freman	19½d
William Barlich	9d
Margery Large	18d
John Thomelyn	14d
John Inthehale	10d
Robert le Waryner	20½d
William Wale	12d
Bartholomew Damarie	18d
Roger Damarie	2s 11¾d
Walter Barlich	11d
William de Westmoncote	3s 5½d

Approved. Total, 18s 9¼d

Upper Slaughter (*Sloughtr Superior*)

165

Walter le Bercare	10s
John de Sloughtr	4s
Robert le Freman	12d
Robert Lysane	11¾d
John Forst	15d
Richard atte Welle	3s 1¾d
Roger le Freman	18d
Alexander de Chaveringworth	9d
John Hesel	19d

Approved. Total, 24s 2¾d

[Membrane 11 r-h col.]

Lower Swell (*Neyreswell*)

166

William le Welsshe	19¼d
John Wade	2s 1d
Stephen Godefrey	17d
Lawrence de Cundicote	20½d
John Robard	21d
Adam de Swelle	23½d

Approved. Total, 10s 7¼d

Broadwell (*Bradewell*)

167

Richard le Crou	20d
Roger Damelin	9d
William le Beo	9d
Robert le Steor	15d
William Loding	16½d
Richard Wylikyn	17d
Richard Wakemon	2s
Robert le Mulleward	6d
John Ferthing	2s 6d
John de Swelle	2s 10½d
John Lowing	2s 4d
Walter Jauemon	2s 2d
John le Rede	2s 3d
Thomas le Palmere	6d
William Amyce	19d
John Thomas	9d
Richard Iwing	15d
John atte Mulne	18d
Walter de Bradewelle	3s 6d
John de Bradewelle	2s

Approved. Total, 32s 11d

Donnington (*Doington*)

168

Adam Roys	10s
Alice Adekines	12d
Agnes Childes	13¼d
Walter Short	20d
Richard atte Mulne	18d
Walter le Bonde	20d
John Bernard	18d
Richard Bernard	12½d[41]
Thomas Daniel	12¼d
Adam Aidewelle	22d
Walter Whyting	18d

Approved. Total, 23s 10d

Adlestrop (*Tatlesthrop*)

169

Reginald Passegaumbe	10s
Agnes Kentes	2s 6d
John Dycon	16d
John Hobbes	10d
John Danyel	18¾d
Walter le Kny3t	3s 6d
Thomas le Horlere	3s 9½d
William Averay	12d
Richard Guie	3s 4d
Walter Knotte	18d
William Blundel	18¼d
Thomas le Kni3t	19½d
John le Graunger	3s
John Coleman	17d
Alan Hacones	16d
Julian la Cartere	2s 2d
Richard Thommes	17d
Walter Haukyn	16d
William Tribe	8d
Alice de Bradewelle	12d
Ralph de Bradewelle	9¼d

Approved. Total, 45s 8¾d

Maugersbury (*Malgaresbury*)

170

Margaret Fakel	10d
Julian Short	3s 4d
Agnes Geffes	15d
John le Freman	22¾d
Thomas Short the younger	3s 0¼d
Walter de Caldewelle	18d
John Huwesone	9d
Alice (*Alica*) Gilberd	2s 0½d
Julian de Bampton	3s
William atte Putte	7¼d
Robert Aleyn	2s 0½d
Walter Henry	2s 7¼d
Nicholas le Palmere	9d
John Sottes	12d
Thomas Gerard	2s 11¾d
Walter atte 3ate	2s 6d
John Mallyn	18½d
John le Palmere	3s 2d
William atte Ston	2s 0½d
John le Dean	19½d
William Hodeknas	2s 0¼d
Walter Batecok	18d
John Gyne	23d

Approved. Total, 43s 11d

Oddington (*Otynthon*)

171

Ralph Broun	2s 1d
Walter le Carpenter	20d

[Membrane 11 dorse]

Also Oddington

Hugh, son of Hugh le Frenshe	12¾d
John de Wappenham	10s
John Inthehale	13¼d
Simon le Bonde	12½d
Alice de Cundicote	6d
John Aleyn	10½d
Richard le Southerne	2s 6d
Joan Baggepayes	9d
Henry Thomas	9d
Cecily la Smythes	12¼d
Anthony (*Antoneo*) de Marsh (*Maresco*)	2s 2d
Richard le Naylere	2s 5¾d
Thomas Inthe [*sic*] Mershe	14¼d
John, son of Geoffrey le Frenshe	9d
Ralph de Compton	2s 0¼d

William le Parys	2s 9½d
Hugh le Broker	2s 11d
Julian, who was the wife of John le Frensh	4s 3d
Walter le Frenshe	16d
William Basset	15d
Walter de Wlverwelle	18½d
John Thomas	2s
John le Heort	2s 10d
John Wylles	3s 6¼d

Approved. Total, 54s 7¾d

Condicote[42] (*Cundicot*)

172

Richard le Freman	19¾d
John Galweyn	3s 6¾d
John Wylles	2s 3¾d
Ralph Galweyn	13¾d
John Galweyn	2s 8¾d

Approved. Total, 11s 5d

Stow on the Wold (*Stouwe*)

173

Richard Godchild	3s 6d
Alexander Bisshop	3s 6d[43]
John Drinkewater	2s 5d
William Rolf	3s 2¾d
Agnes Rolf	9¼d[44]
Henry Haym	20¼d
John de Kirkeby	12d
Paul le Dyere	10s
William Oky	2s
Stephen de Lecch	18¾d
William Saren	14d
John Canoun	12d
Walter le Dyere	5s
Agatha la Dyere	18d
John Basset	5s
John Gerard	15d
Clarice Donnyng	12d
Julian de Swelle	12d
John Mydewynter	2s 0¾d
Richard Welywalshe	12d
William le Rag	9d
Edith, who was the wife of William Roger	2s
John Donnyng	3s
John atte Burne	6d
Richard Sutor	3s 1½d
Richard Basset	2s
Robert Maydegod	5s 6d

Approved. Total, 66s 7¼d

Total of the whole hundred, £38 5s 10¾d

Subtaxers (*Subtaxatores*)

174

Walter de Kyrkeby	10s
Nicholas de Stouwe	10s
Robert de Lynham	12d
John Stone	12d
Michael de Bladynton	12d
Walter de Sherdynton	12d
Henry de Shirebourn	12d
John Villeyn	12d

Total, 26s

Total of the whole hundred with the subtaxers' taxes, £39 11s[45] 10¾d

KIFTSGATE HUNDRED
(*HUNDREDUM DE KYFTESGATE*)

Broad Campden (*Villata de Brodecaumpeden*)

175

Hugh Daudele	4s 5¾d

[Membrane 11 dorse r-h col.]

Also Broad Campden

Roger Est	6s 1½d
Henry Weoleye	5s 4¾d
William de Michelton, chaplain (*capellano*)	6s 8d
William Wattes	3s 5¾d
Simon atte Croyce	2s 1¼d
Richard Alewyn	2s 1½d
Geoffrey Adam	19d
Isabel Collyng	21½d
Joan Geffrey	15¼d
Adam Alisaundre	2s 2½d
John West	2s 8½d
John Inthehale	11¾d
William le Neuweman	2s 2d
John le Stronge	2s 6½d

Total, 45s 7½d

Westington (*Villata de Westynton*)

176

Richard Maunstild	22¾d
William Sparehalf	2s 1¾d
Thomas atte Nelme	2s 1d
Christine Wyllames	4s 2¼d
Thomas Manstild	2s 4¼d
Philip Bovetoune	2s 5d
Matilda Robynes	23¼d
Alice atte Pirie	15d
John le Reve	2s 11¾d
John de Clopton	18d
Reginald Roggers	14½d
William Dychford	18¼d
Roger de Quenton	19d
Nicholas Bailly	21½d
Clarice atte Slough	2s 0¼d
John le Smyth	2s 0¾d
Alex. atte Mulle	2s 5d
Richard atte Hulle	2s 9¼d
William Boltere	2s 0¾d
William Hanecokes	17d
John Weoleye	2s 3½d
Henry le Lech'	18d
Richard Hardyng	20½d
Richard Godrich	2s 3¼d
Alice Cappe	21¼d

Approved. Total, 51s 2¼d

Chipping Campden (*Villa de Caumpeden*)

177

Robert de Haverle	18s 11d
Thomas Bonafaunt	18d
William Mareschal	16½d
Robert Carpenter	18d
William Hewet	2s 5½d
Geoffrey Champioun	2s
Nicholas Masoun	15d[46]

[Membrane 12]

Also Chipping Campden

Philip de Pershore	5s 8½d
Cecily Hallyng	2s 5¼d
William Mareschal	2s 5¾d
William Foliredy	2s 8¾d
Sybil la Fisshere	2s 4¾d
Robert Broun	5s 8½d
John de Rusteshale	6s 6d
Hugh le Clerk	3s
Adam Dyeare	19½d
Robert de Combe	2s 2d
Robert le Factor	3s 10d
Geoffrey le Despenser	6s 8d
John de Muchelton	18d
John Mareschal	15¾d
William Mulleward	12d
Robert de Pechesleye	18d
Richard Foward	14½d
Walter Harding	8s

Approved. Total, £4 8s 10¼d

Subtaxers (*Subtaxatores*)

178

Nicholas de Spechesleye	12d
Philip Calf	12d

[Total, 2s][47]

Total of Chipping Campden vill with the subtaxers' taxes, £4 10s 10¼d

Buckland (*Bokelonde*)

179

William Alibon	2s
Alice Haukines	2s 3½d
Matilda de Hope	2s 2½d
Richard atte Yate	2s 1¾d
Richard Cartere	2s 3¾d
Edith Clementes	2s 10¼d
Walter le Gek	2s 0¼d
Matilda atte Mulle	17¾d
Richard le Braund	3s 8d
John le Gek	2s 10d
Walter Stevenes	2s 6½d
Alice Richardes	3s 5¼d
Robert le Rok	2s 5¾d
John Godewyne	16½d
Sarah atte Welle	2s 5½d
Richard le Rok	2s 9¼d
William atte Churcheye	2s 4d
John Turbut	2s 7¼d
Philip Wygod	22d
William James (*Jacobo*)	2s 4¾d
Julian Henries	2s 8¼d
Robert Wilkines	2s 6½d
Thomas Godrich	16d
Geoffrey Juliane	18¼d
Thomas le White	23¼d
John le Blake	18½d
William Bovetoun	22¾d
Robert Bundy	2s 1d
John de Wormynton	2s 7¼d
John Goddok	2s 7d
Richard Godrich	14d
Richard Inthehale	2s 6d
Matilda Hamptones	2s 8½d
Walter Bovetoun	2s 7½d
John de Baddeseye	2s 7d
Julian Godefray	2s 1¾d
Matilda la Yonge	2s 7¾d

Approved. Total, £4 5s 7¼d

Willersey (*Wylarseye*)

180

William Pak	23¾d

William Cloper	2s 11½d
William Jordan	2s 3½d
Reginald Athelard	2s 11¾d
Nicholas Hayel	2s 1d
Thomas Inthehale	3s 0¾d
Alice la Smythes	22½d
William Marioten	2s 2d
William Geffreis	3s 0¼d
Ranulph Wilkines	2s 10¾d
Richard Binesard	2s 3d
Emma Jannen	3s 1¼d
John Russel	3s 7¼d
Agnes la Persones	2s 9¼d
Agnes Anycen	3s 5d
Matilda Everard	2s 4¾d
Thomas Roberdes	3s 5d
John Hugin	23½d
Thomas Bate	2s 1¼d
Walter Weth	18½d
Robert Weth	20d
Nicholas Weth	3s 4¼d
Nicholas Symondes	2s 3½d
Thomas Rosen	18d
Clar. Matheus	8½d
William atte Forde	4s 6½d
William atte Paston	4s 2¾d

Approved. Total, 70s 2d

Saintbury (*Seynesbury*)

181

William Benethetoun	3s 2½d
Alice Musard	7¼d
John atte Broke	3s 6¼d
William le Cok	2s 0½d

[Membrane 12 r-h col.]

Also Saintbury

Richard de Ullynton	22¾d
Alice Whitbred	3s
Geoffrey de Coleshull	19¾d
John de Touneshull	3s 7¼d
Peter Thurbarne	2s 9¾d
Robert de Honibourn	19¼d
Amice Chapelein	10¾d
Nicholas Margrete	3s 1d
Richard Inthelon	4s 10½d
John Henr	4s 1¼d
William Bonde	5s 11¾d
Nicholas Chamvill	4s 0½d
Matilda Robardes	4s 1d
William le Yonge	3s 9½d
Agnes la Hideman	2s 5½d
William le Hideman	14¾d
John Prodhome	4s 5½d
John Squyer	2s

Approved. Total, 64s 11¼d

Weston Subedge (*Weston sub Egge*)

182

Executors of John Giffard	5s
Henry Abovetoun	21¾d
Thomas Gardont	13¼d
John Robines	14¾d
John Ballard	17¼d
John Hugges	6½d
Alice Ate	4s 0½d
John Reve	19d
Nich. Clerkes	14d
William Huggen	15½d
William Shirlok	22½d
Dyonis. Thomne	2s 0¾d
Robert Laurence	22d
Walter Geffen	11½d
Hugh Foward	12½d
John de Guldeforde	18d
Walter Gardont	16d
William Turney	21½d
Agnes Crisp	2s 2¼d
William Pinel	3s 1d
William Brounyng	14d
Geoffrey Bisshop	2s 9¾d
Geoffrey de Weston	7s 3d
Agnes de Chambre	5s
John atte Grene	4s 6d
William Lovekin	3s 6¼d

Approved. Total, 61s 1½d

Norton (*Norton sub Egge*)

183

Executors of John Gyffard	5s 8¾d
Ralph Kuten	2s 6½d
Robert Belamy	2s 6½d
William Vercare	2s 9d
Richard Watten	20¾d
Edith Cappen	18¾d
Ralph le Eorl	2s 9¼d
Isabel Bladyntones	2s 11¾d
Millicent Waryn	3s 10d
William Gynour	21¼d
Christine la Wedewe	2s 5¾d
Lawrence Jones	2s 6d
John atte Grove	2s 8¼d
John Robardes	2s 7¼d
Millicent Lenay	4s
Hugh Foukes	2s 1½d
Alice Richardes	22½d
Henry Witten	3s 1d

Approved. Total, 49s 6¾d

Cow Honeybourne (*Honibourne*)

184

Robert le Dreu	2s 11½d
John Baroun	2s 4¼d
John le Hogh'de	2s 10½d
Robert Clement	18¼d
Sybil Walteres	2s 4¾d
Reginald Hassewy	2s 2¾d
William atte Pole	2s 9d
Reginald Haukar	3s 1¾d
Nich. Bonde	2s 1¼d
Reginald Bonde	2s 6½d
John Broun	3s 10½d
John Bonde	2s 9¾d
Lawrence Reve	2s 8½d
John Lutteltones	3s 1¼d
Walter Shirebourn	2s 8d
Reginald Duy	20¾d
William Inthehale	2s 3½d
Matilda Willames	2s 7½d
Robert Hauker	19½d

Approved. Total, 48s 3¾d

Aston Subedge (*Aston sub Egge*)

185

John Flemmyng	5s 1¼d
John le Freman	3s 4¼d
Joan Freman	20¼d
Walter atte Yate	2s 4d
Isabel Rogers	2s 4d
Roger de Hudecote	2s 11½d
Adam Heyward	17¼d
Robert Geves	2s 9d
Robert Elisaunt	5s 10¾d
Walter Haukines	12½d
Roger Hideman	2s 5d
Nicholas Maggen	2s 0½d
Millicent la Wydewe	4s 10d

Approved. Total, 38s 2¼d

[Membrane 12 dorse]

Mickleton (*Mukelton*)

186

Gilbert de Seynesbury	2s 4d
Richard le Mey	2s 2d
Nicholas Trapel	2s 5d
John de Seynesbury	22d
John Cartare	4s 6d
John Duy	14d
John Stopel	18d
Richard Cartere	4s 8d
Matilda Chamville	18d
John Eliot	18d
Inag'n Trapel	16d
Richard Gamule	2s
William Fourner	2s 4d
Simon atte Nelme	2s 6d
Nicholas Russel	2s 1d
Richard Palmere	2s
Alex. Palude	4s 6d
William Cromme	18d

Gilbert Walter	4s 6d
Richard Gibbes	4s 6d
Cecil. atte Grene	14d
William Reve	5s
Reginald Broun	20d
Richard Walter	4s
John Fourner	20d
John Helemendon	3s
Emma Watten	14d
John Lenay	2s
Richard Richardes	18d
Richard Taillour	14d
John Hobekines	2s
Nicholas Wilkines	16d
William atte Pleystude	22d
William Russel	2s 2d
Clar. Richeman	16d
William Saad	20d
William Whitbred	2s 2d
Alice Kembestere	6½d
John atte Pleystude	2s 1d
John atte Ston	17¼d
Richard Saad	12½d

Approved. Total, £4 10s 9¼d

Clopton (*Clopton*)

187

John de Clopton	6s 7¼d
John le Yonge	3s 10½d
Alice Proude	7¼d
William Thomen	16¾d
John Thomen	22¼d
Walter Parker	16¼d
Walter Hobekines	22¾d
Robert Clarice	13d
Nicholas Wilkines	2s 8¼d
Ralph le Reve	2s 0¼d

Approved. Total, 23s 4½d

Pebworth and Broad Marston (*Pebbeworth & Mershton Boys*)

188

Thomas Jurdan	2s 4½d
John Martin	2s 6¼d
Robert le Mune	15½d
John Pigod	2s 6½d
Richard Fraunkelein	3s 5¼d
Alice Fraunkelein	20d
William Reve	3s 4¼d
Walter Mareschal	15¼d
Hugh Hereward	3s 2¾d
John Skinar	3s 3d
John Tomasyn	19¾d
Thomas Crisp	2s 11d
William Henries	2s 3d
Alice Beaumond	2s 7¾d
Alice Morice	2s 7¾d
Maurice Wilkines	2s
Edith Cok	2s
William Joce	2s
John Haukar	23d
Thomas Hugin	12d
John Bonde	2s 0½d
Agnes John Broun[48]	3s 0½d
John Hobben	22¾d
Walter de Chambr	3s 7½d
John de la Lee	2s 7d
Richard Richeman	16d
William de Mukelton	2s 3½d
Thomas de Cantellow (*Cantilupo*)	2s 10¼d
William Hichecokes	2s 7¼d

[Membrane 12 dorse r-h col.]

Also Pebworth and Broad Marston

William Busshel	3s 3½d
Hugh de la Bustere	2s 4¾d
John de la Bustere	3s 4d
William Peresson	2s 11d
Roger Haukare	18½d
Henry Jannes	22d
John Inthelon	2s 3½d
Emma Fraunkelein	22¼d
Richard Fraunkelein	12¾d
Nicholas Beaumond	2s 2¾d
John de Brewes	2s 7d
Robert Cosin	3s 5¼d
John le Large	3s 1¾d
Nicholas Beaumound	21¾d
John Dodelare	3s 0½d
John Nichol	2s
Peter Thomen	3s 11½d
John Cosin	3s 4½d
Robert de Garston	2s 8½d
Richard Morice	2s 2d
Henry Beaumond	2s 1½d
Walter Beaumond	15¾d
Hugh Coy	11¾d
Richard Brayn	2s 5¼d
John de Chamber (*Camere*)	3s 0¼d
Margery Catewk	2s

Approved. Total, £6 12s 5d

Ullington (*Ullynton*)

189

William Phelip	2s 1¼d
Stephen atte Yate	2s 0¼d
Robert Blauncheberd	2s
Richard Thomen	20d[49]
Cecily Wilkines	23¾d
Alice Geffen	2s 1d
Agnes Inthelon	21½d
Walter Kayen	12¼d

Approved. Total, 14s 8½d

Long Marston (*Mershton Sicca*)

190

Richard de Campeden	21¾d
Petronilla la Eorles	3s 9¾d
Roger le Plaidour	3s 3¾d
Isabel Shailard	2s 6d
Hugh Richardes	4s 1½d
Julian Anketel	2s 1d
Alice la Mareschal	3s 4d
Walter Jacken	22½d
Christine Walry	15½d
Hugh Wassh	9¾d
William Nichol	2s 6¼d
Adam le Knyt	2s 6d
Roger le Saltmere	2s 8½d
Hugh Stevenes	12¾d
John Haukines	2s 4d
Walter Robines	15¼d
Alice la Taillour	3s 8d
Walter Laurence	2s 2¾d
Hugh Foukes	2s 3¾d
Robert Jurdan	3s 4¼d
Hugh Ernald	2s 7d
Robert atte Were	2s 9d

Approved. Total, 54s 3d

Dorsington (*Dersynton*)

191

Thomas de Peros	5s 0½d
Adam Fraunkelein	2s 8d[50]

[Membrane 13]

Also Dorsington

John Beaumond	2s 5½d
Richard Bourn	2s 9½d
John Balle	2s 7½d
John Wylkines	2s 0¾d
Richard le Grey	2s 10½d
John atte Were	3s 1½d
Henry Balle	2s 5¼d
Henry Edith	2s 8½d
William Wylkons	3s
John Losty	2s 6¼d

Approved. Total, 34s 3¾d

Weston Maudit (*Weston Mauduyt*)

192

Ellis atte Pirie	3s 3d
Agnes la Neuman	21¼d
Nicholas le Baxter	2s 10d
John Dod	2s 10¼d
Reginald de Dersinton	15¾d
Thomas le Gardiner	18¼d

John Godhine	14d
Agnes Lolle	12¼d

Approved. Total, 15s 9¼d

Weston on Avon (*Weston super Abbonam*)

193

Robert le Cok	16¼d
John le Skinnar	18d
William Machen	22¼d
William Abovethetoun	2s 2½d
John de Weston	2s 11¾d
Henry Joce	8d
Hugh le Neuman	2s 0½d
Thomas atte Vloddre	18d

Approved. Total, 14s 1¼d

Willicote House (*Welecote*)

194

John le Ground	3s 8½d
Ralph le Whyte	2s 8½d
William Holtome	2s 8d
Nicholas Hamuld	3s 2½d
John Hugyn	3s 2½d
Joan Hamuld	3s 6¾d
Christine Inthehale	4s 8d
Alice Lucas	3s 0½d
Ralph Lucas	2s 9½d
Isabel Hicken	2s 6½d
William le Prestes	2s 0½d

Approved. Total, 34s 2¾d

Quinton (*Quenton Marmioun*)

195

John Gibbes	15¾d
Margery la Berner	17½d
Henry atte Grene	23¾d
Robert Houdon	2s 0½d
John Nichol	19¾d
William Baret	13¼d
Alice Houwen	3s 3½d
John Watten	2s 8d
William Colynes	20½d
Alice Wygot	23d
Henry Lescy	2s 2¼d
John Ronde	2s 9d
William Randulf	19¼d
William Henries	2s 11¼d
John Huggen	2s 5½d
John Fraunkelein	20½d
Margery Gilben	20½d
Richard Lucas	2s 9d
Johan. Waynepayn	2s 4½d
John atte Grene	3s 4¾d
Richard Ronde	3s 3½d
Walter Rond	12d
Alice la Reven	2s 2½d
Richard Jones	2s 2¾d
William le Ronde	20½d
Thomas atte Halle	2s 8½d
John de Heyforde	3s 6d
William Wygot	2s
John Marmyoun	12s 9d

Approved. Total, 74s 4¾d

Admington (*Adelmynton*)

196

Agnes Cnytes	2s 7½d
Robert Gybben	14¼d
Walter Watten	3s 8¼d
John Warr	3s 8d
Robert Haukynes	3s 4¾d
John le Budel	3s 6¾d
Nicholas Saad	3s 6½d
Sybil Jones	3s 1d
Robert Botyld	3s 2½d
John Lovekin	3s 8d
Richard le Warr	4s 1½d
John Houwen	4s 1½d
Robert le Prestes	2s 6¾d

Approved. Total, 42s 5¼d

Meon Hill (*Mune*)

197

Thomas Wygod	13½d
William atte Hulle	3s 11¾d
John Stephenes	2s
William Watten	2s 0½d
Gilbert Soudun	4s 0¼d
John Bynethetoun	8d
Simon atte Forde	2s 4½d
William Ernald	4s 0½d
Gilbert Wygot	3s 11½d
John Gilbard	3s 0¾d
. . . Westerne	2s 10½d

[Membrane 13 r-h col.]

Also Meon Hill

Robert Hobben	2s 3d
Hugh le Blake	2s
Robert le Blake	4s 7¼d
William le Large	21d
Henry Benet	3s 3½d

Approved. Total, 44s 1½d

Hidcote Bartrim (*Hudycot Bartram*)

198

John de Heyforde	2s 7d
John de Welecote	3s 2½d
Gilbert Bradeweye	2s 2½d
Henry Houwen	4s 5d
John Lauwen	18¼d
William Bourne	5s 2¾d
John Houwen	7¼d

Approved. Total, 19s 9¼d

Lark Stoke (*Stoke*)

199

Christine de Bisshopesdon	3s 6¼d
John de Foxcote	3s 11¾d
John Perkines	23¼d
John Thursteyn	12¾d
Richard Robines	15½d
Geoffrey atte Hulle	8½d

Approved. Total, 12s 6d

Ebrington and Hidcote Boyce (*Ebryhton & Hudicot Boys*)

200

Roger Corbet	11s 1¾d
Thomas Abovetoun	20d
William Benjamyn	2s 0½d
William Stor	3s 0½d
John Fraunkeleyn	12d
Richard le Carpenter	2s 9d
Robert le Crek	2s 2½d
John le Freman	3s 6d
Richard Inthehale	23½d
Thomas de Seleby	2s 4¾d
Roger Godwine	21½d
Adam Aubrey	2s 7½d
John Edith	2s 1¼d
Thomas Watevylle	2s 4d
Emma Inthehale	3s 5d
Thomas atte Hulle	3s 8¼d
Adam atte Hulle	3s 8¼d
Alice Wyllames	2s 9½d
William le Ȝonge	2s 9d
John Adames	19½d
Matilda Flok	3s 7¾d
John le Reve	2s 0¼d
William le Neuman	3s 7d
John de Hudicote	2s 4½d
Richard Thomme	2s 7¾d
Robert Lovekyn	4s 1¾d
Walter Bovethetoun	2s 0½d
Hugh Bourne	2s 11¼d
William le Freman	2s 3d
Henry Hobben	3s 2½d
Isabel Cromme	3s 1½d
John Godknave	3s 3½d
Hugh Inthehale	2s 4¾d

Joan Saleman	4s 1d
Robert le Wodeward	3s 6¼d
John le Gardiner	3s 3½d

Approved. Total, 107s 0½d

Charingworth (*Chaveryngworth*)

201

William Hardepirie	19½d
William le 3onge	21¾d
Christine Heynes	2s 10¼d
Walter le Carpenter	15½d
Christine Barel	12d
William Robardes	19d
John Huggen	23½d
Thomas Alysaundr	2s 7d
Richard le Tayllur	13¾d
William Aylwine	12½d
Robert le Porter	2s 6¼d
Robert Dorset	11¼d
Walter Harding	5s

Approved. Total, 25s 4¼d

Batsford (*Bachesore*)

202

Thomas Golafr	3s 3½d
Alex. Godefrey	15d
William Suette	10½d
Felice Hamond	16d
Adam atte 3ate	2s 1¾d
Adam Wardeyn	19¼d
William Wyot	15½d
John de Foxleye	2s 6¼d
Roger Poundelarge	21½d
John de Hodynton	3s 0½d
Executors of Nicholas Geyneys	12d
John Ponteys	18d
Margery Ponteys	18¼d
Richard Gerveys	2s 0¾d
Margery Ponteys	7¼d
Adam le Skryveyn	18½d

Approved. Total, 27s 4½d

Sezincote (*Schesnecot*)

203

William le Palmere	2s 3¼d
John de Wenlak	3s 2½d

Approved. Total, 5s 5¾d

Longborough (*Longebergh*)

204

Adam Suth	18½d
William Suth	14½d
Matilda South	18½d

[Membrane 13 dorse]

Also Longborough

Thomas le Southerne	9¾d
Richard de Hodinton	5s 2d
William Clement	3s 0½d
John Syward	2s 2¼d
Thomas Martyn	23½d
William Peornele	2s 2¾d
Peter Maggen	16¼d
John Martyn	18¼d
Philip le Smyth	2s 5½d
Thomas atte Croyce	3s 1¾d
Thomas Trewoll	13d
Margery Briddes	18d
Walter Inthelone	3s 6¾d
Peter Inthelone	2s 3¾d
John Heved	20d
Henry Hornewy	19d
Thomas Assewel	2s 1d
John Rolf	23d
John Schursteyn	19½d
Henry Roys	21¾d
Agnes la Wedewe	2s 3¼d
Joan Batille	2s 1¼d
Edith Ferthing	23¾d
John Selyman	20d
Alice Widow (*Relicta*)	3s 0¼d
John Hereward	2s

Approved. Total, 60s 4¼d

Upper Swell (*Swelle Superior*)

205

John le Hayward	16d
Christine la Bourkny3t	2s 6¼d
Henry Kayen	2s 10¼d
Roger le Mulleward	17d
John atte Croyce	2s 9¾d
Richard Inthehurne	2s 10½d
John Batyn	3s 4½d
Adam Inthehurne	23½d
John Inthehurne	22¼d
William de Seynesbury	12d

Approved. Total, 22s

Condicote[51] (*Cundycot*)

206

John de Stonore	5s 4½d
Margery la Chesman	8d

Approved. Total, 6s 0½d

Total of the whole hundred, £73 6s 4½d[52]

Subtaxers (*Subtaxatores*)

207

William de Evnelode	6d
Thomas Beaumund	6d
John Burne	6d
Richard Gatewyk	6d
Richard Prodomme	2s
Thomas Letice	2s

Total, 6s

Total of the whole hundred aforesaid with the subtaxers' taxes, £73 12s 4½d

HOLFORD AND GRESTON HUNDRED
(*HUNDREDUM DE HOLFORD & GRESTON*)

Childswickham and Murcot (*Wykewan [et] Morcot*)

208

Alice atte Brugge	2s 11½d
Ralph Tod	4s 9½d
Richard Berde	3s 10¾d
Robert de Aldeward	20d
John atte More	2s 4d
Robert Druwery	3s 0¾d
Robert Broun	20d
William Joce	6d
Warren de Spellesbur	3s 6d
Robert Rolves	2s 6d
William Jurdan	3s 0¾d
John le Wariner	5s 10d
William le Treuman	2s 10d
Ralph Tod	6d
Joan Berde	2s
Thomas Pereman	2s 5½d
Nicholas le Ʒonge	2s 7¾d
Richard Phelippes	3s 4½d
John de Bremesgrove	23½d
William Hodde	3s 9¼d
Nicholas Hondys	2s 6d
Matilda Toddes	20¼d
Richard le Bedel	19d
Alice Rogers	18½d
Cecily Hobbekines	2s 1d
Richard le Treuman	3s 3d
Matilda Douces	2s 0¼d
William Hondys	2s 9¾d
William Whyting	4s 1d

[Membrane 13 dorse r-h col.]

Also Childswickham and Murcot

Alice Hethe	3s 5½d
Richard Aykewe	16¼d
William Toddes	2s 4½d
John Ingelard	13d
William Abovetoun	15½d
William Berde	5s 2d
William Kembe	3s
Walter Inthehale	3s 4d
William Reynald	2s 9d
Robert Baroun	3s 3½d
Nicholas Baroun	21¾d
Julian Sulewed	2s 9½d
Edith Russel	22¼d
Stephen Gilbert	3s 5d
John Gerard	2s 8d
Thomas King	2s 7½d
Richard Harding	2s 1¼d
John Blyke	2s 6d
Richard Sampson	2s 9d
Agnes de Weston	4s 3d
Walter de Weston	2s 1¼d
Richard de Weston	20¼d

Approved. Total, £6 14s 6½d

Dumbleton (*Dumbulton*)

209

Adam Prouting	20¼d
William Baroun	2s 4d
Nicholas le Eorl	14d
Christine Henries	2s 11¼d
John Helins	2s
John de Northende	15¾d
Walter Tarlewine	5s 2¼d
Cecily Inthelon	2s
Walter atte Grene	4s 1¼d
William Wymark	21¼d
Joan Burgeys	2s 5d
Peter Gilberd	3s 0¾d
Edith Godwines	2s 6d
Joan Hodes	23d
Nicholas Baret	6s
John Monnyng	2s
Robert Baroun	2s 6d
William Heylin	18¾d
Henry Pollard	2s
John le Tayllur	4s 0½d
John Wattes	21¾d
Thomas atte Style	2s 3¾d
Richard atte Orcharde	3s 4d
Richard le Barcour	2s 4¾d
Walter le Bonde	2s 5½d
John atte Grene	3s 3d
Walter Huchenes	23½d
Richard le Colyare	18d
Henry Jop	3s 0½d
Robert le Neuman	2s 6d
Robert Dastyn	7s 2¼d
William Prat	21¾d
William Daston	5s 7d
Matilda Bernardes	6d

Approved. Total, £4 12s 7¾d

Aston Somerville (*Aston Somerville*)

210

Geoffrey Daston	3s 6d
Hugh Reve (*Preposito*)	2s 6¼d
William le Flint	17½d
William Dreu	19d
Sarah Hertes	17½d
Thomas de Bougrave	3s 5½d
Robert Alein	3s 7¾d
Thomas le Bele	2s 6½d
Reginald Henries	21½d
John le Bele	3s 1½d
John le Wyʒte	2s 9¾d
William le Messager	2s 2½d
Thomas Lauwen	18d
John Foules	3s 0½d
William atte Brugge	3s 1½d
John Thomes	16¾d
Alan Chaunterel	3s 11¾d
Thomas atte Strode	12d
Ralph Adam	16¾d
Hugh Kembe	17½d
William Daston	2s 2½d

Approved. Total, 49s 2½d

Wormington Grange/Berry Wormington (*Wormynton Parva cum Lutlynton*[53])

211

Robert de Bodenham	2s 1d
Richard atte Mulle	2s 7¾d
Edith Rolves	14d
John le King	3s 2¼d
Matilda Jones	2s 1¼d
Robert Wylkines	8d
Agnes Wryke	15¼d
William Beaufiz	8d
Nicholas Graunt	12¾d
Walter de Colne	2s
Robert de Knelle	9d
Alice de Colne	6d
Robert Dastyn	6s 10¼d
William Horsnayl	8d
Richard le Wyse	6d
Margery la Carpenter	6d
Isabel Aleyn	6d
Richard Alein	6d
William Miller (*Molendinario*)	6d

Approved. Total, 28s 1½d

[Membrane 14]

Wormington (*Wormynton Magna*)

212

Thomas Cole	21¾d
William Mogg	20¾d
John Houwen	2s 5¼d
Andrew Brant	19½d
John Dabat	2s 8d
William Abraham	12d
Robert de Home	2s 10d
Peter Wyllam	2s 11d
William Huggen	2s 7¾d
Henry Odam	12d
John Huggen	2s 1d
Robert Brant	16d
William Ferthing	2s 7½d
William le Noble	2s 9d
Robert Gouwer	20d
Richard Brant	20d
Richard Bonde	13½d
Richard de Home	3s 1d
Walter Huggen	3s 1d

Approved. Total, 40s 6d

Didbrook (*Didebrok*)

213

Robert Gouwer	2s 8d
William Andreu	2s 8¼d
Alice Colines	20¼d
Richard le Bek	2s 0¾d
Odo de Beckeforde	2s
John le Carpenter	8d
Richard Huwen	2s
Henry Silvestr	2s 8d
Walter Gouwer	15¾d
Walter Osebarn	19¾d

Approved. Total, 19s 4¾d

Coscombe (*Costecoumbe*)

214

Henry Wyrre	9½d
Stephen de Cestecoumbe	8¾d
Margery Uppehulle	6d

Approved. Total, 2s 0¼d

Pinnock, Ford and Hyde (*Pynnok, Forde [et] Hyde*)

215

William Springafeld	7d
John le Sclattere	7d
William atte Mulle	7d
Walter le Treuman	15d
Stephen Inla [*sic*] Hyde	2s 2¾d
Julian atte Hyde	12d
Margery atte Asshe	16d
Christine Inthelone	8d
Henry Goffat	8d
William atte Nasshe	6d
John Thomes	22d
Robert Inthelon	3s 7½d
John Batyn	9¾d
Giles de la Forde	14¼d

Approved. Total, 16s 10¼d

Sudeley (*Sudleye*)

216

Sir John de Sudleie	6s 7¾d
Richard Beauveys	6d
Robert de Tedinton	20¼d
Richard Sparwe	2s 1d
Richard Patyn	20¼d
Henry le Cok	20¼d
Walter le Feye	12d
Richard de Stoke	6d
Thomas le Horsman	6d
Walter Taus	6d
John le Grey	12½d
Robert de Mill (*Molendino*)	12d
Richard de Hullemulle	12d
Richard Clerk (*Clerico*)	3s 6d
Richard le Wheolar	6d
William de Astmer	6d

Approved. Total, 24s 4d

Greet (*Greote*)

217

Richard Dastyn	5s 11d
Robert de Wotton	20d
William de Wotton	22¼d
John Bisshop	14d
Ingram (*Ingrameo*) de Greote	12d
William Gerveys	14¾d
John atte Grene	12d
Robert Bubel	2s 8½d

Approved. Total, 16s 6½d

Gretton (*Gretton*)

218

Roger le Warde	20½d
. . . Mohaud	6d
. . .e atte Grene	14½d
William Ingelard	6d
. . . Notervile	14½d
. . . Bubel	19¾d
. . .to Ayleward	15¾d
. . .r Notervyle	6d
. . .ide Snop	6d
. . . Hobekines	21d
. . . de Bracebrugge	20d

[Approved][54] Total, 12s 6d

[Membrane 14 r-h col.]

Stanley Pontlarge (*Stanleye*)

219

Richard le Bercar	6d
Isabel de Stanleye	21½d
Paulinus le Ȝonge	2s 9¾d
Philip le Kniȝt	2s 11¼d
Walter le Treuman	2s 10d
John Giffard	2s 9¾d
John Wattes	13¼4d
John Paynwyke	18d
John Herbard	2s 9¼d
Robert le Fraunkelein	4s 8d
William Baldrik	17½d
Robert le Fraunkelein	3s 8½d
Ralph Nicholes	2s 11½d
William Osbarn	8d
John Osbarn	6d

Approved. Total, 33s 0¼d

Naunton and Frampton[55] (*Neuton [et] Bampton*)

220

Lord of Aston	2s 8½d
John Adam	12d
Simon le Nevew	6d
John Jones	3s 3d

Approved. Total, 7s 5½d

Toddington (*Tudynton*)

221

William Pynsoun	4s 2½d
William le King	21¾d
John le Tayllur	6d
Matilda la Couherde	3s 1¾d
Alice Alenar	22d
Henry atte Putte	2s 7d
Matilda Upedich	22¼d
John Alenare	2s 3¾d
Philip Miller (*Molendinario*)	3s 3d
John le Bien	2s 10¼d
Richard le Chaumbrer	12d
John Heynes	12d
Christine Whithond	12d

Approved. Total, 27s 4¼d

Twyning (*Twenyng*)

222

John le Mullewardes	3s 1½d
Henry Coppe	2s 0½d
John Wynsoun	8½d
Robert de Betewelle	3s 0¼d
Nicholas le Leornare	8¼d
Henry Botte	15¼d
John le Tayllur	6d
Henry Ordewey	3s
William Lacok	20d
Thomas Anketyl	10¾d
John Louenhulle	21¼d
John le Freman	2s 1¼d
John atte Pyrye	18d
John Pollard	8¼d
Richard atte Lepeȝate	18d
John Hannyg	15d
Matilda la Passour	10d
Adam de Poukethrop	2s 0½d
Henry Pouke	23¾d
Agnes la Leche	12d
Henry Herbarwe	6d
Nicholas Morice	9¾d
Walter de Pauntelegh	3s 6d
Agnes Arkayl	2s 2d
Robert le Crokare	6d
Thomas le Shepherde	9d
John le Crokare	10¼d
Robert de Bybury	21d
John Dod	15d
Robert atte Wode	18d
Anthony Sutor	10d
Nicholas Wade	19d
Geoffrey Baret	12½d
Richard Bone	18d
John Dober	6d
Robert atte Welle	23½d
Amice la Taillur	6d
Thomas Merewy	3s 1¼d
William le Taillur	51s 4¾d
John Dalby	6d
William Bulbat	6d
Richard de Poukesthrop	12¼d
John Huwotes	15d
John Budeles	6d
Philip Pinchoun	12½d
John atte Forde	12½d
Alice Trukeman	12¼d
Alice Keting	12d
Geoffrey atte Stone	12d

Approved. Total, 67s 5½d

Frampton and Naunton[56] (*Freulynton [et] Neunton*)

223

William Gilben	9d
William Mayou	6d
William Hikeman	6d
Roger Mayou	6d
John Nethewarde	4s 9d
Taundy [*sic*]	3s 4d
Richard le Eyr	21d
Henry Bonere	23d
Margery de Aldrinton	5s 10¾d
Alice Perkines	2s
Richard Boner	3s

Approved. Total, 24s 10¾d

[Membrane 14 dorse]

Stanton (*Staunton*)

224

Henry Abovetoun	2s 3½d
Robert Elys	10¼d
Ralph Quenyld	8d
Julian Bonekniȝt	18½d
John Biȝe	2s
Richard le Kniȝt	17d
Walter le Treuman	2s 3d
Richard Dame	10d
John Broun	2s 3¼d
Ralph le Eorl	18¼d
Thomas Ferling	3s 9d
Ralph de Blade	2s 9½d[57]
John Morwy	2s 9½d
Ralph Nicholes	3s 2½d
Ralph Gosselin	2s 4¼d
Ralph Wynsoun	15d
Robert Damedyth	2s 1¼d
Richard atte Broke	20½d
Robert Huwen	21d

Approved. Total, 37s 4¼d

Snowshill (*Snoweshull*)

225

John le Freman	12d
William Morcok	14d
William Broun	20½d
Ralph Michel	20d
William atte Ȝate	14d
Adam le Quarreour	18½d
Sarah de Brokhampton	12d

Approved. Total, 9s 3d

Roel (*Rowell*)

226

Robert Strenet	8¾d
Richard le Hayward	20½d
Richard Benet	6½d
Richard le Cartere	8¾d
William Edward	21d
Henry Kitten	11½d
David Botevylein	13¾d
John Gerard	13d
John Heynes	10d
Henry Jannes	6d
John atte Brok	7½d
John de Sponleye	19¼d
John atte Welle	20½d

Approved. Total, 13s 11d

Hawling (*Halling*)

227

Thomas Hobekynes	2s
Peter Hobekynes	12¼d
Thomas Botevylein	22½d
Ralph le Deye	16d
Robert Henryes	18¼d
Adam Bryȝt	21¼d
John Henryes	9¼d
Richard Hobekines	17d
John Wyot	8d
William le Longe	6d
William Dousing	20½d

Approved. Total, 14s 7d

Charlton Abbots (*Cherleton*)

228

Matilda South	13½d
John Damedith	14¾d
Simon Damedden	16¾d
William Drake	6d
Thomas le Ȝonge	17d
Roger Briȝt	6d
William atte Barr	2s 0½d
Richard Reeve (*Preposito*)	12d

Approved. Total, 9s 2½d

Catesthrop (*Cotesthrop*[58])

229

Ralph de Ennestane	10d
Nicholas le Bercare	8d
Alice la Cartere	7¼d
Nicholas le Webbe	6d
Walter le Frere	6d
Robert Peytevyne	8½d
Henry Richardes	12½d
Richard le Neuman	6d
Isabel Colynes	3s 1d
William le Swon	15½d
Richard le Dur	12½d
William le Dur	6d
Simon de Throp	6d

Approved. Total, 11s 9¼d

Postlip (*Poteslep*)

230

Lady of Poteslep	4s 6d
John Champeneys	6d
Richard de Caumpeden	8¼d
William le Jay	6d
Sir Richard de Cokkebury	3s 5d

Approved. Total, 9s 7¼d

Farmcote (*Farncot*)

231

Roger le Cok	8¾d
John Lambard	12d

[Membrane 14 dorse r-h col.]

Also Farmcote

Sarah Lambard	12d
Stephen le Jet	12½d
William Taundy	10¼d
Ellis atte Grove	6d
Walter Hobbes	14½d
Chad (*Cedom.*) de Francote	2s 0½d
John Wandes	10½d
William le Bonde	8d
John le Wyse	8d
Abbot of Hayles	3s

Approved. Total, 13s 7d

Castlett Farm (*Catteslade*)

232

William de Meosyhampton	5s 2¼d
William de Bedeforde	12d
Nicholas Kivel	6d
John Haukines	7½d
John Miller (*Molendinario*)	2s 11¼d

Approved. Total, 10s 3d

Guiting Power (*Guytyng Poer*)

233

John Mustel	5s 1d
John Hickes	14¼d
Thomas Wattes	3s 3½d
John Hasard	14½d
William Saumoun	12d
William Hasard	3s 1½d
John Wattes	2s 4½d
William le Vycory	8d
Robert Saundres	13d
Thomas Hervy	12¼d
Walter Jackes	3s 0¼d
John Godhale	10½d
John Emmen	15¼d
Richard Huwen	12d
John Brayn	6d

Approved. Total, 26s 8½d

Markdean (*Markeden*)

234

John de Staunton	5s

Total, 5s

Temple Guiting (*Guyting Temple*)

235

John Hobbes	17½d
John Wylles	2s 0¼d
Alice Wyot	19¾d
John Heynes	3s 1½d
William le Brother	2s 3¼d
Richard Alecok	6d
Geoffrey Weccheharm	8d
Walter le Raag	12¼d
William le Reve	8d
Walter Huwelot	3s 0¼d
John le Lord	8d
William de Didebrok	2s 7d

Approved. Total, 19s 7¾d

Kineton (*Kyngton*)

236

John atte Broke	3s 3d
Robert atte Broke	11d
Peter Uppehulle	2s 10¾d
John Payn	18¼d
John Jannes	2s 10d
William Richardes	12d
Robert Wyot	12½d
John le Leue	2s 5½d
Margery Dycones	18d

Approved. Total, 17s 5d

Barton (*Berton*)

237

William Weccheharm	21d
Agnes de Snowdon	2s 10½d
William Weccheharm	2s 7½d
Peter Syward	12d
William atte Broke	6d

Total, 8s 9d

Total of the whole hundred, £40 3s 10¾d

Subtaxers (*Subtaxatores*)

238

Thomas de Newenton	12d
John le Mareschal	12d
Robert de Chaveringworth	2s
John le Graunt	2s

Total, 6s

Total of the whole hundred aforesaid with the subtaxers' taxes, £40 9s 10¾d

BERKELEY HUNDRED
(*HUNDREDUM DE BERKELEY*)

Berkeley (*Vill. de Berkeleye*)

239

Adam Pynel	2s 6d[59]
John Burgeys	6d
Robert le Prestes	22d
Walter le Wodeward	6d
John Noblepas	6d
John Swele	3s
Isabel, widow of Roger Cuppere	2s
John le Webbe	12d
Thomas Sewaker	15d

[Membrane 15]

Also Berkeley

Robert Prykke	12½d
William Bonde	8d
Hugh le Proute	18¼d
William Miller (*Molendinario*)	12d
Thomas atte Halle	6d
John de Fremelode	15¾d
Nicholas le Vygnour	18d
John atte Churche	2s 6¼d
William le Clerk	3s 5¾d
William Judde	5s
Robert Groundy	19¾d
Robert le Shipward	12d
William de Aur	3s 0¼d
Edith, widow of Henry le Gardiner	4s 1d
John Walebrok	6d
Thomas de Malvarne	6d
Henry Swele	6d
William le Smyth	6d
Henry Modybrok	12d

Approved. Total, 44s 6¾d

Vills of Wotton under Edge, Ham, Cam, Dursley, Beverston and Almondsbury with hamlets (*Vill. de Wotton, Hamme, Came, Dursel., Beverston & Almondesbury cum hamell.*[60])

Wotton under Edge Borough[61] (*Wotton Intrinseca*)

240

Isabel de Berkeleye	14s 4d
Maurice de Chepstouwe	5s 0¼d
William Godard	2s
William Pycard	12d
John le Dyeare	2s
William de Almondesbury	12d
John Brevel	6d
Hugh Pydus	2s
James (*Jacobo*) le Mulleward	2s
Walter le Bonde	6d
John le Wese	6d
Henry Snyte	8s
Adam Pynnok	12d
William le Vicory	12d
John le Plomer	12d
John de Aure	12d
Ellis le Bakere	12d
John de Hokesforde	12d
Richard le Smyth	18d
John Geffrey	2s
Thomas Brounyng	2s
Peter le Chepman	6d
Gregory le Hore	12d

Approved. Total, 51s 10¼d

Wotton under Edge Parish outside Borough, with hamlets[62] (*Wotton Forinseca cum hamell.*)

241

Isabel de Berkeleye	10s 1d
Reginald Sake	5s 10½d
Adam Heysogge	5s 3d
Thomas le Hayward	3s 10d
Richard atte Welle	11d
Ellis Reina'	12d
Walter atte Hulle	17¾d
Thomas Fallewelle	3s 7¼d
Thomas Wynegod	14d
Eleanor de Bradeleye	3s 2d
Robert Slydewine	18d
Richard Brounyng	2s 10½d
Adam Josep	2s
Walter le Machoun	16d
Walter Josep	15¾d
Richard atte Broke	4s 11d
Roger de Berleye	5s 1d
Henry le Holdare	15d
Matthew Latyn	4s 4¾d
Roger le Styward	2s 1d
Abbot of St Augustine's	7s[63] 2d
Joan de Kyngeston	2s
Robert atte Halle	12d
Michael Howes	20¾d
Walter Saundres	3s 2d
John le Skay	4s 7d
Roger le Duynysshe	15s 1¾d
Richard de Caumvylle	9s 2¼d
Clar' de Combe	4s 0½d
John atte Chirche	6s 10½d
Nicholas Warderobe	3s 0½d
William Pavy	19¼d
Nicholas Draysid	11d
Nicholas Bernard	13d
Robert le Shephirde	2s 8d
John Cronnok	2s
Nicholas Heynes	12d
Walter Axepode	21d
Adam Edus	2s 9¾d

Approved. Total, £6 15s 1¼d

Uley (*Iwelegh*)

242

Walter Symond	13s 3¼d
John Symond	7s 6¾d
Nicholas Lovecok	5s 4½d
John de Benecoumbe	5s
John de Luyde	6s 1½d
Walter atte Ȝate	4s 5d
Robert Broun	4s 5¼d
William Topyn	2s 7¾d
John Jolyf	12d
John Spyleman	6d

Approved. Total, 50s 4d

Kingscote and Owlpen (*Kyngescote & Oulepenne*)

243

William atte Welle	11s 1¼d
Walter le Duyk	2s 6d
William de Kingescot	3s 5½d
Robert le Bohun	6d
James (*Jacobo*) Jerom	6d
John le Clerk	12d
Hugh le Southerne	9s 3d

[Membrane 15 r-h col.]

Also Kingscote and Owlpen

John Richard	5s 0¼d
John Hobekynes	3s 3½d

Approved. Total, 36s 7½d

Ham with hamlets (*Hame cum hamell.*)

244

Thomas de Berkeley	9s 10½d
Roger Purlewent	2s 2d
Henry Holewey	3s 8d
Thomas Suret	2s 1¼d
Adam atte Welle	2s 8d
William, son of Robert	4s 8d
Thomas Greyel	3s
John Purlewent	4s 8d
Henry Whitemay	3s 10¾d
Robert Bastard	4s 0¾d
William Greyel	2s 8¼d
Adam Perys	2s 10d
Thomas Holeweye	21d
Richard atte Slo	3s 11d
Alex. Dole	2s 6d
William Andreus	6d
Hugh de Costene	2s 6½d
Hugh de Northlon	2s 1¼d
Ralph de Thacham	6d
Walter Snyte	2s 1¼d
William Galiane	6d
John de Lyndeseye	3s 6½d
Walter atte Welle	3s 7d
Roger atte Slo	2s 6d
Nicholas Neel	2s 9d
Richard le Whyte	2s 7¾d
Brother Nicholas de Briȝtebowe	3s 7d
Walter atte Broke	3s 5¾d
Thomas atte Broke	3s 4¼d
Thomas Huwelot	8s 8½d
Richard de Stanforde	2s 6d
Matilda de Stanforde	7s 2½d
Nicholas Iweyn	2s 5d
Abbot of St Augustine's, Bristol	9s 7d[64]
Joan de Kingeston	4s 2d
William Hugynes	15¼d
John le Kyng	19½d
John Coutholf	4s 5d
John Balstake	6d
John Capel	5s 8d
John de Swonhunger	4s 7d
John Everard	5s 5d
John de Egeton	2s
Walter le King	5s 7¼d
John le Serjaunt	3s 5d
Thomas de Crauleye	2s
William Richardes	5s 8½d
John de Potamton	7s 1¼d
William Inthehurne	4s 4d
Edward de Fremelode	8s 8d
William le Swonhunger	2s 4d

Approved. Total, £9 7s 5d

Alkington (*Alkynton*)

245

Thomas de Berkeley	7s 4d
John de Saltmarsh (*Salso Maresco*)	8s 8½d
William Godynow	3s 8¾d
William Inthehurne	2s 9½d
Adam de Mattesdon	4s 6½d
Agnes Godynow	14½d
William Keniltr	3s
Walter Inthehevedfelde	23½d
Walter Huwes	3s 0¾d
Robert atte Hulle	2s 9d
John le Machoun	2s 4d
Adam Daungervile	5s 8½d
Adam Greyel	7s 8¼d
Walter Lotheray	5s 10d
William Pattok	12½d
William Dosy	10d
Walter Toyt	4s 1d
Philip Gibbes	6d
Peter de Stone	2s
William Wyllins	2s 8d
John le Fader	10¼d
Richard Jones	3s 8¾d
Robert le Baylyf	10d
John de Wydyhull	11½d
William Cut	2s 2d
William Kene	8d
John de Staunden	4s 11¼d
Roger Pattok	12½d
Henry le Eyr	6d[65]
William Cnyte	6d
William Bolkard	12d
Nicholas le Swon	2s 10d
Nicholas le Visshare	22d
Nicholas le Proute	9d
William Moryce	6d
Richard Golde	4s
Robert de Asselworth	3s 2d
Henry Broun	12d
Richard Dolling	2s 10d
Walter de Combe	4s . . .[66]
William Golde	4s
John Greyel	6d
Adam atte Cloude	12d
William le Grip	2s
Richard le Ferour	2s . . .½d

Approved. Total, £6 12¼d

Hill and Nympsfield (*Hulle & Nymdesfelde*)

246

John le Fiz [*sic*]	. .[67] 5½d
Matilda, Lady of Hill (*Hulle*)	. . .
William Martel	. . . . . .[68]
Robert Boltupriȝt	. . .
William Boltupriȝt	. .[69]

[Membrane 15 dorse]

Also Hill and Nympsfield

Walter atte Nelme	2s 9½d
Adam Pacy	12½d
Roger le Bonde	2s 9d
John atte More	3s 3d
Robert Sygare	16d
John atte Pulle	3s 2d
Robert le King	3s 6d
William le Knyȝt	4s 7½d
John Malot	2s 8¼d
John Payn	3s 6½d[70]
Robert le Bonde	3s 6d
Hugh, son of Denise	6d
Robert atte Croyce	2s 3¾d
Walter le Mareys	14d
John le Levefrend	2s 9d
William Martel	7s 5d
Nicholas Lydeȝard	6d
Nicholas le Prestes	8s 0½d
Walter le Shephirde	4s 6d
William Fort	22d
Walter Symond	10s
John Giffard	2s 7d
John Batyn	13d
William Payn	19¼d
Philip Payn	2s 3¼d
John Payn the elder	18d

Approved. Total, 104s 10¾d

Cam with hamlets, namely Stinchcombe, Breadstone and Woodmancote (*Vill. de Came cum hamell. viz Styntescombe, Bradeston & Wodemoncot*)

247

Thomas de Berkeleye	6s 8d
Henry de Nasse	4s 10½d
Henry de Came	8s
Robert Passelewe	4s 9½d
Henry le Wodeward	3s 1¾d
Gilbert Godknave	2s 10½d
Roger atte Hulle	2s 2d
William Sperke	2s 2d
John Shidwalle	4s 5¼d
William Wydie	18¾d
Robert atte Style	2s 6d
Richard atte Shote	2s 9¾d
John atte Mulle	4s 11¼d
Richard le Wine	2s
Roger Harding	5s 5¾d
Richard le Reve	4s 5d
Gilbert atte Forde	6s 3¼d
William atte Doune	6s 7½d
Thomas Inthewodende	7s 6¾d
William Soliman	7s 4d
William Hathewy	4s
Reginald Brounyng	2s 2d
Nicholas Topyn	2s 8¼d
William atte Broke	10s 0¼d
John de Milkesham	3s 4¾d
Walter Passage	4s 3½d
William de Astmed	12d
John atte Plaunche	12d

Walter le Wodeward	3s 3½d
Amice la Monek	16d
Walter de Astmed	6d
Robert de Draycot	6d
Thomas de Lillebourn	12d
William le Mortimer	23¼d
William Arnald	12d
Roger le Webbe	6d
John de Longeforde	12d
Matilda Inthehale	6d
Thomas de Bradeston	3s 6d
Richard atte Hamme	3s 7¾d
Gilbert le Whyte	3s 6½d
Thomas Waltres	2s
Thomas de Swynebourne	6s 8d
William Mody	2s 10½d
Robert atte Ȝate	7s 4½d
William atte Marleputte	4s 8½d

Approved. Total, £8 5s 0¾d

Beverston (*Beverston*)

248

Thomas Apadam	7s 1¾d
Alex. atte Nassh	3s 8d
William atte Norcharde	17d
John le Palmere	6d
John atte Nassh	19d
Thomas de Brayforde	12d
Walter Saleman	4s 9¾d
Thomas Saleman	21¼d
Stephen Colles	21¾d
Robert le Hayward	8s 9d
Roger Alfrich	6s 8d
Thomas Testard	8s 11d
Philip Smart	6s
Walter le Wlouke	3s 9d
Robert le Tayllur	5s 3¾d
Richard le Wlouke	19d
John Athelard	8s 10½d

Total, 73s 6¾d[71]

Coaley (*Coueleye*)

249

. . . de Berkeleye	6s 8d
. . . le Wariner	4s 4¼d
. . . le Wodeward	2s 7d
. . . le Hulmonecot	5s 7d
John de Rede	4s
. . . Colles	3s 1d
. . . Inthehale	5s 8d
. . . . . .	4s 10¾d

[Membrane 15 dorse r-h col.]

Also Coaley

William Colynes	8¾d[72]
Walter Coriet	2s 0¾d
Walter atte Hame	4s 4d
Robert atte Fisshwere	3s 9¼d
Nicholas le Brueware	12d
Robert de Coueleye	9s 2¼d
Thomas Rawyne	2s 4d
William Neel	3s 5¼d
William Jurdan	5s 3d
William atte Style	9¾d
John Wylkines	3s 3¾d
Robert Eliot	2s

Approved. Total, 75s[73] 0¾d

Slimbridge (*Slymbrugg*)

250

Thomas de Berkeleye	6s 8d
Nicholas Selewyne	6s 9d
Robert Wynter	6s 6¾d
William le Longe	18d
Gilbert Burel	13d
William de Oldelonde	6s 6¾d
John atte Ȝate	17s 1d
John le Longe	6s 4d
Thomas le Marchal	6d
Joan de Kingeston	8s 7¼d
William Passemer	2s 9d
Adam Broun	15¼d
Walter de Oldelonde	12s 1d
Odo de Actone	11s 11¼d
Edward Golde	3s 9½d
Thomas le Muchele	7s 10d
William le Botyler	3s 1d
Roger le Archer	3s 7d
John de Bradeforde	3s 4d
Roger atte Watere	4s 1d
Agnes de Mattesden	3s 4d
Thomas de Beolegh	3s 4d
Richard le Touchte	7s 6d[74]
Ralph Pulm	2s
William atte Pulle	2s 9d
Thomas Pynel	3s
Roger le Mortimer	3s 4d
Thomas de Beoleyesterte	12d
Joan Fallewelle	2s 4½d
Matilda Culling	6s 1d
John Hard	13d
John Symond	14¼d
Roger Pynel	2s 10d
Matilda atte Grove	3s
Thomas Halling	2s 1¼d
Richard de Worthwode	12d
Thomas le Couherde	12d
Nicholas Kydun	12d
Edith Wynter	12d
Adam le Ȝonge	12d
David ap Gryfith	3s 10½d
Adam Burel	12d

Approved. Total, £8 10s 2¼d

Arlingham (*Erlingham*)

251

Richard de Clyfford	8s 6½d
Walter Wych the younger	5s 6½d
Matilda atte Berwe	5s 4d
John de Symondeshale	3s 4d
Walter Leuward	2s 11¼d
William Pride	12d
John Mey	23½d
John le Hayward	10s
William Janes	13¼d
Robert Bertram	12d
Ellis Huwes	12d
Walter le Charer	2s 11¼d
John de Bolgarston	15½d
Robert Geffrey	3s 11¼d
Robert Cordy	3s 5d
Richard Wych	3s 2d
John le Tayllur	14¾d
Nicholas le Bakare	6d
John de Middelton	2s 0¾d
William Jones	2s 6d
John Warde	12¼d[75]
Alex. atte Slo	2s 8½d
John Bride	22¼d
Richard le Smith	6d
John Stapel	18½d
Robert le Hayward	2s 10¾d
John Fraunkelein	18d
Alice Scot	6d
Robert de Benhale	6d
Robert le Frere	16¼d[76]
Adam Malines	6d
Walter Byl	6d
William Dun	9s 10¾d
Ellen Gevis	7s 7¾d[77]
Richard de Longeneye	2s 11¼d
Walter de Middelton	3s 8½d
John le Frere	4s 4½d
William Saundres	22½d
James (*Jacobo*) de Wylton	5s 5½d
John de Pendok	3s 1¾d
Robert Jurdan	3s 2¾d
Walter Wych	3s 10d
Richard, son of John le Hayward	12d

Approved. Total, £6 5s 3¼d

Ashworthy Farm and Cromhall (*Asshelworth[78] [et] Cromhale*)

252

William Jones	2s 3d

[Membrane 16]

Also Ashworthy Farm and Cromhall

Nicholas le Kyng	2s 9½d
John Alissaundre	5s 5d

Geoffrey de Longeneye	6d
Roger le Hopere	6d
John le Kniȝt	2s 8d
William atte Halle	3s 5¾d
Godfrey Daston	6d
William atte Brugge	6d
Thomas Cole	15d
Henry Fraunceys	6d
Thomas Fiz Williame	2s 7¾d
Adam le Ȝonge	8¼d
William le Hayward	2s 11½d
William de Wauton	6s 2½d
Richard de Budelescombe	12s 7d
Roger Daunt	11½d
Walter atte Halle	5s 7d
John Godwine	13¼d
John Dounatom	2s
William le Botiler	2s 5d
Walter de Whitefeld	2s
William de Whitefeld	21½d
Philip le Botyler	7¼d
Alex. Barbost	6d
John atte Were	8½d
Roger Hobbes	6d
William Whyting	12¼d
Robert Whytimon	22d
Ellis Wylkines	9d
Richard le Crockare	9d
Nicholas Friday	6d
John de Shyneleye	2s 11¼d
Richard Baroun	2s 1¼d
John Jordan	6d
Richard Talebrok	22¼d
Roger le Shephurde	2s 10½d
Robert Baroun	6d
Adam le Taillur	12d
Roger Maunsel	6d
John de Brokeneberwe	10¼d
William Baloun	6d
Robert le Hayward	4s 11¾d
Richard de Shinel	2s 0¾d

Approved. Total, £4 9s 1½d

King's Weston and Elberton (*Kyngesweston & Aylbritton*)

253

Thomas ap Adam	6s 3¼d
Walter Hobbes	4s 3¼d
Robert le Bragelare	17¼d
Anselm de Gorne	3s 8½d
Walter le Bakar	9½d
Walter atte Hulle	6d
Hugh le Knyȝt	2s 8¼d
Stephen le Hunte	18d
Walter Wylkines	17d
Adam le Justare	16½d
John atte Halle	3s
Richard Croceman	15¼d
Simon atte Broke	7s 10d
Hugh Grym	3s 2¼d
Hugh Delling	3s
John le Duyk	4s 3d
Thomas le Mareys	3s 4d
William atte More	3s 4d
John atte Trewe	3s 7d
Walter Duggel	3s 5¾d
Thomas le Gardiner	3s 0¼d
Walter le Carpenter	3s 4¾d
William de Stanberwe	3s 6d
Thomas ap Adam	7s 8¾d
John Champeneys	18s 10d
John Gostard	16¾d
Walter le White	2s
Adam atte Pyle	4s 6d
Adam atte Wode	6d[79]
John Edny	4s 8¼d
Walter Phelippes	3s 7d
Richard West	3s 10d
Roger Stroguyl	5s
John Rolves	21d
Robert le Smyth	2s 7d
William atte Berwe	2s 4d
Nicholas Rolves	20½d
William le Hopere	7¼d
William le White	7¼d
William Stroguyl	19¼d
Robert Heynes	3s 4d
William le Smith	8d
Nicholas Edny	3s 6d
Walter Dauwes	6d

Approved. Total, £7 16¾d

Horfield and Filton (*Horefeld & Filton*)

254

William West	2s 8¼d
William le Ȝonge	15s 5½d
Thomas Russel	6d
David le Freman	16d
Thomas Mayel	2s
John Maydegod	6d
Roger le Bate	2s 9½d
John West	2s 11d
John le Holdare	7¾d
Walter le Portare	2s 8¾d
Richard atte Brugge	2s 6d
John le Sopere	16¾d
Henry de Patepulle	18¾d
Ellis de Filton	6s 8½d
John Aylward	2s 5d
. . . le Fox	12d
Roger atte Brugge	12d
Robert atte Brugge	6d
Edward atte Hulle	2s 2¼d
William atte Hay	5s 0¾d
. . . Beaumond	6d
. . . Rode	3s
. . . Stanleye	2s 0½d
. . . . . .d	4s 0½d

Approved. Total, 65s 6¾d

[Membrane 16 r-h col.]

Almondsbury (*Almondesbury*)

255

Robert Heynes	2s 6d
William Cnyt'	21¾d
Nicholas Brounyg	6d
John atte Wayneȝete	17d
William le Carpenter	11½d
William le Swein	14¼d
Thomas Cnyt	18¾d
Nicholas le Songare	2s 8¾d
William Lateberwe	6d
John Whete	20¾d
Richard le Swon	2s
Thomas Davy	2s 8¼d
William de Stanweye	3s 6¼d
Nicholas le Holdare	6d
Stephen Heynes	6d
Henry Aylwyne	6d
William Smith (*Fabro*)	4s 8d
Agnes le Meregure	6d
John Cromme	12d
David West	20d

Approved. Total, 32s 5¼d

Dursley (*Durseleye*)

256

John de Berkeleie	8s 1¾d
Sir John de Bradeforde	3s 1¾d
Richard le Harpour	4s
William le Tayllur	12d
Hugh Clement	7½d
Roger le Tannar	3s 5¾d
Robert le Smyth	12d
John le Harpour	6d
Walter le Clerk	3s
Thomas le Wodeward	4s 10d
Thomas Attenelme	3s 8¼d
Agnes Atteȝate	3s 3¼d
William le Freond	2s
Robert Attenelme	2s
John le Crone	2s
Richard le Freond	6d
Ralph Potu	6d
Matilda la Tanner	12d
Robert le Gardiner	5s 7d
Nicholas le Stompe	18d
Roger Hathemar	4s
John Dybus	2s
Reginald le Wodeward	6d

Approved. Total, 58s 3¼d

Newington Bagpath and Ozleworth (*Newenton Baggepathe & Osleworth*)

257

John de Berkeleye	13s 3d

Henry Norman	63s 11d
John James (*Jacobo*)	14d
Henry Damejoneson	2s 8d
John le Wodeward	10d
William le Shephurde	4s 7d
Adam Tassot	4s 3¼d
William James (*Jacobo*)	4s 3¾d
Walter le Southerne	5s
Thomas le Southerne	18d
John de Cheltenham	2s
Robert le Rede	3s 2¾d
William le Webbe	12¼d
Thomas le Proute	13d

Alice atte Forde	4s 2d

Approved. Total, 113s

Total of the whole hundred, £92 9d

Subtaxers (*Subtaxatores*)

258	
Robert Groundy	12d
Thomas Page	2s

John de Oulepenne	12d
John de Kyngeston	12d
Peter de Styntescombe	12d
Stephen de Draicote	12d
Walter Pride	12d

Total, 8s

Total of the whole hundred aforesaid with the subtaxers' taxes, £92 8s 9d[80]

CLEEVE HUNDRED
(*HUNDREDUM DE CLYVE*)

Bishop's Cleeve (*Villa de Clyve*)

259

William atte Brugge	2s 4½d
John de Fladebury	2s 10¼d
Robert Thommes	6d
John Benet	18¾d
John le Messager	15d
Samson le Hunte	5s 6¾d
Richard le Mareschal	6d
Gregory de Mareny	5s 3d
John de Clyve	2s 4d
Roger atte Mor	3s 9½d
Peter Janekyn	2s 0¼d
John le Iryssh	2s 4d
William le Droys	2s 6d
John le Gardiner	4s 1d
William Fichel	19¼d
Richard le Hone	3s 0¾d
William Sparke	3s 0¾d
William le Fisshar	2s 6d
William Camel	2s 4¼d
Richard le Chapman	3s 9d
John Huwes	9d
John Billing	19d
John Huwettes	3s 4d
John de Southbroke	2s 1d

Approved. Total, 61s 1½d

[Membrane 16 dorse]

Woodmancote and members (*Wodemancot membr.*)

260

Nicholas Cavel	23d
Walter le Blake	2s
Edith la Kinges	6s 9d
William le Reve	6s 4¼d
Samson Toly	2s 5¼d
William Baldwine	8s 0½d
William le Ussher	12s 1¼d
Edith la Neuman	3s 8d
John Bungy	6s 0¾d
Robert Austyn	23d
John Frewine	6d
John Gamel	5s 0¾d
John de Whitindon	5s 2d
John de Wyke	20¾d
Peter atte Wyke	6d

Approved. Total, 64s 2½d

Gotherington (*Goderynton*)

261

John de St Amand (*Sancto Amando*)	17s 3¾d
Stephen le Routare	2s
Matthew le Calewe	21¾d
John Whythod	9d
Walter le Wetherherde	3s 11½d
William atte Brugge	12d
Margery Stevenes	18d
John Jurdan	3s 6d
John le Prest	15d
Simon Jones	2s 7¾d
John le Freman	4s 6¾d
Peter Balle	12d
John Bele	8s 0¾d
Walter le Eorl	2s 4½d
Katherine Neel	2s 1½d
Samson Knulle	12d
John Hathewy	2s 6d
John Herbert	3s 7d
Richard Roger	2s 10¾d
William Gilberd	2s 7½d
John de Wormynton	22½d
William de Chantmond	2s 5½d
Simon Pendok	19½d
William Pygaz	23d
Richard Berry	2s
Nicholas Dod	3s 4¼d
Richard Beatrich	3s 4½d
Gilbert Berry	3s 6¾d
Samson Boneth	6d
Rector of Cleeve Church	8s 4¾d

Approved. Total, £4 15s 6¼d

Stoke Orchard[81] (*Vill. de Stoke*)

262

Alice Geffrey	2s 0¾d
Henry Droke	2s 1½d
Thomas Jannes	18¾d
Robert Court	3s 8½d[82]
Robert Denys	14¾d
William le Mulleward	12d
John de Home	4s
Alice (*Alesia*) la Archer	5s
Geoffrey le Archer	6s 5¾d
John Mody	10d
Thomas Broun	9d
John Thomes	11¾d
John le Smeth	6d
Margaret Douk	9¼d
Walter Saundres	6d
Richard Wylicok	2s 0¾d
John Tabert	6d
Robert le Webbe	6d
Richard le Chapeleyn	2s 10¾d
Walter Mauger	23½d
John Jannes	18¼d
Nicholas Herbert	14¾d
Walter Thomes	10¾d
Roger le Ȝeman	12d
Henry Cok	6d

Approved. Total, 44s 7¼d

Southam (*Southam*)[83]

263

Richard le Smyth	5s 6d
William Attenelme	2s 3¾d
Matilda la Bonde	2s 6¾d
Nicholas atte Hulle	4s 3¾d
John atte Hulle	3s 3¾d
John Smart	2s
Richard Nichol	4s 10½d
Richard le Marech'	2s 9¾d
Adam le Kniȝt	2s
Robert Lovecok	12d
Thomas de Amondesham	4s 0¾d
Richard Mayou	6d
Walter atte Oke	2s 6d
Gilbert le Bohun	9s 0½d
Reginald, son of Herbert	7s 0¾d

Approved. Total, 53s 10¼d

Brockhampton (*Vill. de Brokhampton*)

264

John le Fisshare	3s 5½d
William le Kniȝt	2s 1d
Richard Pouke	3s 9¾d
Richard Dameysabele	18¾d
John atte Roche	3s 9d
Beatrice de Clyve	5s 1d
John Godwine	4s 9¾d
Richard le Freman	2s 6½d
Philip le Burgeys	2s 0¾d
. . . la Fers	3s 4¾d
John le Wodeward	4s 6¾d
R. . . de Clyve	2s 3d

Approved. Total, 39s 4½d

[Membrane 16 dorse r-h col.]

Stony Cockbury/Rushy Cockbury (*Cockebury & Huntelowe*)[84]

265

John Pyrie	2s 2¾d
Alice Jay	12¾d
Philip de Cockebury	6d
Robert Hywenet	18d
Hugh Coke	12d

Approved. Total, 6s 3½d

Rector of Cleeve Church's Tenants (*Tenentes Rectoris Ecclesie de Clyve*)

266

John le Reve	22½d

Nicholas atte Pounde	19¾d
William Bonsquyer	21¾d
Samson le Wayte	12d
Geoffrey le Whyte	18d
Nicholas le Shephirde	12d
William Cavel	12d
Robert le Euche	9d
William Gerald	6d
John de Wyncheleseye	16d

Approved. Total, 12s 5d

Total of the whole hundred, £18 17s 4¾d

Subtaxers (*Subtaxatores*)

267

John Sampson	12d

William de Fladebury	2s
Richard Bate	2s

Total, 5s

Approved. Total of the whole hundred aforesaid with the subtaxers' taxes, £19 2s 4¾d

BISLEY HUNDRED
(*HUNDREDUM DE BYSELEYE*)

Bisley (*Bysele*)

268

Joan la Bohun	7s 0½d
Hugh de Bysele	2s 0¼d
Adam de Rokwode	6s
Hugh de Lutlerugge	3s 4d
John de Rokwode	18d
William Mile	2s 6d
William de Stancombe	16d
William Hobbes	12d
Richard atte Blakewell	3s
Richard Sebarn	18½d
Richard Perisson	18d
Christine Inthefelde	17½d
William Salaman	2s 6½d
William Rog'	17d
Agnes Roger	20¼d[85]
Miles Sebarn	8d
Thomas Sebarn	15d
Robert Batecok	15d
Ellis de Bisrug	9d
Alex. de Tymbhulle	12d
Henry de Chalforde	3s 6½d
Thomas de Pagenhulle	18d
Henry le Hyne	6d
Robert le Cok	20d
Hugh le Hayward	12d
William Godale	2s 6½d
William Inthecombe	18¾d
Eva la Webbe	20d
Thomas Robert	15d
Walter atte Pirie	16d
Richard de Coppychegrove	2s 0¼d
Richard de Coppichegrove	18¾d
Nicholas de Chircheye	2s 6½d
Ellis Alrich	6d
Henry Alrich	2s
Alice de Strode	2s 2¾d
Richard atte Hulle	12d
Richard Sered	6d
John le King	2s 2d
William de Stonebrug	18d
Richard de Stancomb	20¾d
Ellis Underhulle	12d
Agnes Underhulle	18d
Roger le Duriard	5s
Dyonis. le Duryard	3s 6d
Robert de Hockenhale	2s
Roger Swele	2s

Approved. Total, £4 12s 1¼d

Paganhill (*Pagenhull*)

269

Roger de Dene	2s 2d
Nicholas de la Bourn	20d
John le Smyth	18d
William le Rede	15d
Roger de Seymor	16½d
Margery de Dene	2s 6d
Richard le Clerk	15½d
John le Walsshe	18d
Henry le Fermer	2s 4d
Benedict de Dodebrugge	18d
John Roger	3s 1½d
Robert Selewine	20¾d

Approved. Total, 21s 11¼d

Lower Lypiatt (*Lupog Inferior*)

270

John le Reom	...
Nicholas le Gussh	...
William Bytheweye	...
Andrew de Hathmer	...
Henry Jones	...
William Bygge	...
Robert Upehulle	...
William Jones	...

Approved. Total, 16s 3d

[Membrane 17]

Bidfield (*Dudefeld*)

271

Robert de Sapy	8s 8d
Robert Loverich	18½d
Robert Adm	15½d
Richard atte Hasele	4s 0½d

Approved. Total, 15s 6½d

Middle Lypiatt and Tunley (*Lupeyate Superior & Tonleye*)

272

William Maunsel	8s 0¼d
Margaret Maunsel	2s 6d
Margaret Ferr	2s 6¼d
John in the Felde	2s
Richard de la Frith	3s
Sarah de la Frith	3s 6¾d[86]
William le Proute	3s 1d
John de la Broke	15d
Alice in the Coumbe	2s 6½d
Robert Willames	18d
John de Clyveshale	4s 1d
Hugh Ferr	3s 3¾d
Henry de Clifford	13¾d

Approved. Total, 39s 4¼d

Sapperton (*Saperton*)

273

Henry le Heose	11s
William de Island (*Insula*)	8s 1½d
Richard Leg	12d
Walter atte Forde	2s 8½d
Anselm Pegoys	21½d
Nicholas Pegoys	16d
Matilda la Smyth	22d
John Gille	9d
William de Haille	3s 9½d
Alice la Reve	15d
Ralph Cherug	20d
William Tote	4s 3½d

Approved. Total, 39s 7¼d

Frampton Mansell (*Frompton*)

274

William Maunsel	4s
Margaret Maunsel	18d
William Porter	2s 0¼d
Henry Bletȝ	15d
Henry Michel	20d
John Pethet	12d
Alice atte Steorte	18d
Philip Stouk	18d
Richard de Chirinton	22d

Approved. Total, 16s 3¼d

Througham (*Troham*)

275

Robert Stonȝate	16d
Richard Stonyate	2s

William Pagenhulle	18d
Robert Howel	2s
William Crech	18d
Richard Pagunhulle	19d
Richard Clyvehale	3s 6d
John Coliar	20d

Approved. Total, 15s 1d

Winstone (*Wyneston*)

276

John de la Hyde	16d
John Haiward	2s 2½d
John Noble	2s
Thomas Noble	3s 5d
Robert atte Brugge	8d
Walter Cok	15d
Robert Coliar	2s 7¼d

Approved. Total, 13s 5¾d

Edgeworth (*Eggesworth*)

277

Peter Helioun	5s 6d
William Leyr	16d
William Porter	14d
Walter Knyt	12d
John Nyng	6d
John Prodomme	18½d
Matilda Chysewelle	14d
Robert Onerton	3s 7d
Richard atte Halle	18d
Walter Skede	2s 8¼d
Agnes Westwode	22d
Walter Pog	20d
William Westwode	2s 6½d

Approved. Total, 26s 0¼d

Wishanger (*Musardere Wyshangre*)

278

Edmund de Wodestoke	18d
John Clement	18d
Nicholas Larch	18d
William Smalrugg	2s 2½d
John Alayn	18d
Richard Yonge	9d
Robert de Mercombe	12d
William Sodgrove	18d
Brother Michael	2s 10d
Henry de Cronham	12d
Clarice atte Hulle	6d
William Rolves	12d
Godfrey Aleyn	15d
William Honicombe	2s 6½d
Thomas Deuenet	6d
Peter Horsman	2s 6d
William Elys	15d
Richard atte Fortheye	15d

Approved. Total, 26s 1d

Painswick (*Payneswyk*)

279

Robert With'	2s
Agnes Chesecombe	12d
Robert Gerard	3s 0¼d
Walter atte Halle	2s 8d
John Chudde	12d
John Bonehull	2s 6½d
William in the Felde	9d
John Pigaz	12d
Alice de la Strode	4s
Richard de la Strode	2s
Reginald Eltre	12d
Henry Skyuerel	3s
Alice Phelippes	3s
William Scrich	22d
William Brok	9d
Henry Godde	18d
William Blakeman	3s
Alice Walssh	18d
Golda Leggetr	6d
Roger Worich	2s 1d

[Membrane 17 r-h col.]

Also Painswick

Nicholas Hamond	15d
Reginald Broune	3s
Alice Judde	18d
Ellis Hamond	18d
William atte Putte	12d
John de Batecombe	12d
Nicholas Cromplyng	18d
Alice Segrym	18d
John Blisse	18d
Lettice in the Combe	2s
John Knyt	15d
Richard Eylof	3s
John West	2s 0½d
Richard atte Wode	12d
James (*Jacobo*) Skyuerel	12d
John Colines	12d
John Skyidel	2s
John Segrym	14d
Richard Godman	22d
Richard Colynes	12d
Nicholas Berde	12d
Nicola Cromplyng	15d
Walter Peseforde	2s 2¼d
Richard Rog'	21d
Richard Whelar	18d
Ellis Whelar	3s
Julian Pural	12d
Richard atte Mulle	22d
Richard Kyng	4s 0¼d
Gilbert Chapman	2s
Robert Salcombe	2s
Richard Salcombe	3s
Richard Tideshulle	18d
Alice Hare	3s
John Chagge	18d
Thomas Gurdlar	18d
Simon Whiston	2s 6d
Reginald Whiston	15d
John White	2s 3d
Reginald Cuppe	15d
John Brocworth	8d
Walter Rog'	12d
Robert atte Castle	12d
William Damesele	16d
Margery Bernard	22d
Walter atte Strode	3s
Simon atte Strode	18d
John Salecombe	4s

Approved. Total, £6 2s 9¾d

Total of the whole hundred, £22 4s 6¾d

Subtaxers (*Subtaxatores*)

280

John de Cotes	12d
Thomas de Eggesworth	12d
Robert Crouste	12d
John de Frompton	12d
Henry Batecoke	12d
Henry de Strodforde	12d
Osbert de Sponbedde	12d

Total, 7s

Approved. Total of the whole hundred aforesaid with the subtaxers' taxes, £22 11s 6¾d

BLEDISLOE HUNDRED
(*HUNDREDUM DE BLIDDESLOWE*)

Alvington (*Alvynton*)

281

Walter Kech	6s
John Frend	2s
John, son of John	21¾d
Margery la Deye	3s 8d
Brice Shonyn	8d
John Ivor	2s
John Spyneye	6d
Adam Broun	12d
Lucy Godefray	23¾d
Matilda Godewyne	15½d
Richard Morice	18d
Adam Smith (*Fabro*)	12d
William Hathewy	12d
Alice Roddok	21d
Nich. Richeman	3s
Walter Godefray	20d
William Tamar	2s
Nicholas de la Heose	6d
Robert Ely	12¼d
Joh. Shonyn	18d
Walter Richeman	2s 6d
Adam Richeman	2s
Nicholas Bou	6d
William Hondy	3s
Adam Wilekynes	2s 6d
John Croudar	12d
Alan Swon	12d

[Membrane 17 dorse]

Also Alvington

William Andreu	2s
Adam Rudar	12d
Walter Sebarne	12d
Agnes Morice	18d
Philip Clerk (*Clerico*)	12d
Walter de Hill (*Monte*)	2s
Robert Balle	12d
Robert Pakkar	18d
Geoffrey Gategrove	12d
John Smith (*Fabro*)	6d
William Kyng	10d
William Gorwy	12d
Philip Motoun	6d
William Webbe	3s 6d

Approved. Total, 67s 8¼d

Aylburton (*Ailb'ton*)

282

Ellis de Ailb'ton	3s 5¼d
William Wodeward	6d
Matthew Swele	15d
John Palmer	20d
William Bussard	15d
Henry Miller (*Molendinario*)	6d
Richard Cartere	12d
John Shipman	23¾d
Sybil Machen	12d
Isaac atte Broke	15d
Philip Cornon	20d
John Yawan	3s
Roger Oriel	6d
John Benet	2s
Thomas le Clerk	6d
William de Hill (*Monte*)	3s
John Yawan	2s
Matthew Yawan	3s
Walter Moul	4s 4d
William Benet	11d
Richard White	3s 4d
Christine Swele	14d
William Shypmon	20d
John Pride	6d
William le Gosherde	16d
Nicholas de Hill (*Monte*)	2s
Walter atte More	16d
Thomas Riche	12d
William, son of Adam Benet	20d
Henry Reve	3s 6d
John Bokerich	6d
William Wale	12d
Joan la Bruthr	6d
Ralph Smith (*Fabro*)	12d
John White	2s
Thomas Spicer	6d
William Cradok	9d
Richard Moul	12d
Ellen Moul	2s 6d
William Wale	18d
Ellen Morice	6d
Sir Adam Sampson	2s

Approved. Total, 66s

Lydney with members (*Lydeneye cum membr.*)

283

Gilbert Talbot	4s 9d
Henry de Nasse	4s 1d
Ralph Dody	6d
Walter Pesshoun	20½d
Ralph Moul	6d
Joh. Folnord	15½d
John Carpenter	6d
William de Court (*Curia*)	6d
Joh. Spiring	12d
William Hokstar	6d
John Edy	23½d
Thomas Odyn	7½d
Thomas Goky	6d
William Poche	6d
William Bonde	9d
Walter de Foxleye	7d
John Frer	11½d
Philip Pesshoun	15d
William Webbe	12d
Richard Home	15½d
Peter Basshelegh	12d
Walter Loksmyth	6d
Matilda Achard	6d
John Mareschal	6d
John Poche	6d
Walter Jurdan	6d
John atte Walle	16¾d
Henry Partrich	6d
Adam Perkyn	12d
Walter Edy	6d
Richard, son of Thomas	13d
John de la Hurste	14¼d
William Leulyn	3s 4d
Philip St'newall	2s 2½d
Richard Frer	12d
John Hurlond	9d
Richard, son of Richard	6d
Walter, son of Stephen	4s 3½d
John, son of John	2s 6¾d
John Snel	6d
Philip, son of Thomas	19½d
William atte Gorste	2s 1½d
Alexander Hurlond	13¼d
Peter Shephurde	6d
William Waryn	3s 10½d
Ellis Gardiner	6d
John atte Churche	12d
Walter atte Hurste	3s
Reginald Waryn	12d
Richard Rede	2s
Gilbert Kyne	2s 2¾d
Walter Heme	3s

Approved. Total, 71s 0¼d

[Membrane 17 dorse r-h col.]

Awre with members (*Aure cum membr.*)

284

Thomas de Berkeleye	4s 3¾d
John de Berkeleye	2s 1½d
John de Aure	18d
John de la Boxe	2s
Walter Lauwes	6d
Hugh le Knyt	6d
Robert le Knyt	16d
Stephen le White	6d
John le Cok	6d
Richard le 3onge	6d
Hugh le Bonde	6d
Robert, son of Walter	6d
Richard Baderon	6d
Thomas le Grovare	6d
Richard Leward	6d
John le White	12d
John Palefray	13¾d
William Beke	6d
Walter le Skinnar	2s
William Menske	16¼d
Henry Seybryght	6d
Henry Martyn	6d
Robert de Blidd	13¼d
John Wylkines	6d
Adam Reynald	12d
John Bonde	6d
Henry Endas	15d
Hugh de Crykfeld	6d
John Torry	6d
John Smith (*Fabro*) de la Boxe	6¾d
John atte Pulle	6d
Richard atte Boxe	12¾d
Humphrey atte Boxe	9d
Thomas atte Home	6d
Henry le Waleys	2s 8d
Richard Wydie	6d
John Brounyng	15½d
Walter Arnolf	6d
Richard le Palmere	6d
Walter de la Hulle	18¾d
Walter Wylly	6d
John Smith (*Fabro*)	12d
William Goceline	7d
Adam Eliot	19½d
Adam Smalpront	19d
John, son of Robert de Aure	17d
Walter de Westfeld	2s
Henry de Haggelowe	6d
John de Wylington	6s 7¼d
William Taillur	15d
Roger atte Felde	12½d
Robert le Carpenter	6d
Jurdan atte Hulle	6d
Henry Crompe	14¼d
John de Nasse	2s
William Leulyn	7s
Richard de Midwey	4s
Adam Whyteking	3s
William Smith (*Fabro*)	3s 3¾d

Approved. Total, 78s 7½d

Total of the whole hundred, £14 3s 4d

Subtaxers (*Subtaxatores*)

285

Nicholas Ragoun	12d
Roger de Bliddeslowe	12d
Walter de Auste	12d
John Baderoun	12d
Thomas le Forester	12d

Total, 5s

Approved. Total of the whole hundred aforesaid with the subtaxers' taxes, £14 8s 4d

DUDSTONE HUNDRED
(*HUNDREDUM DE DUDDESTON*)

Brookthorpe (*Brocthrop*)

286

John Bonde	18d
Robert Colston	7½d
Robert Oswold	16d
Walter Meriet	9d
Richard Meriet	14¼d
Robert Danyels	9¼d
Gilbert in the Felde	10d[87]
Geoffrey in the Felde	8½d
Robert Bysshop	8¼d
Richard Fox	7¾d
Henry Joene	14d
William in the Felde	12¼d
Agnes Lok	6½d
Thomas Bigge	14¼d
Walter de Hewergh	2s 0¼d

Approved. Total, 14s 11¾d

Tuffley (*Toffeleye*)

287

Richard Barlich	12d

[Membrane 18]

Also Tuffley

Walter atte Wode	8d
Matilda atte Wode	9¼d
William Stroyl	2s
Nicholas le Eorl	14d
Dionis. de Sudgrove	2s 0¾d
Robert Glede	12¼d
Walter le Mulleward	6d
John Gery	9d
Simon Tancard	2s 2d

Approved. Total, 12s 1¼d

Upton St Leonards[88] (*Upton*)

288

William le Conestable	22d
Ralph le Palmer	22¾d
William Hynderling	2s 4d
William Phelip	15¼d
John Short	21¼d
Matilda Curteys	6d

John de ȝareforde	9d
Ellis de Byleye	9¾d
Walter Short	16d
Richard Adames	13¼d
John le Bonde	9d
Robert Okholt	12¾d
Richard de Whaddon	22½d

Approved. Total, 17s 3½d

Saintbridge (*Sendebrugge*)

289

Philip le Hayward	10d
Henry le Daunsare	15¾d
John le Daunsare	6¼d
William Uggel	13¼d
Robert atte Buedelesmull	15d
Geoffrey Fisher (*Piscatore*)	9d
Robert Foket	9d
John Wymond	10½d
William Gerald	6d[89]
Thomas de Mattesdon	2s 3d

Approved. Total, 10s 1¾d[90]

Sneedham's Green (*Snedham*)

290

Nicholas le Murye	21d
Richard Axtel	21d

Approved. Total, 3s 6d

Elmore (*Elemor*)

291

John de Gyse	7s 4d
Beatrice de Gyse	6s 9¾d
John atte Polle	15¼d
William Phelipp	6d
Richard le Brok	22d
John Jannes	6d
William le Reve	17d
Matilda Dauwe	9d
William le Brok	7¼d
John Lok	6d
Adam Garlek	16d
Agnes Jip	18d
William Caam	12½d
Richard Garlek	11d

Felic. Umfray	9¼d
Adam Umfray	11¾d
Walter Nichol	11½d
William le Cok	9d
Adam le Holdare	13¼d
Richard Rauel	6d
Adam Bollok	6d
Henry de Polle	16¼d
William Prat	6d
William Hatholf	9d
Margaret atte Welle	12d
William atte Broke	9d
Robert Halyday	8d
Matilda Arnewy	10d
William Godrich	12¼d
Richard Godrich	13½d
William le Brok	6d
Walter Eolf	9d
Walter de Shirne	9d
Robert Dabitot	12½d
Robert atte Welle	9d
William Bullok	6d
John Chynoun	6d
Adam Inthehale	6d
Richard atte Polle	9d
Henry atte Polle	9d
Walter le Deye	9d
Walter le Graunger	9½d
Adam Michel	8d
John le Shirreve	7¼d
Henry le Brok	8d
John le Hopere	6d
Robert de la Berwe	6s 4¼d
William Dake	6d
John Wattes	6d
Nicholas Dake	6d
Johan. la Swones	6d
Thomas Cronnok	6d
Reginald atte Hulle	9½d
Alice de Holteleye	14¾d
John de Holteleye	11¼d
William de Holteleye	9½d

Approved. Total, 63s 3d

[Membrane 18 r-h col.]

Hempsted (*Heyhamstucode*)

292

Walter Reod	2s 7¼d
Walter le Smyth	2s 3¾d
John le Mariner	6d

Richard le Archer	13d
Robert Cary	6d
John Inthehurne	17¼d
Nicholas Stephenes	9d
Aldith la Mulleward	6d
John Davy	12¼d
William le Taillur	15¾d
Richard Cade	16¼d
Alex. Gladewyne	11¼d
Roger Keys	2s 2¾d
Isabel Alayn	20d
Henry Rogers	2s 9d
John Cade	20¾d
Walter Henry	9d
John le Wheolare	18d
Robert Rogers	16¼d
Henry Dake	18d
John de Staunton	9d
William le Smyth	2s 2d
William Kylthorn	9d
John le Bacare	21½d
Simon Cary	14d

Approved. Total, 34s 5d

Longford[91] (*Longeforde*)

293

Robert Lethenard	2s 1¼d
John de Bures	3s 11¾d
William Fynam	2s 11d
William Ingeleys	18d
John atte Welle	16½d
Walter Stephenes	15¼d
Alice la Brewes	21d
John Shonyn	14½d
Walter Isaak	20d
Matilda la Gode	6d
Simon Somer	6d
John le Skylfole	2s
Henry Bishop	14¼d
William le Murye	6d
Johan. Holdeborowȝ	6d
Robert Rynde	15d

Approved. Total, 24s 3d

Sandhurst[92] (*Sonthurste*)

294

John de Wylington	5s 9¼d
William atte Morslade	22¾d
Agnes la Webbe	6d
John Mayou	14¼d
Alice la Palmere	9d
Emma la Priour	12d
Walter le Mulleward	6d
Adam Martin	6d
William Shonyn	9d
Roger Martin	9d
Henry Martin	6d
Walter de Cheltenham	4s
John Sparwe	6d
Walter le Hore	6d
William le Rioun	6d
Walter le Hopere	6d

Approved. Total, 20s 1¼d

Abload's Court (*Abbelode*)

295

John le Murye	12d
Thomas Godsuein	6d
Walter Mile	6d
William le Murie	19d
Walter Godrich	6d
Walter le Bonde	9d
John Perys	9¾d
William atte Letwine	2s 3½d
Walter Shonyn	6d
William le Couherde	2s 0¼d

Approved. Total, 10s 5½d

Over (*Overe*)

296

Alice atte Wode	16d
Alice Harald	10½d
Robert Golde	19d
Gilbert le Hayward	9¼d
Alice atte Bruggende	9¼d
Reginald de Durhurste	4s 3½d
Ralph le Wheolare	8s 1d

Approved. Total, 17s 8½d

Linton (*Lylleton*)

297

Richard le Swein	9d
John Fyge	6¾d
Walter Adames	9d
Richard le Wyse	14½d
Henry de Vernhale	12d
Thomas Passeavaunt	14d
Robert de Seydon	8d
Roger Whitemay	4s 0½d

Approved. Total, 10s 1¾d

Highnam (*Hynehome*)

298

Geoffrey le Clerk	18¾d
Roger Ingulf	9d
William Ingulf	2s
John Inthefelde	2s 0½d
Thomas Inthehale	6d

[Membrane 18 dorse]

Also Highnam

Alex. le Mortimer	8d
William Maynard	6d
William le Fisshare	6d
Richard atte Ston	13½d
John de Cheddeworth	3s
Thomas Spark	9d
Julian Scitur	6d
Alice la Frensshe	6d
John le Swon	8d
Walter le Smyth	6d
Simon le Skinnare	9d
John de Merheye	6d
William Edrich	6d
Thomas de Wyggemor	12¾d
William Baldwine	6s

Approved. Total, 23s 4½d

Highleadon (*Hynelden*)

299

Nicholas le Frensshe	18d
Edith Hendy	6d
Matilda Barfot	2s 11¼d
Walter Barfot	20d
Robert Bytheweye	21d
John le Ȝonge	9d
Walter le Northerne	6d
Robert le Walsshe	2s 8½d
Walter Hykes	12d
Agnes atte Stile	12¾d
John de Leden	2s 2d

Approved. Total, 16s 6½d

Lassington (*Lassyndon*)

300

Agnes la Freman	22d
Robert Herbert	9½d
Walter le Clerk	6d
Matilda de Prestebury	9¾d
Hugh Hamelyn	9d
Henry de Coluerlowe	13¾d
John Cof	6d
Lawrence de Marcle	11¼d
Richard Maynard	15d
Matilda Elys	6d
Peter de Helioun	7s 5d

Approved. Total, 16s 5¼d

Hartpury (*Hardepirie*)

301

John le But	12¾d
Alice de Hale	12d

Marg. Cole	6d
William de Hale	16d
John Perys	9d
Margery la Clerkes	2s 3d
John Pope	12d
John Kiniot	13¼d
Walter Thomas	6d
John de Sladebrugge	2s 1d
John le Hayward	8d
Gilbert atte Lamputte	10d
John atte Snede	2s 2d
Richard atte Snede	2s 4¼d
John de Rodleye	9d
John atte Hulle	16½d
Adam le Founare	14¾d
Richard atte Style	17d
Henry Russel	6d
Walter Aylet	15¼d
Edith Test	8d
Walter Osbarn	12¼d
Edith la Forester	11¾d
John de Cattesberwe	16¼d
Hugh le Longe	6d
John de Hale	11d
John de Blakwelle	9d
Walter Caty	8d
Richard Belle	16d
William Partrich	11¼d
John Child	6d
John atte Grove	14d
Edith de Wolstonesmede	6d
Thomas Thoky	20d

Approved. Total, 37s 1¼d

Morwent (*Marwent*)

302

Henry de Comleye	3s
Adam Inthehulle	11d
Henry de Dygelesworth	6d
Richard le Barcare	2s 2¼d
Thomas de Aldelond	12d
John de Marwent	9d
John le Cnyte	6d
Robert le Cnyte	12d
William Bisshop	8d
John Partrich	12¾d
Edith de Marwent	2s 2d
William le Horsman	12d
William le Hopere	9d
John atte Lone	2s 0¼d
Lyena[93] atte Elme	10¼d
Robert atte Mor de Wodetoun	16d
Robert atte More	6d
John le But	10d
Robert de Goldhulle	5s 4½d

Approved. Total, 26s 5d

[Membrane 18 dorse r-h col.]

Preston (*Preston*)

303

Roger le Mulleward	12½d
Matilda la Wyth'	20¼d
Alice atte Hulle	10½d
William Henr'	15d
William le Ȝonge	15¼d
Walter Ȝongeman	10½d
Hugh Jones	15½d
John Inthefelde	4s 2¼d

Approved. Total, 12s 5¾d

Maisemore (*Mayesmor*)

304

Walter Loverich	15d
John le Rede	10d
Alice Saundres	12¼d
Walter Wyth'	17d
Henry Russel	9d
William le But	2s 0¼d
Petronilla la Gode	15¾d
William Seward	12¾d
Walter Seward	18¼d
Walter le Bole	15½d
Walter atte Hasele	2s 0¼d
Richard de Seydon	14¼d
Stephen Godynowȝ	9d
Walter Segrym	9d
Robert Ewet	6d
Adam le Bays	10d
William Pope	6¼d
John Hewet	10d
Robert le Kyng	12¼d
Robert atte Wyneȝard	10d
Richard le Hayward	3s 6d
Walter le Clerk	12d
William de Stokwelle	2s 1d

Approved. Total, 28s 3½d

Barnwood (*Bernewode*)

305

John Richardes	8d
William le Mey	6d
Agnes Arnewine	6d
John Mosechat	17d
John le Reve	6d
John Shot	9d
Henry Wygot	8d
Reginald de Cleyforde	18d
Thomas Honsum	3s 6½d

Approved. Total, 10s 0½d

Wotton St Mary Without[94] (*Wotton*)

306

Alice la Brewes	15¼d
Walter Tod	8d
Thomas Kewer	6d
Walter atte Stone	10d
John Shot	8d
John le Eyr	9d
Walter de Gryneshulle	12¾d
John Flory	12½d
Henry Patrik	5s
Walter de Ruyton	12d
Nicholas Bursy	6s 7d

Approved. Total, 19s 4½d

Brockworth (*Brokworth*)

307

Henry Baret	12¼d
Robert Lethenard	3s 8¾d
William le Vicaryes	3s 1d
Richard le Wodeman	6d
Robert de Brewes	16¼d
Alice Ingrith	20½d
Robert Ingrith	2s 1d
William Prodhome	16¼d
John de Wyke	13¼d
Robert Cutel	10d
Gilbert Ingrith	18d
John de Cheltenham	18½d
Gilbert de Wolmer	6d
William de Brocworth	3s 1d
Simon Passemer	2s
Gilbert Rundulph	10d
William Droys	12d
John le Cok	12d
Alice Droys	20d
Henry de Brocworth	4s 4d
John le Reve	6d
Richard Ernesse	6d
Robert de Wyke	8d
Gilbert le Notte	12d
William le Thecchare	16d
William le Wondar	12d
Simon le Burgeyse	6d
Robert le Bayllif	6d
John Arnald	2s 6d
William de Pyncote	6d
Robert le Tuekele	12d
John le Bouere	15¾d
William Kiniot	12d

Approved. Total, 46s 6½d

Down Hatherley (*Dounhatherleye*)

308

John de Annesleie	5s 1¾d
William Gilberd	16½d
Godric (*Grico.*) le Hayward	2s 1¼d

[Membrane 19]

Also Down Hatherley

John Sewyn	10d
William Davy	15½d
Thomas le Hayward	2s 0¼d
Adam Sewy	8d
Roger Mayflin	18d
Ralph de Wylington	2s 6½d
William Hathewy	2s 0½d
Robert de Goldhulle	7s[95] 9d

Approved. Total, 27s 3¼d

Badgeworth (*Beggeworth*)

309

John le Strange	17d
Thomas Simond	9d
Margery atte Bruggende	8d
Reginald le Mulleward	6d
John[96] Gabbe	8d
William Kyng	14d
Henry de Penhoo	13½d
Andrew Inthelon	6d
Alan Gabbe	8d
William Colpek	7¼d
William Gabbe	18¼d
John atte Tounesende	6d
Peter de Hathleyewode	15¼d
John le Gnat	7¼d
John de Byngham	7¼d

Approved. Total, 12s 6¾d

Bentham[97] (*Parva Bentham*)

310

Fulk Fiz Waryn	4s 1d
Beatrice le Hunte	20¼d
William Chaplain (*Capellano*)	20¼d

Approved. Total, 7s 5½d

Little Shurdington (*Parva Shurdinton*)

311

Henry Cropet	9d
Thomas le Shephirde	6d
William Lambart	20¼d
William Gernoun	9d
Alice Osbarn	6d
Matilda la Heort	8d
William le Hunte	8d
Walter le Hornar	8d
Thomas Lambart	2s
William Craucoppe	6¾d
John Mautravers	3s 4d
Richard Damedith	15¼d
John Galewy	8d

John Bobbe	15¼d
Richard Sewyn	6d
Agnes la Kinges	16¾d
John Hykeman	16¾d
Ellen Cole	9d
John Sewyne	12½d

Approved. Total, 20s 4½d

Bentham[98] (*Magna Bentham*)

312

John Harding	15¾d
Thomas Motty	6d
William Sewyn	12d
Richard le Masoun	3s
Walter Kybe	12d
Alice Cutul	6d
William Rolph	2s 2¼d
William Coterel	6d
Thomas de Foxcote	6d
Thomas Stephenes	6d
Thomas Rondulph	18½d
John le Cnyte	9d
Richard le Gnat	10d
John le Fendur	9d
John Husk	13¼d
Robert Gille	12¼d
Richard Broun	12d
Robert atte Grove	19d
Christine la Mulleward	6d
William de Bentham	12¼d
Walter Godale	14d

Approved. Total, 22s 3¼d

Little Witcombe (*Parva Whyticombe*)

313

Thomas le Smyth	14d
John Wroggy	10d
William de Briddelep	17d
William Fode	9d
Thomas le Wolm'e	9d[99]
Richard le 3onge	10d
Isabel de Sothereye	12¼d
Walter Aylrich	8¼d
John Hickes	10d
Thomas Roberd	18¼d

Approved. Total, 9s 9¾d

Crickley (*Crecleye*)

314

John de Crecleye	18d
William Rundulph	12d
John le Clerk	12d

Approved. Total, 3s 6d

Shurdington (*Magna Shurdinton*)

315

Edith atte Chircheye	9¼d

[Membrane 19 r-h col.]

Also Shurdington

William le King	13¼d
Ralph Clef	10¼d
John le Brid	18¼d
Walter Veysar	6d
Alice la Semes	12¼d
Robert Arnald	6d
John Rolph	18d
Henry Wylkin	18¼d
Richard atte Pleystude	12¾d
William atte Pleystude	6d
John Crysp	19d
John Top	6d
Henry atte Tounesende	6d
Agnes la Hayward	6d

Approved. Total, 13s 11¼d

Great Witcombe (*Magna Whytecombe*)

316

John de Whytecombe	12½d
John Sely	10d
Richard de Salcombe	14d
Henry Lyne	20½d
Geoffrey Mogge	12¾d
Gilbert Keys	16d
Henry Alfrid	12½d
John Gernun	15¾d
Thomas Strene	6d
William Martin	14d
William Keys	18¼d

Approved. Total, 12s 8¼d

Bishop's Norton (*Norton Episcopi*)

317

Reginald le Shephirde	8¼d
William Pelie	6d
William Inthehale	12d
Richard le Westerne	12d
John atte Welle	10d
John atte Grene	18½d
Marg. atte Fenne	9½d
William Hamond	12½d
Richard Hamond	10½d
Simon atte Chircheye	11d
John atte Hulle	12¼d
William Edrich	10d
Richard Halling	15d
John le Eorl	6d
Marg. atte Orcharde	6d

Simon de Mickeleie	12½d
Walter le ȝonge	8d
Richard Baldwine	12¼d
William le Eorl	10½d
Richard de Harnhulle	13¾d
Philip atte Strete	8d
Richard atte Strete	6d
Walter atte Strete	6d
Walter, son of Nicholas atte Strete	8d
John atte Grene	9d

Approved. Total, 21s 1½d[100]

Prior's Norton (*Norton Priori*)

318

Walter Russel	15½d
Walter Inthehale	6d
Isabel Bat	15¼d
John le Sclattar	12¾d
Richard le Swein	6d
Dyonis. Nicholes	13½d
Robert atte Mulle	19¼d

Approved. Total, 7s 4¼d

Brickhampton (*Bryththampton*)

319

Richard de Bryghthampton	3s 3d
Richard de Shenyndon	14¼d
John le Carpenter	12d
Ellis atte Grene	10¾d
John Sage	4s 7d

Approved. Total, 10s 11d

Parton (*Parton*)

320

William atte Tounesende	13¾d
Robert le Chapman	9d
Agnes Hundy	15½d
John Elys	19¼d
Adam atte Broke	13¾d
Richard Brounyg	16d
William le Smyth	21¼d
Robert le Eyr	6d
Walter le Brewere	14d[101]
John le Brewere	16d

Approved. Total, 12s 0½d

Pirton (*Pyriton*)

321

John de Piriton	2s

Alice de Piriton	12d
William atte Elme	8¾d
Gilbert Wade	8¾d
Agnes la Longe	14d
John Simond	12½d
Peter le Gray	9d

Approved. Total, 7s 5d

[Membrane 19 dorse]

Churchdown (*Chirchedon*)

322

Richard Pouke	12d
Christine de Begworth	7½d
William Hog	12d
William atte Strete	7¼d
Alice de Longforde	15¼d
Richard Posth	12½d
John Corndan	9d
John Godsueyn	9¾d
Walter le Longe	11d
Walter Takebat	6d
Agnes la Longe	6d
Walter le Rede	6¾d

Approved. Total, 9s 7d

Noke Court (*Oke*)

323

William Laurence	13d
John Ives	8d
John le Bonde	9d
Geoffrey le Mulleward	12d

Approved. Total, 3s 6d

Hucclecote[102] (*Hoclicot*)

324

Richard le Palmer	6d
Walter le Hunte	9d
Walter Pouke	12½d
John Henr'	13¾d
Margery la Palmere	6d
John Albard	6d
Walter le Morman	10d
Richard Seod	11d

Approved. Total, 6s 2¼d

Hucclecote[103] (*Wodehoclicot*)

325

Alice la Palmere	12½d

William Walteres	14d
Robert de Cromhale	6d
Walter Wruyte	11d

Approved. Total, 3s 7½d

Elm Bridge (*Elmebrugge*)

326

John le Kinge	2s 2d
Simon de Elmebrugge	7¼d
Alice Batecok	6d

Approved. Total, 3s 3¼d

Brook Street (*Brokstret*)

327

Nicholas le Chamberlein	8s
Adam de Clive	3s 6d
John le Dyeare	2s

Approved. Total, 13s 6d

Whaddon (*Whaddon*)

328

William Haukin	14¼d
John le Cumper	15d
Margery la Cumper	9d
Richard Dabetot	5s 0½d
Thomas le Clerk	9d
Thomas le Cumper	9½d
John de Horsforde	14d
Julian Cumper	6d
John Bruggeman	9d

Approved. Total, 12s 2¼d

Total of the whole hundred, £35 15s 7½d

Subtaxers (*Subtaxatores*)

329

Robert Richeman	12d
William de Piriton	12d
Thomas Passemer	12d
John atte Pleystude	12d
John Fraunkeleyn	12d

Total, 5s

Total of the whole hundred aforesaid with the subtaxers' taxes, £36 7½d

BOTLOE HUNDRED
(*HUNDREDUM DE BOTTELOWE*)

Upleadon (*Ledene*)

330

John le Stonheware	21½d
Lawrence de la Hay	18d
Hugh le Frend	17d
Henry Fymon	19¼d
William de la Hale	2s 2d
Felic. de la Hulle	11d
Nicholas de Waryhulle	12½d
Alice la Smyth	12d
John Aylȝot	17¼d
Siward Michel	9d
John atte Rok	12d
Henry le Bonde	4s
William atte Hay	3s
John le Portman	3s

Approved. Total, 24s 7½d

[Membrane 19 dorse r-h col.]

Rudford (*Rodeforde*)

331

Richard Caty	2s 0¼d
Walter atte Croys	9¾d
William le Northerne	16d
William Tony	12d
Adam Caty	16d
Thomas Dodde	11½d

Approved. Total, 7s 5½d

Tibberton (*Tyberton*)

332

Thomas le Blount	6s 3d
Adam Fraunkeleyn	12d
Christine Cuggel	2s 9¾d
Walter Vobe	18½d
William Vobe	18¼d
John Thoky	13d
Thomas le Hunte	2s 9d
Margery Thomes	18½d
William Pirk	19d
Adam Boter	18½d
Adam Pirk	15d
John le Moul	9¼d
Matilda Wynyng	2s 0½d
Alice Brid	18½d
Stephen Stour	13¾d
Ellen Dyne	12d
Walter Dyne	9½d
Agnes de la More	12½d
Edith Broun	12¾d
Walter Saundres	5s 7d
Gilbert atte Pole	5s

Approved. Total, 42s 10¼d

Huntley (*Hunteleye*)

333

Robert de Sapi	6s 9d
Margery Hannyle	2s 0½d
Robert de Hannyle	3s 2½d
Gilbert, son of Peter	2s 1d
Walter le Hullare	13d
Walter de Hannyle	8s
John de la Pole	14d

Approved. Total, 24s 4d

Taynton (*Magna Teynton*)

334

John de Bures	8s
William le Valence	15½d
Gilbert Miller (*Molendinario*)	2s 0½d
John de Byfar	6s 6d
John Pennesone	18d
Walter de Houwenhulle	15d
William Prithel	9½d
John de Ledbetare	2s 6½d
Thomas Kyngot	12½d
John atte Grave	9d
Richard le Baillyf	2s 7d
Henry le Clerk	11d
Richard atte Grove	3s 0¾d
William Heregoud	9½d
Walter Fotich	15½d
Adam le Budel	12d
Henry Yblessed	12d
William Hendy	14d
Adam de Chelenhed	7½d
John Coly	3s

Approved. Total, 41s 1¾d

Little Taynton (*Parva Teynton*)

335

Bevis (*Bogon.*) de Knouille	4s 3d
Walter Gerald	12¼d
Henry Gerald	18d
John le Ridare	17d
Adam Playche	2s 9½d
Nicholas le Cartere	8d
John de Crauenhulle	20d
John Kingot	2s 0½d
Adam Ceny	3s

Approved. Total, 18s 4¼d

Newent (*Neuwent*)

336

John Payn	19d
Roger de Mammcliue	6¼d
Roger le Chesare	6½d
Edward le Mercer	6d
Roger le Webbe	16d
John Hobyes	12d
Walter le Dyear	6d
William Wynter	13d
John de la Hulle	6d
Peter de Hewe	13d
David Baker (*Pistore*)	6d
Richard Flawe	6d
Walter Maynard	2s 1½d
Walter de Compton	12d
Thomas Coppe	12½d
John de Hertelaunde	10d
Stephen atte Byrche	6d
Alice Bytheweye	18½d
Robert de Hewe	7d
Dyonis. atte Pirie	6d
Thomas atte Halle	18d
John de Ardarne	2s
Henry de Bradenore	18d
John de Staurton	3s 0¼d
Geoffrey Winter	2s
Adam Barefot	5s
John de Farleye	6½d

[Membrane 20]

Also Newent

Henry Bytheweye	6½d
Gilbert de Caple	19d
John de Caple	18½d
William atte Brome	6d
John Broun	6d
John de la Home	18d
Richard atte Cros	20d
William Fekard	6d

Roger Coppe	12½d
William Emelot	18d
Henry[104] Emelot	7d
John de Plodye	18½d
Richard de la Plodie	12d
Walter de Farleye	2s 2¼d
Robert de Farleye	10d
Robert atte Birche	7d
Hugh le Swon	18¼d
Nicholas Bodde	6d
Henry le Tilar	12d
Adam Ely	13d
Thomas de la Hulle	18½d
Richard de Olbrok	20d
Richard de Hertesleye	18½d
Lucy de Sotherbe	2s 2d
Sybil Davy	6½d
John Jones	18½d
John atte Shawe	9½d
Walter de Sterteden	9¼d
William de Bolesdon	5s 0½d
John, son of *Ros'*	6¼d
John atte Halle	6d
Thomas de Killecot	9d
Robert atte Norcharde	18½d
Richard Wymond	2s 2d
Thomas atte Cros	16½d
William Hyne	20d
Agnes la Crompe	7½d
Robert atte Newe	3s 3¼d
Richard le Holdare	7d
Walter de la Hulle	7½d
Richard le Budel	6d
John Dylewy	7d
Roger le Waleys	11d
John Cok	7½d
Walter atte Putte	9d
Henry Smith (*Fabro*)	13d
Peter le Cok	2s 8d
Thomas Athelard	14½d
William Coppe	7d
Geoffrey le Crompe	7d
John Hyne	12¼d
Edith la Bonde	7d
Henry Bisshop	6d
Agnes Anketel	6¼d
Reginald le Corvyser	9d
Richard de Hertelaunde	4s 0½d
Edith Bollok	7d
William de la More	7½d
Alice atte Chapele	18½d
Owen (*Audeen'*) de Ocle	2s 1d
Richard de Craswalle[105]	6s
John atte Slouȝ	18½d
Nicholas de Commodewe	12½d
John Bytheweye	3s
Thomas de Hewe	6s
Robert Ely	16d
William le Reve	2s
Nicholas de la Hoke	15d
Nicholas de Sterteden	2s 0¼d
Walter atte Hoke	6d
Richard Mile	2s 6¼d
Randolf de la Polle	6½d
John, son of Peter de Ocle	2s 0½d
Isabel Gardyn	6d[106]
Matilda de Ocle	12d
Margery atte Mere	7d
John atte Grene	11d
John le Waleys	9d

Total, £6 19s 6¾d[107]

Oxenhall (*Oxenhale*)

337

William de Grandison (*Grandissono*)	6s 0½d
Roger atte Ȝeldhalle	12d
William Cok	9¼d
William de la Hulle	12d
Roger le Mareschal	4s 1½d
William Hathewy	2s 0½d
William atte Ȝeldhalle	7d
Julian la Cartere	18¼d
Luc. atte Shute	10d
Emma la Whyte	2s
William James	9¼d
Geoffrey le Gondre	9d
Christine la Smythes	7d
Adam Houwe	2s
John Wynter	3s 0½d
Richard Hathewy	10d
William atte Grove	12d
Walter de la More	21d
Robert atte Strete	10½d
William le Palmere	4s
John atte Strete	4s
William de la Pykedok	4s
Walter de la Ȝeldhalle	3s 6d

Total, 47s 0¼d

[Membrane 20 r-h col.]

Kempley (*Kempeleye*)

338

Henry le Grey, knight (*milite*)	10s
John Jakes	2s
John atte Pyrie	18d
Adam de la Felde	20½d
Gilbert le Pouwer	6d
John le Frensshe	12d
John Geffrey	21¼d
William Pouwer	12d
Robert le Marchald	6d
John atte Wode	6d
Richard atte Brok	12d
Robert de la Hulle	3s 6d
John Seysel	19d
Richard P'utout	3s 3½d
William le Gardiner	3s 6d

Total, 33s 4¼d

Bromsberrow (*Bromesberewe*)

339

William de Whitefeld, knight (*milite*)	4s 6½d
Richard de Langeleye	18d
Appelon Toney	3s
Walter Dyke	12d
William de Bernwode	13d
Roger de la Hethe	2s
Roger Cheverel	2s 1d
John Henries	2s 1d
Walter atte Grene	2s 2d
Edith la Mulleward	6d
Walter Aubrey	5s 6d
William de Chelenhed	13d
John de la Hacch	3s 3d
Robert atte Grove	5s
Richard le Mulleward	13d
Thomas Aspilon	2s
William Russhel	16d
Henry atte Broke	20d

Total, 40s 10½d

Pauntley (*Paunteleye*)

340

William de Whitinton, knight (*milite*)	6s 0½d
Felic. de Hewe	2s 6d
Matilda Godefray	12d
Henry Syward	2s
Hugh de Ruyleye	2s 2d
Felic. Cobbe	12d
John de la Hulle	4s
John de Ketford	6d
William de Salbrok	6¼d
Richard Godefray	12½d
John de Solers	18d
John Aylmer	6d
Walter Frannceys	15½d
Thomas atte Oncheve	18d
Nicholas le Walsshe	3s
William Bleyth	17d
William Bleyth the elder	8d
Peter atte Shawe	6½d
Robert Boton	12d
Henry atte Wode	13½d
Reginald le Frere	19d
John Crok	3s
William Wardelok	12d
William de Clynegrove	6d
Richard Syward	5s 6½d
Thomas atte Oncheve	3s
Walter de Solers	2s

Approved. Total, 49s 11¼d

Total of the whole hundred, £23 9s[108] 6¼d

Subtaxers (*Subtaxatores*)

341

Adam de Ocle	18d
William de Ketford	12d
Reginald de Combwell	18d

John de Ocle	18d
Henry de Hertelaunde	18d
John de Barbe[109]	18d

Approved. Total, 8s 6d[110]

Approved. Total of the whole hundred aforesaid with the subtaxers' taxes, £23 18s[111] 0¼d

HENBURY HUNDRED
(*HUNDREDUM DE HEMBURY*)

[Henbury] with hamlets, namely Charlton, Lawrence Weston and Stowick Farm (*cum hamelett., videlicet Chorlton, Weston & Stowyk*[112])

342

Joachim atte Tounesende	51s 6¾d
Walter Smith (*Fabro*)	5s 8¾d
Thomas le Parkar	2s 10¼d
Nicholas Furnel	12¼d
Robert le Hokar	2s 10¼d
Stephen Dod	16¼d
William Aylward	22¾d
Richard Joye	3s 0¾d
Robert le Kyng	8d
John atte Wode	2s 3¾d
Thomas Hathewy	15¾d
Alice de Sautemareys	4s 8½d

[Membrane 20 dorse]

Also [Henbury], Charlton, Lawrence Weston and Stowick Farm

Thomas le Veym	2s 4¼d
Walter Grym	12¾d
Richard atte Pyle	2s 6¾d
Henry Caneday	14¼d
Ellis le Mayster	12¾d
John Weaver (*Tixtore*)	22¼d
Henry Mattok	8d
Walter Coudrich	21d
Walter Auctips	3s 6d
Nicholas Shordefold	8d
Robert de Elmelegh	15d
Walter atte More	2s 9¾d
Adam Goldwyne	3s 10¼d
Edith Mattok	2s 9d
Christine de Fisshpulle	6s 3¾d
John Gamel	12d
Alice Bondy	3s 9¾d
William Chytne	13¼d
John Isgar	12d
Agnes Lenegod	12d
Adam atte Weye	8d
Walter Duggel	22¼d
Robert le Palmere	2s 1¾d
William Judde	12d
Walter atte See	16d
Richard de Belers	4s 4¾d
William Kynewyne	22¼d
Richard atte Mulle	12d
William le Ȝonge	2s 1¾d
John de Bradelegh	5s 4¼d
Robert Davy	8d
Ellis de Wyke	2s

Approved. Total, £7 5s 3¾d

Yate and Itchington (*Yate & Ichenton*)

343

John de Wylington	8s 3d
John de Bromcroft	4s 6¾d
Alice de Blakeneye	12d
William le Brok	10½d
Thomas Ady	13¼d
John atte Forteye	19d
Thomas Gorwy	8d
Richard le Bostare	13d
Simon Russel	8¾d
Walter Kynseth	2s 6¾d
Walter le Hert	9¼d
Nicholas le Brode	8d
Walter de Stanburn	22¼d
John Broun	8d
Thomas le Graunt	3s 3¾d
Roger Osward	6d
Robert Morgan	8d
William Gewy	8¾d
John Wyth'	15½d
Hugh Betherigge	2s 5½d
Edith atte Wode	10¾d
Thomas atte Nasshe	19½d
Thomas Dolling	22¾d
William Stintescombe	15d
Philip le Slegh	13¼d
Robert Godgrom	8d
Thomas atte Heth	22¾d
Robert atte Hulle	18d
Thomas le Cartere	15d
Walter le Swon	6d
William atte Burcholte	8d
Thomas Bonebrok	12d
Thomas Upehulle	5s 3d
Roger Raybon	5s 0¾d
Roger le Gay	21d
John Wynebek	2s
William le Holdare	6s 9d
Geoffrey, son of Joan	7s 0½d
Richard Heynes	7s 0¼d
John, son of Joan	3s
Thomas Jones	3s 3d
Julian Barry	3s 9¼d[113]
Roger Davy	2s 0¾d
Roger Bolt	2s 5¾d

Approved. Total, £4 19s 0¼d

Aust with Redwick (*Auste cum Hamel. de Radewyk*)

344

Roger Cantok	6s 9d
Adam le Catour	4s 5¼d
William Wytfeld	10¼d
Edith Belech	21¾d
Hugh West	2s 9d
William Russel	19¼d
Widow of William Lacy	2s 3¾d
Thomas de Monenuth	2s 1¾d
Richard le Harpetre	21d

[Membrane 20 dorse r-h col.]

Also Aust with Redwick

Walter Hauyes	22¾d
Joan Churcheman	2s 3d
Robert Martyn	3s 1¼d
Alice Golde	15d
Robert Burgate	20½d
Reginald atte Trewe	17½d
William de Corsham	6d
Matthew Olet	8¼d
Robert Heryng	6d
John Eliot	18d
Matilda Isgar	16¼d
Walter Algar	15d
William Aylrich	8½d

Approved. Total, 42s 7d

Westbury on Trym with Stoke Bishop and Shirehampton (*Westbury cum hamelett., vz. Stok & Hampton*)

345

Prioress of the Blessed Mary Magdalen	3s 8½d
Thomas de Elleb'ghe	2s 5½d
Adam atte Hay	17½d
Richard de Blakeneye	15d

Robert Jordan	7¼d
William Masoun	22¼d
Adam le Parcare	3s 4¼d
Thomas Somer	2s 1¾d
William Tridelaunde	10¼d
William Longe	21¼d
Walter atte Pyle	3s 8½d
William Lambard	6¾d
Walter de Asshton	8¾d
Thomas Sely	6d
Robert atte Ston	7¼d
Thomas Richeman	6¾d
John Joye	8d
Thomas Dammesele	6d
Hemmyng atte Cote	13¼d[114]
William Godefray	14¼d
Robert Fouk	19¾d
Thomas Batyns	6¾d
Hugh Davy	6d
Walter Hemyng	13d
Robert atte Pleystude	2s 4¼d
John le Foghelere	6d
John Elyot	7¼d
William Warr	7¾d
John Celar	6s 7¼d
Robert Hemyng	8d
William de Avene	16¾d
William Hykedon	2s 6d
John le Rede	16¾d
William Gregory	2s 1¼d
William le Botiller	2s
Geoc' Reynny	10s

Approved. Total, 64s 1¾d

Stoke Gifford and Easter Compton/Compton Greenfield (*Stoke Giffard & Compton*)

346

Margaret Giffard	12s
John Stoyl	9s 2½d
Richard Lovel	2s
Thomas le Eyr	2s 9d
Ralph le Fox	3s 11¼d
Richard Stoyl	5s 0½d
Roger atte Style	3s 3¼d
John Wymond	3s 0¾d
Thomas Gabbe	3s 8d
John Buggegod	2s 7¼d
Gilbert Lewelyn	5s 1¾d
Richard le Pope	4s 6d
John le Brok	12d
Thomas Segare	3s
Thomas Gilbert	2s 0¼d
Walter atte Wode	5s 0½d
Reginald Buggegod	8s 4½d
Walter Pope	4s 3¼d
William Hereward	5s 3d
William atte Dych	18¾d
Isabel Richeman	2s 9½d
Richard de Thorndon	5s
Robert atte See	2s
Isabel Syward	18¼d
Gilbert de Dane	2s 10½d
William de la Marche	3s 7½d
Robert Eliot	2s
Reginald Ryvet	12d
William Elyot	12d
John Nayl	5s
Walter le Baylly	15s

Approved. Total, £6 9s 6¼d

Total of the whole hundred aforesaid, £24 7d

[Membrane 21]

Subtaxers (*Subtaxatores*)

347

John de Gydeforde	2s
Florence (*Florentine*) de Stoke	4s
Robert Mattok[115]	12d
Richard atte More	2s
Robert Gustard	2s[116]

Total, 11s

Total of the whole hundred aforesaid with the subtaxers' taxes, £24 11s 7d

TEWKESBURY HUNDRED
(*HUNDREDUM DE TEUKESBURY*)

Tewkesbury (*Villa de Teukesbury*)

348

Simon de Yerdeleye	21d
John Aleyn	6d
Ellis de Boys	8¼d
William de Pulle	21½d
Thomas atte Lone	15d
John Guyge	2s 0¼d
John Toulemounde	3s 2½d
Peter Brutoun	2s 10d
Henry Hughesone	16½d
Roger de Pershor	2s 2¼d
Richard Norreys	10¾d
Walter de Pulle	3s 1½d
John Streyt	2s 4d
Edith Ferrour	18¼d
Richard Whyroun	2s 5d
Simon de Fladebury	7¾d
Nicholas de Morton	23s 8d
Nicholas de Walton	12½d
John Portreve	2s 0¾d
Walter Deyare	4s 0½d
Gunilda Mareschal	13½d
John Spycer	5s 3½d
Sarah de Morton	2s 0½d
Richard Pany	3s 11¾d
William White	11¼d
Robert Goldsmyth	16¾d
John Broun	14s 2d
Alice Ryndecombe	3s 0½d
John Lorymer	3s 8d
Philip Knyt	2s 5½d
John Russel	5s 3½d
Richard Snel	2s 10¾d[117]
John de Kemeseye	13d
Ralph Fisshere	2s 1d
William Botiller	19¾d
William Pyg	19¾d
Richard Cokes	4s 6¾d
Richard Foliot	4s 10d
Walter Taillor	6d
Robert Mouget	21¾d
Henry Jurdan	12d
John Barbour	2s 1d
Stephen de Longeneye	2s 7½d
Robert Wych	6d
Richard de Tedrinton	2s 1¼d
William Guyge	2s 2d
John de Walton	4s 0¼d
Walter Dudecote	12d
Walter Mongondy	8d
Walter Galeys	2s 3d
John Deyere	7s 2d
James (*Jacobo*) Taillor	3s 0½d
Richard Gole	2s 9½d
John Athelam	25s 9½d[118]
Philip Taillor	3s 0¾d
John Tannare	3s 1¾d[119]
Robert atte Wode	6d
Henry Tannare	2s 0½d
William Smale	2s 0¼d
Christine Portreve	5s 3d
John Glaswryght	2s 6d[120]
Adam Breghenok	12d[121]

Approved. Total, £10 6½d

Subtaxers (*Subtaxatores*)

349

William Elyot	12d
Richard Lovecok	12d
Nicholas de Manygforde	12d

[Total, 3s][122]

Total of the whole vill aforesaid with the taxes of the subtaxers, £10 3s 6½d

Kemerton (*Kenemarton*)

350

Alice Beuchaump	4s
Alice Morice	3s 0½d
Agnes Reve	3s 1d
Thomas Bacoun	2s 8½d
John Ler	18d
Thomas Maister	2s
Nicholas Baum'	2s
Christine Pinchaste	2s 8d
John Wenge	2s 6d
William Canoun	18d
Robert Meth'	5s 10d
John Benet	18d
Nicholas Snytȝ	2s
Felic. Pany	12d
Richard Savernag'	12d
Simon de Dene	2s
John Dansleye	20d
William Faukes	2s 10d

[Membrane 21 r-h col.]

Also Kemerton

Alice Morewyne	3s 8d
Thomas Hugge	2s 5½d
William Jon	18d
William Lepare	2s
Richard Hoede	3s 9¼d
William Gabbe	18d
John Walkare	12d
Richard Athelwyne	2s
John Knyt	18d
Henry Reve	18d
Robert Englysshe	18d
William Moryce	15d
Nicholas Osbarn	12d
Richard Baddare	15d
William Reod	12d

Approved. Total, 71s 0½d

Aston on Carrant (*Aston super Carent*)

351

Robert Eorl	2s 0¼d
John Bermo'	2s 1d
Agnes Strach	2s 4¾d
Thomas Damagas	2s
Thomas Ponlyn	2s 6d
Robert le Yonge	2s 8¾d
Robert Welsshe	15d
William Olifer	12d
Margery Selewyn	18d
Adam Stevenes	12d
John Vauch	20d
Thomas Wade	3s 6d
William Godman	4s 0¼d
John Grom	9d
Robert Simond	18d
John Lovecoke	3s 4d
William Sely	2s
Robert Hickes	2s 0¼d
Walter Robard	2s 1d
Nicholas Welar	9d
Matilda Palefray	18d
Agm' Yonge	21d
Agatha Curteys	14d
John Thomas	2s 2¾d
Isabel Jones	12d

Approved. Total, 47s 9d

Shenington (*Shenyndon*)

352

Richard Abberbur	7s 9d
Ellis Sor	2s 4½d
William Whistowe	4s 2d[123]
Elizabeth de Wykham	2s
John Holdar	12½d
John Richeman	12½d
Robert Turch	19½d
Agnes Colines	21d
William Cavel	13d
John London (*Londino*)	11d
John Gonne	9¼d
William Palmar	6d
John Wyllames	18¼d
Richard Colver	13½d
Henry Hendy	12d
Walter de Portenhale	19½d
Robert Batyn	17d
Robert Prudemay	2s 2½d
Robert Palmer	12d
Alice Jannes	2s 0¾d
William Bochard	21d
Margery Hobbes	9¼d
Walter Huwelot	8d
John Ives	6d

Approved. Total, 40s 8¼d

Clifford Chambers (*Clyfford*)

353

Christine atte Yate	15d
Geoffrey Sibili	16¾d
Nicholas Cartere	6d
William Hichekokes	18¼d
William Mareschal	12d
Luc. de Cumpton	22d
Henry Huwes	12d
John Frensshe	15d
Richard Graunger	2s 0¼d
Walter de Norton	17d
John de Shokareswelle	20¼d

Approved. Total, 14s 10½d

Lower Lemington, part of[124] (*Pars de Leymynton*)

354

William Waltres	2s 11d
Richard Holdar	12d
Henry Wattes	21¼d
Walter atte Yate	2s 10d
Robert de Derne	21d
John Bynchaunt	6d
Robert Pirie	9d
William Bocher	10d
Richard atte Walle	12d

Approved. Total, 13s 4¼d

Bourton on the Hill, part of[125] (*Pars de Borton*)

355

Richard Geffes	22¼d
John Palmar	21¾d
Richard Champeneys	6d
John Clement	2s 4d
Hugh Freman	6d
Matilda atte Welle	6d

Approved. Total, 7s 6d

[Membrane 21 dorse]

Taddington (*Tadynton*)

356

John Adekyn	20¾d
Nicholas Goldewelle	21d
John Machen	2s 10½d
Henry Roberdes	21d
John Wodeward	2s 0¼d
John Perky	6½d
John Wetherherde	2s 4¾d
Peter Bryd	18d
John Bryd	2s 0¼d
Matthew le Grey	21d

Approved. Total, 18s 4d

Stanway (*Stanweye*)

357

Thomas Bovetoun	13¾d
John Mulleward	15½d
John Walkar	18¼d
John atte Nelme	12¼d
Richard Inthehale	21d
Richard Ferling	2s 7¼d
Henry Jannes	23¼d
Robert Jannes	2s 3¼d
John Grey	15½d
Richard Freman	3s 11½d
Henry Dake	12d
John Pirye	18¾d
Robert Bovetoun	2s 6d
John Henteloue	2s 0¼d
Robert le Grey	18¼d

Approved. Total, 27s 4¾d

Alderton (*Aldrynton*)

358

Amice Wymot	4s 1¼d
Thomas Keys	18½d
Hugh Tagyan	18¾d
Hugh de Blakwell	2s 6¼d
Richard le Norable	4s 3¼d
Philip Bakare	9d
William Westmancote	18d
Margery de Belkeforde	6d
William Rogers	12d
William Rolves	9d
John Baroun	23¼d
Simon Cokkebury	10d
Walter Bartram	18¼d
John Pannyng	15d
Sir William Maydenes	15¼d
Nicholas Hayward	2s 2d
Alice de Dumbleton	2s 1¾d
Richard Nyng	6d
Hugh Thomas	12¼d
John Besemaunsel	5s

Approved. Total, 36s 1¾d

Didcot Farm (*Dydecote*)

359

Robert Robardes	4s 0¼d
John Duky	2s 7d
John Hegges	2s 7¼d
Stephen Waddare	15¼d
John Bythetoune	12½d
Henry Stake	2s
William Wylemot	22½d
Adam Mayster	18d
John Baroun	12d
Robert Reve	3s 6d

Approved. Total, 21s 4¾d

Washbourne (*Wassebourn*)

360

Henry Machen	2s
Sarah de Wasshebourn	18d
Julian Chapman	2s
Richard Balle	9d
Richard Baldrich	16d
John Inthehale	19d
Richard Swon	6d
Matilda Knyt	23¼d
Nicholas Mey	2s 6d

Approved. Total, 14s 1¼d

Ashton under Hill, part of[126] (*Pars de Aysston*[127])

361

Robert Stacy	3s 11¼d
Robert Yonge	3s 1½d
Alice Bayllyes	18d
Alice Crodwy	2s
John Perys	20d
Walter Hegges	2s 6d
Thomas Toldas	12d
John Pate	2s 7½d
Walter Kent	2s 8¼d

Approved. Total, 21s 2½d

Prescott (*Prestcote*)

362

Richard atte Hasele	15d
Thomas Rede	20¾d
Robert Masoun	2s 2¼d
John Masoun	12d
Thomas atte Welle	6d

Approved. Total, 6s 8d

Dixton (*Dyclesdon*)

363

John de Dyclesdon	6s 11d
John Freman	18d
John Wydeneye	6d

[Membrane 21 dorse r-h col.]

Also Dixton

William Mulleward	17½d
Philip Alvard	9d
Nicholas atte Chircheye	6d
John de Cokkebury	22¼d
Hugh Horsman	18d

Approved. Total, 14s 11¾d

Oxenton (*Oxindon*)

364

John Wysman	18¼d
Alice Jannes	3s 0½d
Alice Toyt	6d
Geoffrey Valeye	18d
Robert Adames	9d
William Mareschal	9¼d
Agnes Brautmes	2s 6¾d
Robert Valeye	2s 10½d
John Pain	18d
John Symond	20d
William Henryes	2s 3¾d
Christine Leyres	6s 4¼d
Walter Joye	18d
John Cosyn	2s
Simon Longe	18d
Nicholas Smyth	4s 8¼d
Thomas Bocher	2s
Margery Illuk	6d
John Spicer	2s 8¼d
John Chaunterel	18d
Roger Trappare	2s
Robert Tymmes	4s 10¼d
John Taillor	12d
John Leyr	2s 1d

Approved. Total, 51s 8¼d

Northway (*Northeye*)

365

Robert Cole	2s 8¾d
Thomas Balle	2s 6¾d
Stephen Palmere	2s
Thomas le Reve	2s 6d
Agatha la Sage	2s 9¼d
William Newe	2s 10d
Thomas Swon	18d
Robert Cartere	20d
Richard Neghebur	18d
Nicholas Kene	2s 6d
Petronilla Rede	2s 8½d
John Cole	2s 10d
William Carent	2s 9d
Robert Skotard	12d
Alice de Wasshebourn	2s
Matilda Balkereve	2s 10d
William Palfray	20d
John Palmer	3s 3½d
John Mondy	16d
Richard Kene	12d
Thomas atte Grene	12d

Approved. Total, 44s 11¾d

Pamington (*Pamynton*)

366

Henry Bolm	2s 9d
Edith Rolves	2s 10d
Thomas Lerneg	2s
Stephen Knyt	2s 10d
William Holdernesse	2s
Alice Mathemo	3s 9d
Edith Burgeys	6d
Geoffrey atte Broke	6d
Robert Mundy	18d
Simon atte Broke	2s
Adam Perys	18d
Nicholas Untowe	2s 8¼d
John Gerveys	3s 6d
Thomas Bole	3s[128]
Roger Mundy	4s 6d
Stephen Colynes	6d
Matilda Crouke	2s
Thomas Luce	3s
Samson Thomas	3s 6d
Samson Martyn	3s

Approved. Total, 47s 10¼d

Natton (*Natton*)

367

Thomas Drake	2s 5½d
Nich. Smith	20d
John Balle	2s 6¾d
Adam Bele	18d
Robert Hardhed	2s 6d

Approved. Total, 10s 8¼d

Fiddington (*Fydynton*)

368

William Harlot	18d
Edith Knyghtes	4s 2d
Richard Clerk	2s 0¾d
John Harlot	6d[129]
Odo de Acton	4s 0½d
John atte Brugg	12d
William atte Mede	18d

[Membrane 22]

Also Fiddington

Richard Janekynes	3s 6d
Stephen Crouke	2s 3d
Henry Horsman	18d
John Housmo'	20d
Adam Housma'	12d
Robert Veysy	2s 2½d
William atte Maple	18d
John Drake	3s 10¼d
John Smether	18d
Robert Newe	12d
Robert Vader	18d

Approved. Total, 36s 8½d

Tredington (*Tredynton*)

369

John Knyt	2s 8½d
John Taundy	6d
Walter Partrich	6d
Stephen Lucas	5s 0½d
John Balle	12d
Margery Jankynes	2s 0¾d
Richard Midewynter	20d
Thomas Wylkynes	9d
John Taundy	12d
Thomas Perys	12d
William Reve	2s 6d
Richard Henryes	2s 3d
Henry Cartere	2s
Thomas Lucy	12d
Julian Rychemanes	2s
William Robard	9d
John Rolves	18d
William Swon	2s 3½d
Alex. Balle	3s 3d
Robert Alston	3s 0½d

Approved. Total, 36s 9¾d

Stoke Orchard, part of[130] (*Pars de Stokearch'*)

370

Thomas Monnyng	21½d
William Herbard	12d
Nicholas de Alre	3s

William Rolves	12d
Richard Gorewy	12d
John Rolves	20d
John Marcer	6d
Henry Newe	18d

Approved. Total, 11s 5½d

Boddington, part of[131] (*Pars de Botynton*)

371

John de Bures	12s 8d
William Ives	12d
John Holdar	8d
Richard de Norton	12d
Richard Hokewon	12d
Reginald Bakar	12d
Emma Hayward	2s 11d
Roger Harnhulle	12d
Adam atte Nasshe	12d
Robert Alvard	12d
Adam Whityngton	8d
Robert Pipar	6d
John Paternoster	6d
Richard de Hayteleye	22d

Approved. Total, 21s 9d

Forthampton (*Forthampton*)

372

John Vynch	5s 6d
Adam Wyth'	5s 0½d
John atte Chirche	3s 3d
John Pope	18d
John Hamond	20d
Geoffrey White	12d
William Soty	17d
John Urban	6d
John Kyng	18d
Andrew atte Hulle	9d
John atte Cross (*Cruce*)	9d
Robert Sevar	2s 1¾d
William atte Croyce	18d
Alice Abel	12d
Richard atte Wode	18d
William Bonde	16½d
Robert Quenhulle	21d
John Lerl	2s 5½d
Nicholas Sevar	18d
John atte Wode	20½d
Richard atte Croyce	12d
Richard Balle	12d
Thomas Pope	6d
Alice Balle	9d
William Hikemones	12d

Approved. Total, 42s 0¾d

Mythe Hook (*Muthehok*)

373

Adam Asshecrofte	3s 5½d
William atte Hulle	16d
William Hok	12d
William Dober	6d
Henry atte Wode	2s 9d
Robert Hayward	2s 2¼d
William Eeode	9d
Philip Hok	6d
Christine de Cors	2s
Henry atte Were	6d

Approved. Total, 14s 11¾d

Southwick (*Sothewyk*)

374

Walter de Shipton	2s 6d
William Goule	18¾d

[Membrane 22 r-h col.]

Also Southwick

John Walsshe	18d
John de Clyve	19½d
Richard de Clare	4s 1d
Dyonis. Montar	12d
Richard Bygge	19¼d
William Geffrey	6d
Stephen Trokkar	6d
John Athelham	2s
Henry Scot	19½d

Approved. Total, 18s 6d

Walton Cardiff (*Walton Kerd'*)

375

Richard Balkereve	22d
Christine Bastard	20d
William Baldwyne	12d
William Rolves	2s 0½d
Nicholas Bonde	12d
John Davy	23d
William Jones	22d
Nicholas Taundy	18d
Henry Cok	12d
Nicholas Davy	20d
William Felice	3s 4d
William de Kerdyf	2s

Approved. Total, 20s 9½d

Total of the whole hundred, except the vill of Tewkesbury,[132] £35 13s 8½d[133]

Subtaxers (*Subtaxatores*)

376

Robert de Aldrinton	6d
William de Wasshebourn	6d
Richard de Walton	6d
Henry Launde	6d
John atte Halle de Shenyndon	18d

Total, 3s 6d

Total of the whole hundred aforesaid with the vill of Tewkesbury and the taxation of the subtaxers, £46 9d[134]

WESTMINSTER HUNDRED
(*HUNDREDUM [DE] WESTMONAST'*)

Hayden (*Heydon*[135])

377

Margaret de Heydon	21¼d
John Barard	2s 2½d
John Duyk	3s 6½d
John Falawe	22¼d
Adam Brusse	2s 4½d
Thomas Barard	3s 4¼d
Henry Broun	8½d
Reginald Holewey	3s 3¼d
Robert Postoly	2s 1½d
John de Beggeworth	3s 11d
Peter de Wigebrugge	23d
John Mustel	7s 3½d

Approved. Total, 34s 4d

Boddington[136] (*Botynton*)

378

Alice de Botynton	3s 7½d
John de Bures	3s

Approved. Total, 6s 7½d

Elmstone Hardwicke (*Herdewyke*)

379

Robert Crouk	4s 6d
Is. Gery	14d
Henry Holewey	17¾d
Manor of Herdewyke	20s 8d
Robert Gilbard	3s 0½d
William[137] Lovecok	6s 1½d
Robert Warrok	3s 2d
John Aytrop	2s[138] 8½d
William atte Rogere	12¼d
Robert Kyng	13½d
William Smart	10½d
John atte Halle	7d
William Gery	14½d
Robert de Stok	17¾d
Reginald atte Roche	16d
William Hosebonde	26d
Reginald Hayward	4s 2¼d
Adam Goderobard	19d
Emma Dawede	13¾d

Approved. Total, 59s 6¾d

Deerhurst Walton (*Walton*)

380

Ralph de Walton	3s 2d
John Walton	4s 0¼d
Is. Pauncefot	8s 9d
Richard Olifer	3s 11¾d
Walter Tof	2s 2d
Walter atte Stone	12¼d
Ralph Olifer	3s
Adam Surpayn	8¾d
John Smart	8d
William de Kenmerton	5s
Ellis Jay	11½d
Richard Cartere	4s 1d[139]

Approved. Total, 37s 6½d

Evington (*Yevynton*)

381

Robert Boulyng	7s 3¾d
William Deverous	2s 4¼d
John Snel	15¾d
William Ofthehulle	3s 2d
Robert de Apperleye	5s 2¾d
Is. atte Stokke	2s 9½d
Nicholas Northerne	10½d
Richard Smart	21¾d

[Membrane 22 dorse]

Also Evington

William Wyffeld	9s 4d
John Alrue	3s 7d
John Derneforde	3s 3½d
Richard atte Mulle	22¼d
John Inthehale	15¾d
Thomas de Comenore	2s
Ralph Orpede	12½d
John Peyt	7½d
Isabel Nightegale	6½d

Approved. Total, 48s 5¼d

Tirley[140] (*Trynleya*)

382

Robert de Dene	8d
William le Whyte	3s 10½d
William Bele	2s 4¼d
Ralph Persones	21¾d
Nicholas Cuyot	12d
Nicholas Prat	4s 5¼d
Reginald atte Toune	5s 1¼d
Margery Savage	4s 4¼d
John Savage	2s 8d
John Roger	11½d
Peter Hasting	3s 2d
Walter Smyth	15¾d

Approved. Total, 31s 8½d

Corse[141] (*Woderowa & Cors*)

383

Reginald Forester	2s 1d
John Mariner	2s 0½d
John May	2s 0¾d
William Russel	5s 2d
Julian Wych	6¼d
Nicholas Webbe	6¾d
Matilda Henries	2s 6d
Richard de Bakehouse (*Furno*)	2s 0½d
John Flesshewar	2s 3½d[142]
Thomas Fytheler	6¼d

Approved. Total, 19s 9½d

Bourton on the Hill[143] (*Bourton*)

384

Ralph de Bereforde	5s 11¼d
John de Perham	8s 9¾d
Robert Huwes	4s 3½d
Walter Maunsel	3s 4¼d
Reginald Calema'	2s 5½d
Matilda Sexsy	9s 5½d
Richard Alberd	13¾d
Walter Elyot	4s 3¾d
A stranger (*Extraneo*)	6s 8d

Approved. Total, 46s 5¼d

Moreton-in-Marsh (*Morton*)

385

Thomas Fraunceys	16d
Giles de Alre	10¾d
John in [the] Corner (*Angulo*)	22¾d
Richard Mayster	18d

Thomas in Thechurcheye	12d
John Bernard	2s 11¾d
Ralph Gybnille	22¾d
Nicholas Clerk (*Clerico*)	12d
William de Hallyng	13¼d
John Purrok	3s

Approved. Total, 16s 7¼d

Coldicote (*Caldecote*)

386

John Roberdes	2s 11¾d
Simon de Caldecote	2s 8d

Approved. Total, 5s[144] 7¾d

Lower Lemington[145] (*Lemynton*)

387

John Page	2s 0¼d
William Wattcote	2s 0¾d
William Bermynton	2s
Henry Bermynton	12d
Margery Freman	12d

Approved. Total, 8s 1d

Sutton under Brailes (*Sutton*)

388

Lawrence de Sotton	4s 3¾d
Roger Basset	5s 5¼d
Robert Godwy	3s 8½d
John Horry	12d
John Inthebroke	18¾d
Thomas Horry	8s 7¼d
William Lovecok	7s 9¾d
Henry Whyte	22¼d
Roger Gorewy	18d
William Fraunkelein	12d
John Pertrich	3s 6½d
John Becoues	5s 2½d
Stephen Wise (*Sapiens*)	4s 9½d
Thomas Syward	2s

Approved. Total, 52s 4d

Todenham (*Todeham*)

389

John Tymmes	4s 3d
Ellis Robyn	4s 6d
Nicholas Bonde	4s 0¾d
William Bonde	6s 8d
Robert Wythege	8s 1d
John Wylkynes	4s 0½d
Nicholas Aspilon	2s
Walter Colles	5s 9¾d
Henry Mylksop	7s 10¼d
John Crom	2s 2d
John Bryan	21d

Approved. Total, 51s 2½d

[Membrane 22 dorse r-h col.]

Wightfield Manor and Apperley (*Wyghtfeld & Apperleye*)

390

John de Helioun	7s
John de la Grove	24s 6d
Alice atte Pole	6¾d
Henry Palmare	7½d
Robert Palmar	6¾d
Richard atte Grove	19d
Walter Heope	7¾d
John de Colseyche	2s 2d
John atte Welle	10½d
Adam Rondulf	13½d
Richard Apperleye	7s 4¾d
Simon atte Birche	19¾d
John Thedrich	15¾d
William Lethenard	3s 10¼d
Lawrence Inthehulle	21¼d
Robert Gerald	12¼d
Robert Somet	7½d
Thomas Walsshe	8d
Walter Budele	7d
Nicholas Fyng	8¼d
John Marchald	10¾d
Thomas Sheld	13d
Dyonis. Stacy	7½d
Simon atte Pleystowe	6½d
Hubert Gerald	13½d
Robert de Apperleye	11¼d[146]
Julian de Apperleye	8d
Richard Clerenon	8¼d

Approved. Total, 65s 9¼d

Corse[147] (*Woderewe & Cors*)

391

William Wyse	12¼d
Isabel Rondulph	9¼d
Robert Bonde	2s 2¼d
William Hawe	8¾d
Walter Tolly	2s 3½d
Richard Seody	3s 2¾d
Robert Cors	2s 0½d
Walter Neucome	5s 0¾d
John Tully	3s 4d

Approved. Total, 20s 8d

Hasfield (*Haffeld*)

392

William Taillor	8½d
Maurice Bercar	2s 2d
John Large	12¼d
John Martyn	12d
John Wyse	2s 9d
Thomas Datecley	18¼d
John Arblaster	3s 10¾d
William Marchale	2s 10d
Margery Wygemor	4s 0½d
Walter Prat	10½d
John Eliot	8½d
Margery Hognes	15¼d
William Admond	16¼d
John Wygemor	18¼d
William Druet	2s 1¾d
John Sely	3s 1½d
John Wylch	16½d
John Prodhome	6½d
Peter de la Toune	2s 8d
Richard Silvester	18½d
William Saleman	10½d
Clement. Pauncefot	11s

Approved. Total, 48s 11¼d

Total of the whole hundred, £27 13s 8¼d

Subtaxers (*Subtaxatores*)

393

Hugh Mustel	12d
Thomas Underhull	12d
William de Teukesbury	10s
Ralph Pouwer	12d
Nicholas de Stokwell	10s
Thomas de Caldecote	½ mark

Total, 29s 8d

Total of the whole hundred aforesaid with the subtaxers' taxes, £29 3s 4½d

TIBBLESTONE AND DEERHURST HUNDRED
(*HUNDREDUM DE THEOBALDESTON & DERHURST*)

Deerhurst (*Vill. de Derhurst*[148])

394

Thomas Hanecok	13d
William Inthehale	9½d
John Scriveyn (*Scriptore*)	9¾d
William Sley	23½d
John Cartere	12d
William Wyghtfeld	5s
Walter atte Style	6d

Approved. Total, 11s 1¾d Proved.

Leigh (*Leye*)

395

William Orpede	18¾d
John de Frompton	19¼d
John Yonge	12d
Walter Oliver	2s 3d
John Huweson	6d
John Fletare	6d

[Membrane 23]

Also Leigh

John atte Stokke	6d
John Gabbe	2s 6d
Agnes Haukynes	9d
John de Parys	6s 6½d
Adam Saundres	6d

Approved. Total, 18s 3d Proved.

Uckington (*Okynton*)

396

Henry Newe	15d
John de Okynton	2s 9¾d
Walter Sley	6d
Agnes White	18d
Henry Cockus	12d
Richard Jones	14½d
William Jones	2s
Is. Binn	9d
William Lovecok	2s 7½d
Robert Gabbe	2s
Nicholas de Dene	6d
Robert Odde	2s
Adam de Dene	3s 6½d
Matilda la Reve	12d
Roger atte Halle	5s 5¼d
Henry Saleman	6d
Reginald le Yonge	6d
Robert Boulyng	12d

Approved. Total, 30s 1½d Proved.

Staverton (*Staverton*)

397

John Sage	4s 2d
John Cley	6d
John Walsned	11¾d
Adam de Hawe	12d
Henry atte Wode	9d
Thomas Webbe	6d
John Alvred	6d
John Gonnor	6d

Approved. Total, 8s 10¾d Proved.

Preston on Stour (*Preston*)

398

John de Yate	4s 0½d
Walter Clarice	12d
Godfrey Mercer (*Mercatore*)	2s 3½d
Walter Inthehurne	6d
William Spark	6s 11½d
Henry atte Grene	2s
Isabel Byseleye	12d
John Ilger	12d
William Botte	2s 11d
William de Alscote	2s
Felic. Culne	4s 8½d
William atte Barre	3s
John Miller (*Molendinario*)	6d

Approved. Total, 31s 11d Proved.

Alstone (*Alscote*)

399

John de Geydon	5s 10½d
William Thechar	12d
John Bonde	12d
Alice Geffen	5s 4¼d
William Waryn	2s 7½d
John Gatebrugge	6d

Approved. Total, 16s 4¼d Proved.

Little Compton (*Cumpton*)

400

William Clement	19½d
Henry de Sewell	12d
William Cok	18d
Richard Penyard	17¼d
Thomas Thedrich	6d
Thomas Ingram	2s 9¾d
Alice atte Grove	6d
John Chichely	6d
Richard de Cumpton	3s 1¼d
Drogo Bercare	9d
William atte Yate	14d
William Hervy	12d
John Wych	2s 6½d
John Eyforde	6d
John atte Welle	6d
John atte Mulle	6d
William Fraunkelein	18d

Approved. Total, 21s 5¼d Proved.

Coln St Denis (*Culne*)

401

Richard Derneforde	2s 5d
Adam de Leden	15¾d
Henry Wylykin	21¼d
John atte Watere	2s 4d
John Swon	12d
John Asshe	3s 4¾d
William de Leden	6d
Robert Edward	6d

Approved. Total, 13s 2¾d Proved.

[?] (*Caldecote*[149])

402

Richard Barbast	2s 9¾d
Millicent Herry	12d
William Abovetoun	6d
William Inthehurne	12d
Henry de Leden	2s 7¼d
John atte Stille	9d
Richard atte Mede	18d
Adam Robert	12d
John Hert	20d
Adam atte Hulle	3s 4½d

John atte Mulle	9d
Richard Freman	3s 3¼d

Approved. Total, 20s 2¾d Proved.

Haw (*Hawe*)

403

Walter Passour	4s 10d
Nicholas Gautroun	6d
Walter Jory	9d
Richard atte Watere	3s 5¾d
Walter Reve	9d
John de Hawe	12d
Reginald Cok	12d

Approved. Total, 12s 3¾d Proved.

Tirley[150] (*Trinleye*)

404

John atte Elme	2s 4d
John atte Toune	6d
Richard Blebury	12d
William Heort	23d
John . . .hull	12d

[Membrane 23 r-h col.]

Also Tirley

Thomas Bernard	12d
Walter Coleseye	6d
John Colecombe	6d

Approved. Total, 8s 9d Proved.

Woolstone (*Wolston*)

405

William Balle	3s 1d
John atte Putte	6d
Henry Alvred	3s 2¼d
Alice Kent	12d
William Pygas	6d
Alice Goldyng	12d
Agnes Wykewane	3s 10¼d
John Droys	6d
Richard Swalewe	9¾d
Henry Yonge	12d
Alice Jannes	3s 9¾d
Hewelina Ballard	6d
Walter de Leden	21d
Walter Frensshe	6d
Eugenia (*Eugenna*) Mulward	3s 3¾d
Matilda Wade	12d
Walter Broun	9d
Philip Persoun	12d

Approved. Total, 28s 0¾d Proved.

Welford on Avon (*Welneforde*)

406

Richard atte Strete	3s 6d
Geoffrey Cavel	12d
John Broun	18d
Geoffrey de Welneforde	4s 1¼d
Margery Wylkynes	2s
William Muridale	12d
George atte Grove	6s 8d
Cecily Willyames	3s 3½d
Robert de Mersshton	6d
William Cavel	6d
John Aldewyne	12d
Gregory Wyllames	3s 6¾d
Richard Spye	6d
Roger Skynnar	16¾d
Robert atte Halle	6d
John Neweman	3s 1¼d
William Geffe	15½d
Walter de Cantellow (*Cantilupo*)	7s 5¾d
Alice Bor	18d
Nicholas Lymeseye	6d
Walter Hycon	6d

Approved. Total, 45s 4¾d Proved.

Prestbury (*Prestebury*)

407

Roger atte Halle	4s 1d
William Bacoun	2s 2½d
Robert Blount	3s 11¾d
Robert Bacoun	3s
William Vynt	12d
John de London	2s 0½d
William Thurkel	3s 0¼d
Alice atte Stile	6d
Richard Arnald	8s 2½d
John Aunger	9d
John Bele	12d
Sybil Yonge	3s 2d
Thomas atte Broke	3s 8d
John Tommes	10s 2d
Geoffrey Shot'	3s 0½d
Richard atte Hulle	7s 6¼d
Walter atte Vorke	2s 6d
Simon de Walton	3s 3¾d
Ralph Burel	9d
Nicholas Pope	3s 4¼d
Walter atte Brugg	18d
Walter Kernel	6d
John Pouke	6s 6d
Simon Budel	6d
Richard atte Pounde	6d
William Leulyn	9d
William Blount	15d
Thomas Thenche	9d
William Cartere	6d

Approved. Total, £4 0¼d Proved.

Beckford (*Villa de Bekkeforde*)

408

Walter Cok	23¼d
Matilda Adam	2s 3¼d
Simon Gylot	6s 6d
Nicholas Cokus	2s
William Wat'ot	4s
Ralph Bele	2s 7d
Sarah Gay	6d
Thomas Dyear	2s
Geoffrey Lovecok	7s 0¼d
Peter Gonnyld	2s
Nicholas Hailles	9d
Robert Stronge	6d
Walter Duk	3s 6d
Richard Westho	15d
William Monek	2s 6d
Richard Jones	5s 6d
Roger Swon	4s 6d
John Morewy	3s
William Smythes	6d
Alice Lyncolnes	7s
Nicholas Smith (*Fabro*)	12d
William Vreke	9d
Reginald Comelay	3s 7d
Henry Wilde	3s 6d
Thomas Bossont	4s
Robert Wheolar	6d
Robert Busshel	6d
Agnes Bonamy	8d[151]
Peter Chaplain (*Capellano*)	3s

Approved. Total, 77s 7½d Proved.

Bengrove (*Bayngrove*)

409

Thomas atte Grene	. . .
Simon Notervill	. . .
William Jones . . .	
Thomas de Bayngrove	. . .
William Nichol	. . .
John Bacare . . .	
Thomas de Prestebury	. . .

Approved. Total, 48s 11d . . .

[Membrane 23 dorse]

Grafton (*Crafton*)

410

Henry Page	5s 8d
Richard Wille	18d
Henry atte Hulle	4s 0¼d
Thomas Morwy	2s 7d
John Court	4s 6d
Thomas Maynard	4s 6d
Emma Erl	5s 0½d
Is. Athelard	4s 6d
Matilda West	5s 5½d

Henry Contreton	22s
Thomas Hobekynes	7s
Henry atte Fortheye	5s 2½d
Robert Bysshop	4s 1¼d
Roger de Haylles	20d
Matilda Bernard	2s 9d
Margery atte Fortheye	4s
William Freynsshe	18d
Nicholas Sterr'	6s
Margery Reve	2s 11d
Henry Cadesor	4s 11d
Thomas Deth	6d
Robert Sabine	12d
William Veysy	4s 6¼d
John Est	3s
Nicholas Janoun	6s 8d
Agnes Dobynes	5s 6d
William Court	2s
John Wyllames	6s

Approved. Total, £6 9s 0¼d
Proved.

Ashton under Hill[152] (*Asshton*)

411

Thomas Baldewyne	10s 11¼d[153]
Simon Webbe	6d
Richard Hullok	5s
John Toldas	3s 6d
John Bonde	4s 8d
William Davy	6s
John Lamma'	12d
Agnes Giboȝ	2s 8d
Thomas Baldewyne	6s
Richard Raulyn	5s 4¼d

John Huwet	3s 6d
John Serich	8s 5½d[154]
Walter Skorr	6d
Agnes Court	3s
Richard Alysaundr	6s
Henry Bruthre	10s[155]
Peter Capelory	20½d
Richard le Reve	3s
Alice atte Welle	8s
Henry Bacoun	4s
John Hickes	3s
Matthew Smith (*Fabro*)	2s
Thomas Porter	3s

Approved. Total, 100s 21½d
Proved.

Hinton on the Green (*Villa de Hyneton*)

412

John Aunsy	4s
John Wylkyn	2s 1d
Nicholas Darnel	9d
Geoffrey Profote	5s 4¼d
Nicholas Bernard	12d
Matilda Knotte	2s 1d
William Reve	6s 9d
Henry Duyk	2s 0½d
John Wolf	12d
John Geffrey	2s 7¼d
John Cok	7s 3¼d
Walter Hycoun	3s 3d
William Fladebury	4s 9d
John Abbot	12d
William Miller (*Molendinario*)	6d

Robert Reve	5s 2¼d
Margery Freman	4s
John Cusmer	5s 0¾d
Thomas Cok	18d
John Russel	5s 2d
Philip Lei	12d
Nicholas Leyr	4s 6¾d
Thomas Roger	2s 5½d
Nicholas Ayward, chaplain (*capellano*)	3s 8d
Nicholas Russel	6d
Robert Turbot	18d
Henry atte Yate	12¼d
Robert Aylward	4s 2d
Ellen Noble	2s 6d

Approved. Total, £4 6s 8¾d
Proved.

Total of the whole hundred, £39 10s 2¾d[156] Proved.

Subtaxers (*Subtaxatores*)[157]

413

Reginald atte Touensende	12d
Thomas Prykke	12d
Thomas Odde	12d

Total, 3s

Total of the whole hundred aforesaid with the subtaxers' taxes, £39 13s 2¾d Proved.

WESTBURY HUNDRED
(*HUNDREDUM DE WESTBURY*)

Westbury on Severn with Upper Ley and Lower Ley (*. . .bury cum hamell. Overleye & Neth'leye*[158])

414

Roger Jourdan	6s
William, son of Smith (*Fabro*) [*sic*]	12d
William de Combe	6d
Henry Felch	18d
Roger . . .e Hulle	12d
. . . . . .e	6d
William . . .	2s
. . . Solers	12d
. . . Elemor	6d
. . . . . .on	9s 1d
. . . . . .	6d
John atte Broke	2s

[Membrane 23 dorse r-h col.]

Roger de Borughulle	3s 6d
Richard Leuwyn	6d
William Taillor	2s
Ralph Bongham	12d
Is. Bonghan	2s
Adam Bonghan	12d
Henry Baldewyne	6d
Alice de Astone	12d
Ralph atte Broke	8d
Richard Beregast	2s
Amice Pope	12d
Emma Wodeman	6d
William Inthefelde	2s
Adam Saundres	18d[159]
William Boregast	2s
Robert Charlet	6d
William de Prestebury	2s
Henry Skynnar	2s
Walter Lovecok	6d
William Gamages	6s 8d
Agnes de Arderne	12d
Alice Budel	6d
William Holt	4s
Idonea (*Idania*) Maundvill	18d
John Bruyn	6d
John Maundevill	2s
Robert Frewyne	2s
Richard Coppe	6d
Walter Maundevill	3s
John Hamull	12d
Walter Broun	2s
Stephen Whyteman	3s
Julian Davy	2s

Cecily Longe	4s
Adam atte Broke	12d
Henry Pope	6d
Joseph de Hokkeleye	7s
John Smyth	3s

Proved (*pbat*) total, £4 16s 11d

Churcham with Bulley and Rodley (*Chirchamme cum hamll. Bolleye & Rodele*)

415

Nicholas Kennouwe	3s
Alice de Ocle	12d
Adam atte Grove	2s
Alice Curslith	12d
William Dru	6d
Henry Hayward	2s
William atte Ston'	12d
Margery Hayward	6d [?]
Walter Whiteman	2s
Is. de Dunye	12d
Walter atte Ston'	6d
Walter Bat	12d
William atte Venne	2s
John Joye	12d
Nicholas Hornare	6d
Robert Mop	2s
Robert Hunteleye	12d
Thomas Wysdom	2s
Ellis Whistlare	12d
Richard de Purihale	2s
Adam Tredde	6d
William Smart	2s
Richard Smyth	12d
Richard atte Wode	12d
John atte Wode	2s
William Sismor	12d
Henry Smyth	2s
Thomas Baroun	12d
Justina Baroun	12d
John de Dunye	2s
Nicola Fauconer	2s
Thomas Fauconer	6d
William Baghot	2s
Walter Okholt	12d
Walter Shirreve	12d
John de Syde	6d
Adam Pirk	12d
Henry atte Grene	12d
William Dere	6d
John atte Hulle	12d

Petronilla Hauker	12d
Margery atte Grene	6d
Cecily Haukere	2s
John Mulward	12d
John de Sutton	4s 1d
Walter Hornare	6d
John Hawardyn	12d
John Wylkynes	6d
Philip Hayward	6d
Richard Thomes	18d
Richard atte Hyde	12d
William Anecosesone	6d
William Godʒalde	16d
John Hornare	6d
Thomas de Abbelode	20d
Richard Dolewyne	6d
Walter Heod	18d
Cecil. Gibbes	6d
John Cok	12d
William Colur	12d
Walter Moare	6d
Margery Hed	2s
Henry Snel	2s
Matilda atte Chirche	4s
William Wodeward	4s

Approved. Total, £4 6s 5d

Longhope with Blaisdon (*Villata de Longehope cum Hamll. de Blechedon*)

416

Sarah Talbot	6s 1d
John Broun	12d
Roger Syrema'	2s
Thomas Hunte	12d
John Whyte	12d

[Membrane 24]

Also Longhope with hamlet

Cecily Page	6d
Hugh Hot	12d
Gilbert Whyte	2s
John atte Broke	6d
Cecily Swyft	2s
Roger de Derleye	6d
John Tone	2s
John Gunyld	2s
John Wylkynes	12d

Sybil Hontar	6d
John Rotor	12d
William Jouet	18d
Alice Vox	12d
Walter Shepherde	2s
Walter Honde	12d
Robert Huwelot	6d
Thomas Sabine	2s
John Patyes	12d
Adam Bonde	12d
William Gode	12d
Adam Howle	12d
William Kyng	6d
Margery Alvard	2s
Walter Huwelot	12d
Alice Sermo'	2s
Roger Jourdan	12d
Hugh Sabine	12d
John le Rede	9d
Walter Huwelet the elder	12d
Robert Bonne	12d
Adam Huwet	6d
William Adus	12d
William Somt'	2s
Gilbert Baker	12d
John Clerk	12d
Reginald Eylof	4s

John Hontar	6d
William Maysaunt	12d
Adam Hondes	6d
Adam Godrich	12d
Walter Whyte	12d
Walter Honyma'	18d
John Smyth	6d
Florence Morice	2s
Reginald de Abbehale	4s
Ellis de Blakeneye	4s
William atte Chirche	6s 2d
Roger de Hokkeleye	4s 6d
John le Whyte	4s 2¼d

Proved (*pbat*) total, £4 6s 8¼d

Morton (*Hamell. de Morcote*)

417

William atte Hull	2s
William Sturthup	4s
Agnes Loveman	12d
John Edrich	12d
John Aylmond	3s
Richard Lun	3s
John Lune	12d

William Kech	3s
Alice Frewyne	2s 6d
Walter Danky	12d
Henry Roberd	18d
Roger Budel	12d
William de Upton	2s
Richard Godefrey	2s
William Chauntel	2s 0¼d

Proved (*pbat*) total, 30s 0½d

Approved. Total of the whole
hundred, £15 0¾d

Subtaxers (*Subtaxatores*)

418

Henry de Chaxhulle	12d
Robert atte Strode	12d

Total, 2s

Total of the whole hundred
aforesaid with the subtaxers' taxes,
£15 2s 0¾d

LIBERTY OF ST BRIAVELS
(*LIBERTAS DE SANCTO BRIAVELL*)

Staunton (*Villa de Staunton*)

419

John de Staunton	4s
William Jaan	12d
Philip Jan	18d
Gilbert Smyth	2s 3d
Alice, widow of Philip de Staunton	2s 0¼d
Roger Borrich	21d

Approved. Total, 12s 6¼d

English Bicknor (*Vill. de Bykenore*)

420

John de Bures	3s 6d
John de Lodebrok	3s 3½d
Thomas Gamel	15d
Geoffrey Gamel	2s
Geoffrey Simond	15d
William Fel	22d
William Fissher	9d
Robert Devenyssh	15d
John Monyeye	8¼d
Robert Avenel	17d
Richard Pipar	22d
Walter Kyng	8¾d
Ralph Avenel	15¼d

[Membrane 24 r-h col.]

Also English Bicknor

Thomas Herford	11d
Griffith ap David	12¾d
Peter Devenyssh	18d
Robert Wodyar	8d
Philip de Chapel (*Capella*)	18d
John de Chapel (*Capella*)	2s
Ralph de Bykenor	2s 6d

Approved. Total, 31s 2½d[160]

Ruardean (*Vill. de Ruardyn*)

421

William Hathewy	2s
William Cady	18d
Walter Buffard	6d
Adam Dymmok	6d
Hugh Hobyes	13d
John Baker	18d
William Smythesson	12d
William Waties	2s
William Foul	18d
Adam Smart	4s
William Phelip	3s
John de Houle	3s 6d
Margery Lodebrok	3s 3½d
Peter Kyn	14¼d
Walter Watyes	12d
Robert Billyng	12d
Robert Cat	6d
Walter Broun	7½d

Approved. Total, 29s 8¼d

Mitcheldean and Abenhall (*Villa de Magna Dene & Abbehale*)

422

Reginald de Abbehale	2s 10¾d
William Whyte	16d
Richard Norreys	6d
William Esgar	2s 9d
Hugh atte Walle	7d
Henry Carpenter	6d
John Naillar	18d
William Ely	12d
Nicholas Mody	2s 0½d
Adam de Donynton	2s 6d
William Cut	20d
Henry Boukes	7¼d
William Faucoun	8¼d
Richard de Falleye	12d
John atte Lone	3s 3d
Richard Adam	12d
Philip Dobyn	7½d
Gilbert Holle	12d
John de Hensclep	9d
Walter Carpenter	6d
Richard Naillare	15d[161]
Richard Donyngton	18d
Richard Telon	12d
Henry Holle	12¼d
Philip Cole	12d

Approved. Total, 32s 5½d

Little Dean (*Parva Dene*)

423

Hugh Foer	18¼d
Richard de Wodenham	12d
John de Herford	6¼d
William Hok	12d
Roger Marchal	2s
Hugh Naillar	8d
William Leulyn	3s 8¼d
John Hoke	19¾d
William Mareys	18d
Philip Hok	8¼d
Joseph de Wodenham	7d
Joseph le Hayward	18d

Approved. Total, 16s 3¾d

Northwood (*Hamell. de Northwode*)

424

Agnes de Polton	21¼d
William Cage	12d
Peter Regn'	7¼d
John Helewys	12d
Walter Crabbe	12d

Approved. Total, 5s 4½d

Blakeney (*Hamell. de Blakeneye*)

425

John Brung	8d
Philip de Blakeneye	6½d
Thomas Rosen	6d
Ellis Brung	6d
Peter Hondies	6d

Approved. Total, 2s 8½d

Lea Bailey (*Hamelett de la Lee*)

426

Walter Beg'	12d
Thomas Whitemay	7¼d
Nicholas Lony	12d
Walter Seysel	7¼d
William de Rugge	9¾d
Henry atte Felde	6d

Approved. Total, 4s 6¼d

Total of the whole liberty aforesaid, £6 14s 9½d

Subtaxers (*Subtaxatores*)

427

Adam Rogger	12d
John de Bykenore	12d

Richard Cartere	12d
Gilbert Gamel	12d
John Marky	12d

Approved. Total, 5s

Approved. Total of the whole liberty aforesaid with the subtaxers' taxes, £6 19s 9½d

[Membrane 24 dorse]

THORNBURY HUNDRED
(*HUNDREDUM DE THORNBURY*)

Thornbury (*Thornbury*)

428

Hugh de Audele	20s 2½d
Edith Bedeles	15d
William Whittawar	7½d
Nicholas Pennok	12½d
Nicholas Baker	8¾d
Thomas Froggeforde	6½d[162]
Walter Baker (*Pistore*)	9½d
John Edemay	7d
William Parker	15d
Nicholas Longe	13d
Adam Chese	15½d
Simon le Clerk	8d
Thomas Tannere	13d
John Stanforde	16½d
Agnes Bartilot	9½d
Robert Frensshe	9½d
William Frensshe	10d
William atte Broke	19¾d[163]
Robert Baron	6½d
Nicholas Westbrok	7d
Nicholas Forestar	9¾d
William Inthehale	2s[164] 7d
John Fot	2s 11½d
Robert atte Nelme	8d
John Longe	4s 3d
William Froggeforde	3s 0¼d
John Slymbrugg	8d
Isabel Mareschal	4s 6½d
Thomas Baker (*Pistore*)	2s 8½d
Richard Wrench	11d
John Kayfot	12d
Walter Brag	17¼d
John de Barton	11d
William Tannar	18d
William Bartelot	18d
John Chafaudhey	12d
John Baker (*Pistore*)	14d
John Chese	15d

Approved. Total, 70s 7½d

Hope and Buckover (*Hope & Bokovre*)

429

Elizabeth Chaumberleyn	2s 8d
William Wytenouȝ	6½d
Thomas de Hope	13d
Henry Ody	9d
Thomas Jon'	9d
Adam Pach'	14d
Thomas Cok	10¼d
John de Longe[165]	2s 5½d
William Maunsel	3s
Walter Miller (*Molendinario*)	12d
Walter Huchoun	3s
Adam le White	18d
Robert de Welle (*Fonte*)	2s
Walter de Stanforde	12d
Richard Smyth	2s
John Taillor	18d
Walter Hughe	2s

Approved. Total, 27s 3¼d

Kington (*Kyngton*)

430

Walter de Morlewode	4s 9¼d
Richard Hok	8d
John atte Pleystude	6¾d
Matilda Wylemot	6¾d
John Smyth	23d
William Neucomen	2s 1¾d
William Theyn	21¾d
Robert Smyth	2s 0½d
Richard atte Broke	20¾d
Adam Baroun	7½d
Gilbert Dryu	7d
David Colyar	2s 0¼d
Matilda Lupeȝete	10¼d
Edward Wylles	21¼d
Alice atte More	9d
Robert de Kyngton	2s
Richard Bolecroft	10d
Agnes Wayte	7½d
Simon de Kynton	18d
Nicholas Maliar	7d
Nicholas Lagraste	20½d

Approved. Total, 31s 8¾d

Morton (*Morton Hamelett*)

431

Richard de Stanforde	10¾d
Walter Wyllames	10¾d
William Hirdman	2s 11d
Robert atte Welle	19d
Robert Kyngewell	6½d
John Colimor	12½d
Matilda atte Stone	9¼d
Ellen de Stone	11¾d
William de Wydefeld	17d
Walter de Merch	13d
Matilda Curteys	10¾d
Julian atte More	6½d
Adam Pach'	6½d
John le Whyte	6¼d
Margaret Aylrich	6½d
Richard Cokkebury	9½d
John Gopeshull	13½d
Robert Mildemay	4s 6½d
John atte Fortheye	12½d
Thomas Picher	3s 8½d
Thomas Wyth'	2s

[Membrane 24 dorse r-h col.]

Thomas Bof	8d
Edward le Smyth	11d
Edith Seysel	6½d

Approved. Total, 30s 6½d

Woolford's Mill (*Hamelett de Wolforde*)

432

Walter Miller (*Molendinario*)	6¾d
Gilbert Devenissh	6½d
William atte Croyce	9¼d

Approved. Total, 22¾d

Oldbury on Severn with the Marsh (*Hamelett de Oldebury cum Marisco*)

433

John de Kyngeston[166]	3s 8¼d
Gilbert Dalue	3s 3½d
Edward Hyndewelle	21½d
John Whytyng	8¾d
Robert Kyng	9¼d
Bartholomew Cole	12d
Edward Isaak	12d
John Foulare	2s 7½d
John Saundres	6¼d
Richard Huchones	20½d
William de Merssh	2s 5½d
Edith Payn	9d
William Thomas	7¼d

Walter Pyl	19d
Julian Reve	11¼d
Joan atte Wode	23¾d
Agnes Edwey	7¾d
Bartholomew Sachen	12½d
Albred. Northalle	7d
Edith Huchoun	2s 3d
Agnes Kyntyng	12d
Richard Thorstayn	22½d
Thomas Isaac	11d
William Cole	3s 1d
Richard Dodman	7d
Walter Monek	10d

Approved. Total, 38s 3d

Cowhill (*Couhull*)

434

John Chaumpeneys	3s 8½d
Note[167] de Couhull	7¼d
Felic. Couhulle	7½d
John Ocle	6¼d
John Janyes	8¼d
Richard Janyes	8d
Osbert Mattare	8½d
John atte Welle	7½d

Approved. Total, 8s 1¾d[168]

Falfield (*Hamelett de Falefeld*)

435

Is. de Clare	3s 2¼d
William Heneg	12½d
Adam Fader	8½d
John Fader	20¼d
Robert Whyte	7d
Roes Croudar	6¼d
Stephen Pynchoun	6½d
Edith Suthmor	6¼d
Edith Kynges	7d
John Wyn	8¾d
Ellis Pynchoun	7¾d
Robert Pynchoun	8d
Robert Mildemay	7¼d
Thomas Tailor (*Cissore*)	8¼d
William Payn	2s

Approved. Total, 14s 8½d

Sibland and Oldland (*Sibelond & Hobelond*)

436

Alice Sautemareys	3s 3½d
Walter atte Felde	23¼d
Henry Pof	7¾d
Robert de Sibelonde	2s 5½d
Thomas Edy	9d
Roger Sibelonde	14¼d
Thomas Elyotes	7¼d
Gunilda Hobelonde	7d

Approved. Total, 11s 6½d[169]

Tytherington (*Tidrynton*)

437

William Corbet	4s 2¼d
Richard Silvestr	7½d
Edward Jonson	14¾d
John Waltres	9¼d
William Batyn	21¾d
Roger Heynes	6s 7½d
Roger Amyot	20¼d
William Macy	6½d
John Wallecote	6½d
William Waltres	11½d
John Geffray	13¾d
John le White	13¾d
Thomas Legat	17¾d
John Barrey	9½d
Roger le Whyte	7½d
Thomas Graunger	8½d
William Goldclive	6¾d
John Hobbes	17½d
Thomas Batyn	6¼d
William de Walcote	8d[170]
William Kyng	9d
John Wynebek	7d
William le Yonge	19½d
John Palmer	18d
Edith Amyot	6½d
Henry Rede	8d
William Westerne	7½d
John Davy	9d

Approved. Total, 36s 2d

[Membrane 25]

Rangeworthy (*Rungeworth Hamelett*)

438

William de Borugh	3s 7½d
James (*Jacobo*) Belsire	2s 2d
Richard Hobekines	6d
John le Monek	9¼d
Robert Shoreuen	7½d
William Wytemare	11d
Walter Willy	7½d
Margery Shoreuen	9d
Roger Shoreuen	14d
Roger Brodhok	18d
James (*Jacobo*) Reynald	12d

Approved. Total, 13s 7¾d

Gaunts Earthcott (*Rouerdecote*)

439

Roger le Freman	2s 1¾d
William Mattok	9d
John Chop'	8½d
Walter Rycheman	8d
Edward Schaldem'e	14¼d
John atte Reode	9¾d
Edward le Gome	6½d
John Teste	9¾d
Walter le Stronge	18¼d
Ellis Dodynge	9d
Robert le Eir	8d

Approved. Total, 11s 2d

Iron Acton (*Acton Hamelett*)

440

John de Acton	4s 5¼d
William de Scotes	10d
Henry Rede	6¼d
Odo de Acton	2s 8d
Richard Simound	19d
John Ferthing	9d
John de Couhull	15½d
Richard le Mattare	20½d
William le Rede	2s 7¼d
Thomas Intheheth	9d
William Wytemay	8¾d
Robert Grene Wernel [sic]	7½d
Roger Batecok	6½d
Henry Moddesdon	2s 9¼d
Geoffrey de Moddesdon	7¼d
Henry Coppare	13d
John Tredelas	8¼d
Roger Carpenter	6½d
Thomas Margan	6½d
Henry Wytemay	8½d
Walter de Lynton	7d
Luc' atte Mulle	16½d
Adam Polyng	11½d[171]
Odo Fraunkhome	7d
Henry Taillor	6d
Hugh Poling	12½d
Roger le Yonge	14¾d
John Whitemay	9½d
Roger Whitemay	10d
John Mattare	8½d
John le White	11d
Walter Miller (*Molendinario*)	9½d
John Rogers	6¼d
Walter de Lyntone	7¼d

Approved. Total, 37s 5d

Cote (*Cote Hamelett*)

441

Roger Cantok	3s 7d
William de Cote	2s 3d

Thomas de Cote	18½d
Walter de Cote	15¼d
William de Cote	7¼d

Approved. Total, 9s 3¼d

Marshfield with hamlet (*Marsfeld cum hamelett*)

442

John le Henne	3s 2d
Richard Dyear	3s 1d
John Flek	15d
Gilbert Yonge	15d
Agnes Horleport	2s 5½d
John de Bradewell	5s 2d
Edith atte Stile	5s 5d
Jordan de Shadewelle	7s 3½d
William Hagide	2s 9d
William Ywell	2s 1¼d
Richard Jardyn	4s 1¼d
Is. de Estwell	3s 3d
Roger Rog'	2s 7¼d
Edith Fich	2s 9d
John atte Bern	2s 9d
Gilbert atte Stile	4s 8d
Robert atte Fenne	9s 8d
Matilda Skimere	15d
William Bonde	3s
Gunilda Rolves	15d
Matilda atte Tounesende	2s 2d
Simon Bryan	18d
Gilbert Garsoun	18d
Richard le Gold	2s 6d

Approved. Total, 76s 10¾d

Ayford Farm (*Heyforde*)

443

Lettice de Heyforde	6s 8½d
Richard Neuman	9s 7d
Thomas Prestes	3s
Simon Marges	18d
Christine de Gaunteswell	2s 6d
Nicholas Packare	3s
Richard Mansshupe	18d
Thomas Pope (*Papa*)	18d

[Membrane 25 r-h col.]

Thomas le Pestour	3s
William de Daunteseye	5s 10d
Henry Devenissh	18d
Robert de Saltforde	8s 6d
Gilbert Bruselaunce	3s 9½d
Gilbert Peres	15d
Matilda Bruthere	15d
Ralph Molin	3s
John Waylaway	18d
Ralph le Cartere	2s
Thomas Mess'	5s 2d
William Schym	3s 1½d
William de la Glyse	3s 11½d
Gilbert Shail	4s 4d
Thomas atte Heth	5s 0½d
Walter Miller (*Molendinario*)	18d
Robert Bartelot	18d
Matilda Trous	12d
John de Gaunteswell	18d
John Shym	5s 3½d
Nicholas Alisaundre	11s 1d
Alex. de Heidon	11s 6d

Avyd. atte Boyg'	15d
Thomas le Graunger	8s 3d
Robert le Yonge	6s 9½d
Thomas atte Mulle	9s 4d
Robert Wynel	8s 6d
Peter de Pellardeswyke	9s 8½d
Adam Chapman	9s 8½d
Robert Montayn	7s 6d
John Chapman	3s 2d
Richard de Okforde	6¼d

Approved. Total, £9 7¾d

Total of the whole hundred [£29 19s 11d][172]

Subtaxers (*Subtaxatores*)

444

Thomas de Tyldesleye	2s 2d[173]
Stephen Beaubras	12d
Philip le Longe	12d
Walter le Masoun	12d
Nicholas atte Grove	12d
Roger atte Castel	12d
Robert Daau	12d

Approved. Total, 8s[174] 2d

Total of the whole hundred with the subtaxers' taxes, £30 8s 1d

SWINESHEAD HUNDRED
(*HUNDREDUM DE SWYNESHEVED*)

Bitton (*Button*)

445

Edmund le Blount	3s 4d
Alice la Blount	13s 1½d
John atte Brogge	20d
John Vauntour	12d
John Gibbes	9½d
Henry Colynes	2s 0¼d
John Chivaler	6½d
Robert Perkynes	12d
Richard Dameanneys	19½d
John Inthehurn	12d
John de Malvarn	12d
John de Kyngton	2s
John Marmyoun	2s 4½d
William Blount	18d
Peter Bercar	10s

Approved. Total, 42s 11¾d

Upton Cheyney and Beach in Bitton (*Upton & Bech in Button*)

446

John le Hopere	14d
Thomas de Staunton	2s 8d
Robert de Launcesdon	12d
John de Cottenham	18d
Roger atte Elme	18½d
Alice atte Grove	15d
Robert atte Bech'	2s 0½d
Roger ate [sic] Fortheie	3s 0½d
Richard Hamond	18d
Thomas Lokhamond	12d
Roger Heort	3s 6d
William Vikeries	12d
Stephen Crauel	2s 2d
John Flie	18d
Robert Poyntel	12d
Thomas Barouns	2s
Thomas Morwe	12d
John Marmyoun	14d

Approved. Total, 30s 0½d

Hanham Abbots and Oldland (*Hanam et Oldelonde in Button*)

447

Sir John de Button	6s 8d
Stephen de la More	3s 4d
John Sautemareys	6s 8d
Nicholas de Bakhous	6s 4d
Robert Sygge	18d
Robert Burnel	12d
John Trabes	4s
Richard Galiar	5s
William Poddyng	12d
Hugh Payn	6s 8d
Roger de Doverleye	4s 3d
Gilbert atte Hulle	12d
John le Bercar	14d
William atte More	12d
Alice Duraunt	12d
Robert le Beek	12d
William Marchald	18d
William de Kyngeshull	14d

[Membrane 25 dorse]

Also Hanham Abbots and Oldland

Thomas Holeweye	2s 9d
John Doverleye	2s
Richard Wildegos	12d
Robert Stork	8d
Roger Berde	8d
Roger Smith (*Fabro*)	16d
Richard atte Wode	12d
Robert atte Wode	12d
Walter atte Soler	2s 4d
John Fox	12d
John le Man	14d
Richard atte Gorste	2s 4d
John le Frensshe	12d
Adam Grymesbur	18d
John Joye	12d
Walter de Pavely	3s 0½d
John Wade	12d
Margery atte More	2s 10d

Approved. Total, £4 22½d

Winterbourne (*Wynterbourn*)

448

Adam atte Luyde	20½d
John Wade	15d
William Campe	20d
William de Holurst	22½d
John Adames	12d
Thomas atte Hurn	12½d
William Dypere	2s 2d
John de Cam'e	21d
Robert Campe	18d
Roger atte Croyce	12d
Nicholas atte Hull	18d
Walter atte Lepeyate	3s 1½d
Walter P'trich	18d
John Temes	21¼d
Margery la Mohoun	18½d
Philip de Cerne	2s 8d
Adam atte Fortheie	20d
William Hogyn	18d
Geoffrey Segar	14d
Robert Hikkes	8d

Approved. Total, 32s 0¾d

Hambrook (*Hambrok*)

449

Richard de la River	3s 4d
John Aueray	2s
John de Hambrok	2s
Adam Honypyn	2s 6d
Nicholas Mussegros	12d
John Richardes	18d
Simon Freman	8d
William Hompyn	2s

Approved. Total, 15s

Hempton, Woodlands and Frenchay in Winterbourne (*Hempton, Wodelond & Petshawe*[175] *in Wynterbourn*)

450

John de Brokeneberwe	3s 6½d
Lawrence Pesshoun	9d
William atte Wode	10d
Reginald Pesshoun	18d
William Lyngyur	12d
John Smith (*Fabro*)	8d
Walter Austyn	18d
William Henries	8d
Alice Denis	2s
William Wideweson	12d
William Kyng	18d

Approved. Total, 14s 11½d

Approved. Total of the whole hundred, £10 16s 11d

Subtaxers (*Subtaxatores*)[176]

451

Henry Chaun	12d
Richard Pesshoun	12d

Total, 2s

Approved. Total of the whole
hundred with the subtaxers' taxes,
£10 18s 11½d[177]

LANGLEY HUNDRED
(*HUNDREDUM DE LANGELEYE*)

Rockhampton (*Rokhampton*)

452

Robert Rendema'	2s 6d
Hugh Sevare	14d
Adam Peres	14½d
John Robardes	3s 6½d
Matilda la Broune	2s 6d
John le Reve	2s 6d
Adam Shipward	12d
Matilda Passour	18d
Richard de Brughampton	2s 0½d
John le Cartere	12d
Thomas le White	12d
Richard Cole	12d
John Uppehull	2s 0½d
Adam atte Fortheye	2s 6d
Gunilda Prauns	12d
Richard Prentiz	6½d
Henry Broun	12d
Peter Pirling	2s 0¼d
Richard atte Fortheye	3s 4d
Thomas Pirling	18d
John Abbod	20d
Amice atte Newetoun	6½d
William atte Newetoun	16d
Adam le White	12d
John de Brughampton	12d
John Sake	12d
Philip Passour	12d
Robert le Lange	6½d[178]
Adam Pyffing	12d

Total, 43s 11¾d

[Membrane 25 dorse r-h col.]

Littleton upon Severn (*Lutleton*)

453

Richard Rolves	3s 4d
William Adam	18d
Richard le Boys	12d
John Edward	2s
John Wylkines	6½d
Thomas Huwelot	12d
John le Smyth	15¼d
John le Shepherde	2s
William Sewy	14¼d
William Henries	18d
Thomas Longe	20d

Approved. Total, 17s

Over (*Overe*)

454

Thomas ap Adam	6s 3d
William de Over	3s 0½d
Walter Sperman	2s
Robert de Stotfold	12d
William Baldwyne	22¾d
Robert Leche	12d

Approved. Total, 15s 2¼d

Frampton Cotterell (*Frompton Cote'l*)

455

John de Wylinton	6s 4¾d
Walter Gasselin	6s 8d
Thomas Alfard	2s 2d
Thomas atte Wode	13d
William Miller (*Molendinario*)	2s
Roger Miller (*Molendinario*)	9¼d
Julian Henries	16d
Henry le White	2s 6d
Emma atte Lepeȝate	14d
John Scriveyn	18d
Stephen atte Pirie	15½d
John Whites	8d
Nicholas Hardheved	12d
Nicholas Brounes	12¾d
William Clerk (*Clerico*)	12d
William Smith (*Fabro*)	9¼d
Walter Motoun	3s 4d
Hugh Sherston	12d
James (*Jacobo*) Som'	11d

Approved. Total, 36s 7½d

Alveston (*Alweston*)

456

Margaret Garyn	3s 1d
Reginald Lovekyn	20d
Fulk de Berleye	12d
John Miller (*Molendinario*)	18d
Thomas le Coliare	18d
Constanc. Corbet	20d

Approved. Total, 10s 5d

Tockington (*Tokynton*)

457

Sir Hugh Poynz	4s 0½d
Roger Stok	2s 2d
Robert Bosse	16d
Edward de Overe	18d
Thomas atte Pulle	12d
John Salaman	20d
William Grasmere	12d
Walter Gustard	9¼d
John atte Pulle	8d
John Parchmenter	12½d
Henry de Bridge (*Ponte*)	7d
Thomas Sewy	12d
Walter Stok	12d
William Taillor	8d
Walter de Bridge (*Ponte*)	6½d
Walter Richeman	12d
John Dag'	8d
John de Hostbrugg	9d
John Morice	16d
Peter de Mayne	14d

Approved. Total, 23s 10¾d

Olveston (*Olveston*)

458

Richard Belers	3s
Richard atte Home	18d
Thomas de Overe	12d
Thomas atte Walle	12½d
Osbert Riche	22d
Robert de Leye	8d
John Godhine	12d
John Tony	9d
William Brockfre	12d
John Nichol	12d
John Sexteyn	8d
Reginald Shirwold	6½d
Philip de Craddich	12d
John Regnald	12d
John atte Grove	8d

Approved. Total, 16s 8d

Doynton (*Doynton*)

459

Reginald Reod	2s
Walter Esegar	12d

William le Monner	20d
John atte Welle	15d
John Adames	18d
John le Porter	9d
John le Welshe	15d
John Pig	12d
Robert Stony	2s
Geoffrey atte Merssh	12d
William le Reve	4s

[Membrane 26]

Also Doynton

Roger Belle	2s
William Cotel	18d

Approved. Total, 20s 11d

Approved. Total of the whole hundred, £9 4s 8¼d

Subtaxers (*Subtaxatores*)

460

John de Weston	12d
John de Alkeleye	12d

[Total, 2s][179]

Approved. Total of the whole hundred with the subtaxers' taxes, £9 6s 8¼d

GRUMBALDS ASH HUNDRED
(*HUNDREDUM DE GRYMBALDESASSH*)

Dyrham and Hinton (*Derham & Henton*)

461

Theobald Russel	5s 2d
William Reeve (*Preposito*)	2s 2d
John Borard	13½d
Roger Sporon	11d
Adam Hereward	2s
John Smith (*Fabro*)	12d
Adam atte More	15¼d
John de Staunden	4s 1¼d
Robert Cope	9d
John Parys	9¾d
John de Weston	12d
William Sporon	13¼d
John Crouste	2s 0½d
William Cope	12d
James (*Jacobo*) Thomas	2s 0½d
Roger Thomas	12¼d
Roger Henries	2s 3d
Christine atte Broke	12d
Ellis Billek	9½d
William Hardyng	5s 4d
John Ynon	5s 6d

Approved. Total, 42s 4¾d[180]

Dodington (*Dodyngton*)

462

John de Berkeleye	2s 8¼d
John Anekyn	10¼d
Hugh Samuel	2s 1¼d
Adam Alwold	10¾d
Adam Samuel	18½d
Adam Balrich	15d
Thomas Leueson	12½d
Walter Don	23d
Philip le Hunte	3s 8d

Approved. Total, 15s 11¼d

Acton Ilger (*Acton Ylger*)

463

Henry atte Nasshe	17d

Approved. Total, 17d

Great Badminton (*Badmynton Magna*)

464

Thomas le Botiller	6s 11d
Thomas North	20¼d
Richard Gren	3s 4d
Gunilda la Frenshe	12¼d
David atte Croice	23¼d
John le Vernoun	2s 1¼d
Robert de Fortheie	11¼d
Ralph North	12½d
Roger le Kyng	2s 2d
Robert le Bonde	9d
Ralph Symondes	2s 11d
William Reod	20¾d
John Adames	9½d

Approved. Total, 27s 3¾d

Tormarton (*Tom'ton*)

465

John de Wylyngton	5s 1½d
Dyonis. de la Rivere	4s 11½d
Adam Edward	3s 1½d
Margery Wattes	2s 6¾d
William atte Sherde	18d
William Huyting	2s 6½d
John atte Welle	22d
Adam Huyting	2s 2d
William Goldyng	2s 4¾d
Roger atte Hole	19½d
Thomas Bog	2s 3½d
John atte Croyce	12¼d
Robert Uppehulle	2s 1d
John le Buedel	3s
Alice Colines	12¼d
William Arthuyr	19½d
Robert Broun	21½d
Henry, servant of Prior of Bradestok	5s

Approved. Total, 45s 8d

West Littleton (*Lutleton*)

466

John de Wylington	5s 5¾d
Richard atte Welle	2s 7½d[181]
John Lamberd	2s 6d
Amice la Frye	3s 0½d
Christine Bakere	2s 2d
Richard le Yonge	2s 6d
Johan. la Whyte	2s 4d
Alice Wade	14d
William le Yonge	2s 3¼d
William Godrich	2s

Approved. Total, 26s 1d

Acton Turville (*Acton Turvill*)

467

William Darches	3s 7¼d
Dyonis. de la River	2s 6¼d
Stephen Batyn	2s 3¾d

[Membrane 26 r-h col.]

Also Acton Turville

Richard Aylwy	18d
Matilda la Clerk	12d
Hugh Carpenter	18d
John Gylemyn	21d
Thomas atte Well	2s 0½d
Thomas Hobbes	2s 6½d
Ralph le Botiller	2s

Approved. Total, 20s 9¼d

Codrington (*Godryngton*)

468

Roger le Monek	12½d
Robert atte Norcharde	19½d
Cecily Pyn	8½d
Hugh Wat'schop'	15d
Ralph Pyn	13¾d
Nicel' Sewy	15¼d

Approved. Total, 7s 0½d

Wapley (*Wappelegh*)

469

Gilbert de Stanshawe	2s 4½d
Joachim atte Wode	9¼d
William Bouryng	10d
Roger atte Ynne	2s 1d

John atte Wode	12d
Walter de Wappelegh	14¼d

Approved. Total, 8s 3d[182]

Old Sodbury (*Villata de Sobbury Magna*)

470

Matilda Cotel	3s
Richard atte Norchard	9d
Nicholas Uppedoune	17d
Roger atte Wodelonde	20¾d
Matilda atte Wodelonde	13d
Richard Miller (*Molendinario*)	19d
John le Sawyare	22¾d
Ralph Russel	13d
Henry Couherde	2s 4d
Isabel de Leygrave	16d
Roger Peytevyn	14d
Richard atte Nasshe	16d
Robert de Leygrave	21d
William de Keynesham	13d
Simon Upedoune	18d
William le Proute	12d
Henry atte Mulle	21d
Hugh Hamond	20d
Thomas le Fox	13d
Stephen Danyel	18d
Peter Smith (*Fabro*)	15d
Robert Sutore	9d
Nicholas Phelippes	2s
William de Kenegrave	18½d
Henry, servant of Prior of Bradenestok	6s 3d
Thomas de Lokynton	5s
Roger atte Broke	4s 3¾d
John le Fayre	5s 0½d

Approved. Total, 56s 8¼d[183]

Tortworth (*Torteworth*)

471

Joan, who was the wife of Nicholas de Kyngeston	8s 9¾d
John Hermo'	2s 3d
Ellis Wirlok	12d
Walter Mariesone	2s 5d
Roger Wirlok	15d
William le Mars	2s 5d
Robert le Cok	16d
William Doresewell	21¾d
William atte Halle	20¾d
John Gocheye	15d
Adam le Webbe	6d
Roger de Northrudynge	22¾d

Approved. Total, 26s 8d[184]

Charfield (*Charefeld*)

472

Joan, who was the wife of Nicholas de Kyngeston	5s 5¼d
William Bryd	2s 1d
Thomas Byboys	2s 1½d
Robert Loreweng	2s 4¼d
Alex. Southwode	12¾d
John Badmynton	2s 0¾d
Adam Sparke	12d
William Carter (*Carectario*)	3s 2¼d
Edward de Aure	9d

Approved. Total, 20s 0¾d

Wickwar (*Wykewarre*)

473

John de la Warre	8s
John Adekyn	18½d
William Mulleward	2s 10d
Richard Harry	3s 5¼d
John Gros	12d
Andrew Dydenham	2s 8d
Robert Herries	6d
John de Chilton	2s 10½d
Robert Baroun	3s 10½d
John Wassemere	12d
Henry Squyer	2s 0¾d
Simon Suthinton	6d
John atte Cornere	12d
Roger Denys	3s 2¼d
John le Machoun	6d
John Denys	19¾d
Henry Inthehurne	12d
John Hopere	12d
William Mom'ay	2s
John le Reve	12d

Approved. Total, 41s 7½d[185]

Boxwell (*Boxwell*)

474

Robert Doun	3s
Henry West	2s 3¾d
William atte Mulle	2s[186]

[Membrane 26 dorse]

Also Boxwell

Richard Welhull	2s 4½d

Approved. Total, 9s 8¼d[187]

Leighterton (*Ley3terton*)

475

Thomas Hamput	3s 0½d

John de Walutton	23½d
John atte Bury	3s 0½d
William Hamput	12d
Ralph le Hopere	23½d
Edward le Carpenter	2s
Gilbert atte Cheore	6d
John Bailly	6d
William Alfred	12d
Robert le Carpenter	9¼d
William Deye	15d

Approved. Total, 17s 0¼d[188]

Hillsley (*Holdesleye*)

476

William Simonis	2s 3d
Adam Person	17½d
William Cosyn	9d
Thomas Waleys	9½d
John de Watershipe	6d
John de Sobbury	6d
William Preostes	8d
Margery de Hildesleye	6d

Approved. Total, 7s 5d[189]

Horton (*Horton*)

477

Roger de Middelton	2s 9d
Richard de Bolton	12d
John Lamberd	2s 6d
William Herdewyke	12d
Hugh Wythenhull	12¾d
Adam Lyoun	2s 4d
John Benet	12d
Adam Saloman	18¼d
John Clerk (*Clerico*)	6d
Richard le Kyng	8¾d
Adam le White	12d
Robert Benet	2s 4½d
William Lamberd	6d
Jordan Lovecok	9d
William le Lech'	3s
William Bobernot	4s 3d

Approved. Total, 26s 3¼d[190]

Hawkesbury (*Hauekesbury*)

478

Matilda atte More	2s 6d
Thomas Danyel	6d
Simon Pape	3s 4d
Henry Topyn	20½d
John Bygo	6d
Thomas Proute	12¾d
Robert Bercare	6d
William Trussebury	12d

Approved. Total, 11s 1¼d[191]

Little Badminton (*Badmynton Hamell.*)

479

John de Hall (*Aula*)	3s 2¼d
John atte Horne	6d
Gilbert Ma. . .te	9¼d
John le Vernoun	6d
William Sewy	9¼d
Nicholas atte . . .ve	18½d
Richard le Eyr	2s 0¾d
John Ingan	9d
Richard Colewich	3s 2¼d

Approved. Total, 13s 3¼d[192]

Hawkesbury Upton and Saddlewood (*Upton Hamel. & Selwode*[193])

480

William Wodecok	3s 2¾d
Walter le Yonge	2s 1¾d
Alex. Wodecok	9d
William Payn	16½d
William Budel	15d
Thomas Irlond	6d
John le Webbe	9d
Richard le Yonge	18½d[194]
Walter Damanneys	2s 4¼d
Gilbert Longe	9d
Robert Shepherd (*Bercario*)	2s 4¼d
John Hikeman	12d

Approved. Total, 18s[195]

Tresham (*Tresham Hamel.*)

481

Lawrence de Tresham	3s 2¼d
Roger Joye	3s 2¼d
Henry Carter (*Carectario*)	12d
Walter Broun	2s 6½d
Richard Packare	2s 2d
Ralph Wymbleye	18d
Ellis Knyt	6d

Approved. Total, 14s 1d[196]

Kilcott (*Killecote Hamel.*)

482

Robert Capoun	2s 3d
. . . Springadieu	9d
William Bobel	12d
Robert Waryn	14¾d
William . . .erma'	12d

Approved. Total, 6s 2¾d[197]

Inglestone Farm (*Ingaueston*)

483

John atte Steorte	20¾d

[Membrane 26 dorse r-h col.]

Also Inglestone Farm

Ellis le Nethere	9d
John Moryn	20½d
John Fowelare	19¼d
Robert le Cartere	19¼d
Robert Aylward	12d
William Hathemere	13½d

Approved. Total, 9s 6¼d[198]

Didmarton (*Budem'ton*)

484

John Torpyn	5s 2d
John atte Slo	2s
John le Brok	15¼d
William Batyn	9d
John de Killecote	6d
John le Fowelare	17¼d
John Neweman	12d
Thomas Waleys	16¼d
Walter Smith (*Fabro*)	12d
Roger atte Stile	6d
Roger Rogers	4s 1¾d
Adam Webbe	12d
Nicholas de Wyke	12d
Walter Carter (*Carectario*)	20¾d

Approved. Total, 22s 10¼d

Oldbury on the Hill (*Oldebury*)

485

Nicholas Burdoun	9s 8¾d
John Wodecok	2s 2¼d
Richard Whitemey	17¼d

Approved. Total, 13s 4¼d[199]

Alderley (*Allerleye*)

486

John de Chausy	4s 8¼d
Nicholas Chausy	3s 3d
Nicholas Adam	2s 0½d
Alan inthe [*sic*] Fen	2s 10¾d
John Inkepenne	3s 3d
Hugh Marmyoun	15d
Nigel Bovetoun	15d

John Veysy	6d
Robert Woderove	2s 3d

Approved. Total, 21s 4½d[200]

Little Sodbury (*Sobbury Parva*)

487

Jordan Bisshop	3s 10d
Adam Chinne	2s 2d
William le Crokker	3s 3¾d
William Bisshop	3s
Henry Whitele	5s 2d
John Fraunkhome	15d
Thomas le Man	8d
John Herbard	8d

Approved. Total, 20s 0¾d[201]

Wick Wick Farm (*Wykkewyk*)

488

John de Wykkewyk	3s 10¾d
Philip Selyman	2s 2¼d
John de Wykkewyk	3s 11¼d

Approved. Total, 10s 0¼d[202]

Total of the whole hundred, £27 19s 8¼d[203]

Subtaxers (*Subtaxatores*)[204]

489

William de Remmesbur	21d
Nicholas Wynebaud	21d
Thomas atte Hulle	12d
William de Dodem'ton	12d
Ellis de Chalkeleye	12d

Total, 6s 6d

Approved. Total of the whole hundred with the subtaxers' taxes, £28 6s 2¼d[205]

PUCKLECHURCH HUNDRED
(*HUNDREDUM DE POKELCH'CHE*)

Pucklechurch (*Vill. de Pokelch'che*)

490

Gilbert atte Rode	2s 11d
William West	2s 2d
John Broun	19½d
Julian Noteprat	12d
Hugh atte Watere	6d
John Crompe	12d
Walter Carpenter	15¾d
Roger Cok	17d
Thomas Janekynes	2s 6d
John Trut	18d
John in the More	18d
William Holdelond	6d
Adam in the More	6d
John Peseleye	6d
Reginald Tethingman	12d
Agnes Thothyngeman'	12d[206]
Thomas Vachour	17d
Walter Tethingman	23d
Alice Aleynes	12d
Adam atte Croice	18d
Robert Wyly	2s 3d

Approved. Total, 29s 0¼d

Westerleigh (*Westerley Hamel.*)

491

Robert . . .bo	6d

[Membrane 27]

Also Westerleigh

Richard atte Lude	8s 6d
John de Nubbeleye	12d
Alice Est	18d
Dowsabel (*Dulcia*) Uppehull	4s
Alice Carpenter	2s 3d
Nicholas de Radeforde	2s
John Parch	6d
Thomas de Radeforde	6s 9d
Adam Andreu	12d
Roger Willam	6d
John atte Strete	6d
William Ferthing	6d
Thomas Walters	4s 3¾d
Walter Blakbergh	2s
Thomas Chaynel	16d
John de Shyrugg	2s

John Rogers	2s 2d
Alice la White	2s 1¾d
William Haywodeby	16d
Richard atte Assh	21d
William Nicholes	6d
Nicholas de Wotton	20d
Alan de Enefeld	20d
John Hopere	12d
John atte Venne	6d
Adam Reol	6d
Thomas atte Stor	2s 6d
Thomas Okeford	2s 6d
John Lyner	6d
William atte Stiyle	6d
Robert Pitman	6d
Thomas atte Berewe	12d
John atte Berewe	12d
Thomas Peris	12d
Richard Dudemor	3s 3d
Julian Shirugg	6s 3d
Thomas atte Hulle	4s
William Cerpe	6d
John de Chist'le	3s 6d
Thomas Chist'le	3s 6d

Approved. Total, £4 5s 10½d

Wick (*Wyk Hamel.*)

492

Thomas Uppehulle	12d
John Bot	13d
John Turner	6d
John Wolmer	2s
Edith Grenewey	6d
William atte Beche	6d
Robert Uppehey	4s 3d
Robert Berdesey	15d
William Carpenter	5s
John de la Pleystude	6d
John atte Forde	6d
William Neweman	6d
William Blakpol	12d
Rees Colswayn	2s 1d
William de Horston	12d
William Clerk (*Clerico*)	6d
John Russel	6d
Robert in the Wolde	13d
Robert Randolph	13d

Approved. Total, 24s 10d

Siston (*Syston Hamel.*)

493

Peter Corbet	3s 5d
Thomas Broun	6d
John Wolshawe	6d
John Balle[207]	6d
Adam Bercar	7s 8d
Richard atte Croyce	7s 10d
Richard Warmeleye	10d
John Holbrond	9d

Approved. Total, 22s

Cold Ashton (*Coldaston Hamel.*)

494

Stephen Gorslade	16d
Walter Kyng	11d
Richard Partrich	6d
Richard Bitheweye	6d
Richard Coluerwelle	8d
Adam atte Mulle	6d
Matilda Hors	6d
Ellis de St Albans (*Sancto Albano*)	2s
Simon Turnay	18d
John Coubrugg	9d
Thomas Flemyng	10d
John atte Rugg	11d
Walter Palmar	6d

Approved. Total, 11s 5d

[Membrane 27 r-h col.]

Tenants of the Rector of Pucklechurch (*Tenentes Rectoris de Pokelch'ch*)

495

Alan de Peseleye	2s 6d
Robert Derneforde	3s 3d
William atte Stote	12d
John atte Halle	3s 3d
Adam Mody	12d
Robert de Leye	12d
William atte Rode	6d
Matilda Holebrok	6d
Joh. de Warmeleye	5s 3d
John de Nastcombe	3s 6d
Isabel Phelippes	2s 7d

Approved. Total, 24s 4d

Approved. Total of the whole
hundred, £9 17s 5¾d

Subtaxers (*Subtaxatores*)

496
William Mohoun 12d
Roger de Frompton 12d
William Wasteville 12d

[Total, 3s][208]

Approved. Total of the whole
hundred with the subtaxers' taxes,
£10 5¾d

CHELTENHAM HUNDRED EXCLUDING ANCIENT DEMESNE
(*HUNDREDUM DE CHELTENHAM PRETER ANTIQUUM DOMINICUM*)

Swindon (*Villata de Swyndon*)

497

Alice Moryn	15s 2½d
Walter Bernard	2s
Simon le Reve	3s
Gilbert Aldride	18d
Walter Stratt	9d
Robert Umfray	2s 7¼d
Robert Brok	23d
Henry Budel	2s
John Lewyn	12d
Nicholas Kymat	2s 6d
William Gibbes	2s 5d
Robert Hayward	15d
Henry Hevene	3s 3d
Matilda Kymat	8d

Approved. Total, 40s 0¾d

Leckhampton (*Lekhampton*)

498

John Giffard	6s 9d

Robert de Prestebury	5s
John Gode	3s
John Clycle	2s
Hugh Couherde	6d
Walter de Bradewell	5s
John Brademay	12d
John Regnaldes	2s
John Belamy	18½d
Richard atte Chirche	18d
William Wolvrich	11d
John Slo	18d
Walter Strongener	12d
William Epres	13½d
Matilda atte Hull	. . .d
John Houwes	. . .d
Simon Willames	20d
John Amyat	3s 6d
William Martin	15½d
Thomas atte More	2s
John Taillour	12d
Alice Deye	12d
John de Elkeston	4s

Approved. Total, 48s[209] 7½d

Total of the whole hundred, £4 8s 8¼d

Subtaxers (*Subtaxatores*)

499

William Whymely	12d
William Lavender	2s
Thomas Spark	12d

Total, 4s[210]

Approved. Total of the whole hundred with the subtaxers' taxes, £4 12s 8¼d

WHITSTONE HUNDRED
(*HUNDREDUM DE WHISTON*)

King's Stanley (*Stanleye Regis*)

500

Hugh de Dodebrugg	3s 11d
Alice Pynnok	2s 5½d
John Notelin	4s 1½d
Henry le Kyng	15d
Richard Baxfeld	6d
William Songare	14d
Alice Beaumanere	15¼d
Roger Tailor (*Cissore*)	20d
William de Spenser	21d
Margery le Despenser	17¾d
Walter Pickestret	8¾d
Dyonis. Gornay	23½d
Thomas, son of the Clerk (*Clerici*)	17¼d
Margery Broun	12d

[Membrane 27 dorse]

Also King's Stanley

John atte Chambr	3s[211]
Amice de Wolb'we	22¼d
Richard, son of Dunstan	18d

Approved. Total, 31s 0¾d

Leonard Stanley (*Stanleye Sancti Leonardi*)

501

John de Berkeleye	8s 11¼d[212]
Henry atte Stompe	14d
John de Cors	18¾d
Maurice de Berkel.	21¾d
Gilbert de Coln	2s 1d
John Hewekin	2s 6½d
Adam Coppare	2s 1¼d
Adam atte Hulle	7¼d
Walter Coppar	2s

Approved. Total, 22s 9¾d

Frocester (*Froucestr*)

502

John atte Fortheye	2s 10½d
John de Bradefelde	21¾d
John Robardes	2s 3¼d
John de Bykenoure	2s 1¾d
Walter Wodecok	3s 6¾d
John Hawekin	9½d
William Couherde	14¼d
John Donyngton	13¼d
Seycel. Jones	2s
William Richard	15d
John atte Yate	2s 11¼d
Thomas Top	5s

Approved. Total, 26s 11¾d[213]

Alkerton (*Alcrynton*)

503

John de Gloucestr	4s 10d
Hugh Baloun	16d
Henry de Wyke	22¾d
William Petit	9½d
John Godman	14¾d
Robert Bercar	16¾d

Approved. Total, 11s 5¾d

Frampton on Severn (*Frompton*)

504

Robert, son of Payn	11s 6½d
John Dopping	19d
Miles de Stoke	20d
Thomas Hany	12¾d
Robert Whete	11¾d
William de Bolesdon	3s 10½d
Peter atte Parkende	22d
John Locar'	3s 1½d
Nich. de la Newelonde	13s 10¾d
William Carpenter	2s 4d
John Flory	3s 3d
William Tailor (*Cissore*)	12d

Approved. Total, 46s 1¾d

Saul (*Salle*)

505

John de Frethorn	18¼d
Agnes Ho. . .	21¾d
Richard Dunstall	22¾d
Richard . . .apel	2s 0¾d
Robert L. . .ge	21d
William B. . .as	16¼d
John . . . Chirche	21¾d
Ralph Ward	9½d
Robert le Eir	21¾d
Geoffrey de Frethorn	5s 1¼d
Nicholas de Salle	12d
Simon de Fremelode	13¼d
William Benet	2s 3¾d
Edith Gilberdes	16¾d
Gilbert de Cromhale	18d

Approved. Total, 27s 2¼d

Longney (*Longeneye*)

506

John Wilkines	4s 3½d
Walter Agne	2s 10½d
John Willames	2s 10½d
John Clench	2s 1½d
John atte Waterende	22½d
Walter Phelippes	22d
Nicholas atte Grove	15¾d
Walter Graunger	2s 0¾d
Robert Stevenes	11½d
Edith atte Hull	22¾d
Stephen Graunger	5s 0¼d
Stephen Rolves	10¼d
Robert Agne	16¾d
William Arneyate	10¾d
John Eolpʒ	16¾d
Stephen Wymond	10¼d
John Huthemere	2s 2¾d
Matilda Lof	10½d
Richard atte Hall	2s 10½d
Alice de Norton	17½d
Thomas de Colethrop	14½d
Ellis . . .	12d

[Membrane 27 dorse r-h col.]

Also Longney

Walter le Bruthere	12d
Roger Haukin	21d

Approved. Total, 44s 11d

Hardwicke (*Herdewyke*)

507

John le Clerk	6d
Marg. de Colethrop	13½d

John le Botiller	6s 8d
John Chamberleyn	20d
Agnes de Shottor	12d
Walter Capel	2s 0¼d
John atte Broke	2s
Walter atte Felde	2s 10½d
John Bodde	9d
Agnes Crom	7½d
Agnes de la Felde	22d
Walter Coppe	9d
John, son of Robert de la Felde	4s 2¾d
John, son of *Clar.*	9¼d
Nicholas de Seysedon	2s 9¼d
Alex. Pynnok	14½d
Walter, son of Richard de Stand	10¼d
John Locar	2s 2d
Simon Maynard	2s 3d
William Hardyng	17d

Approved. Total, 37s 5¾d

Haresfield (*Harsefelde*)

508

John de Bohun	10s 7d
John atte Brugg	7d
Walter Carpenter	2s 3¼d
William Yonge	18¾d
Eleanor, who was the wife of Herbert, son of *Joh.*	3s 9¾d
Walter atte Forde	15½d
John atte Hay	2s 3¾d
Walter Dru	21¾d
Henry Yonge	9½d
Robert Tailor (*Cissore*)	22½d
Roger Jones	9½d
Robert Kateline	14¾d
Nicholas Spaket	12d
John Partrich	16½d
Felic. Pie	19¾d
Gilbert Pie	15d
Richard Shern	21d

Approved. Total, 35s 11¼d

Harescombe[214] (*Harsecombe*)

509

John Organ	16¼d
William Sered	2s 0¾d
Richard Maynard	21¾d
Roger Hayward	16¾d
Hugh atte More	22¾d
Alice Bigge	15d

Approved. Total, 9s 9¼d

Quedgeley (*Quedesleye*)

510

Edmund le Freman	14½d
William Brayn	16¾d
Nicholas Wyndowe	6¾d
Walter Broun	16¾d
Agnes Colines	16¾d
Thomas Cok	21¾d
William Strode	16¾d
Nicholas de Wyke	12d
Walter Meriot	21d
Richard le Smethe	14d
John le White	10¾d
Alice Carter	16¾d

Approved. Total, 15s 4½d[215]

Moreton Valence (*Morton*)

511

Sir Richard Talebot	14s 3¾d
Reginald atte Welle	21¾d
William atte Croice	12d
John le Walshe	4s 3¼d
Richard Tenold	14¾d
Robert Mordestreit	22½d
Henry Neweman	12d
Isabel Bonde	20d
Robert Cocus	12d
Robert de Ebbeworth	9½d
John Ingelond	22d
Roger Pricke	12d
Philip Cagel	21½d
Thomas Craft	12d

Approved. Total, 34s 7d

Eastington (*Estynton*)

512

John le Freman	2s
John Martin	2s 10½d
Thomas Gardiner	12d
Thomas Holdere	2s 2d
Robert le Frend	14d
Henry Reve	21¾d
John Adames	6d
Thomas Cobbe	22d
Stephen Bercar	13¼d

Approved. Total, 14s 5½d

[Membrane 28]

Wheatenhurst (*Whitenhurst*)

513

Earl of Hereford (*Herford*)	7s 7d
John Muchele	12d
Richard Broun	2s 0¾d
Philip Palmere	15d
Matilda Meriot	2s 8½d
Agnes Messager	15½d
Roger atte Hull	2s 3¾d
Ralph Trocy	2s 9¼d
William Parker	2s 6½d
Walter Whithorn	2s 1¼d
Robert Rolves	2s 9½d
William Walkere	15d
Walter Haiward	3s 9¾d
Walter de Wynhull	18d
William Willing	21¾d

Approved. Total, 36s 9½d

Oxlinch (*Hoxlynge*)

514

John Spilman	4s 1d
Henry Glasiare	3s 9¼d
Henry Edolph	12d
Walter de Pedesmor	15d
Richard Page	18d
Richard atte Hoke	3s 6½d
Henry Ket	3s
Richard Bernard	4s 9d
William Mersman	15d
Rees de Pedesmor	3s 3d

Approved. Total, 27s 4¾d

Stonehouse (*Stonhous*)

515

Margaret Giffard	8s 3d
John Lesoy	3s 6d
Walter Daniel	2s 10½d
William de Stonhous	3s 6½d
John Parker	21d
William atte Putte	2s 0¼d
Richard Songare	18d
Stephen Houwes	2s 0¼d
Adam Priour	15d
Adam Silvestre	2s 7d
William de Malden	22d
John Wolfrig	4s 5d
Walter de Sothery	20½d
John Soutere	18d

Approved. Total, 38s 9d

Total of the whole hundred, £23 14d[216]

Subtaxers (*Subtaxatores*)

516

William Davy	12d
Henry de Clyfford	12d

| Richard Viel | 12d |
| John Clauylle | 12d |

Total, 4s

Approved. Total of the whole hundred with the subtaxers' taxes, £23 5s 2d[217]

Overall total of the twentieth in the County of Gloucester, except for the [taxation] boroughs and the lord king's ancient demesne, £826 8¼d[218]

[Membrane 28 dorse]

William Tracy and Robert de Aston, assessors and collectors of the twentieth granted to the king by the laity . . . the County of Gloucester, sent these 28 rolls, delivered under his seal by the hand of Peter de Eggesworth, the 15th day of June in the second year of the reign of King Edward the Third after the Conquest [1328].

[Membrane 29]

The total of the twentieth . . . County of Gloucester from both the [taxation] boroughs and the lord king's ancient demesne, and from the aforesaid county combined (*de comitate com' predicti*) – £1000 17s . . .[219]

NOTES

1. Stained.
2. Stained.
3. Stained.
4. No heading.
5. Rubbed.
6. Omitted.
7. Omitted.
8. Omitted.
9. *Vide* 509.
10. *Vide* 288.
11. *Vide* 306.
12. *Vide* 293.
13. *Vide* 294.
14. Omitted.
15. Interlined between Mareschal and Dyeare.
16. '1' repeated.
17. Omitted.
18. Omitted.
19. 'Nicholas Aleyn' later addition.
20. Omitted.
21. *Vide* 87.
22. *Vide* 86.
23. Entry interlined.
24. Entry later addition.
25. *Vide* 102.
26. *Vide* 100.
27. Forename and surname reversed.
28. Changed from 6d.
29. Changed from 6s or 7s.
30. Changed from 11¾d.
31. Repeated and struck through.
32. *'Fifide'* inserted here as if to divide list into two: *vide* 126 and 127 below. I have treated 116 as one list because only one total sum given.
33. Officer of Knights Hospitallers, cf. Rudder, *New History*, p. 617.
34. Changed from 17d.
35. Valentine?, *vide* Martin, *Record Interpreter*, p.464.
36. Later addition.
37. Cherlton heading and Tetbury total interlined, splitting one list into two.
38. Total interlined.
39. Total interlined.
40. Changed from William; latter underscored with five points but not erased.
41. Entry interlined.
42. *Vide* 206.
43. Changed from 3s 7d.

44. '½d' erased.
45. Repeated and erased.
46. 5 in of membrane left blank after this entry.
47. Omitted.
48. 'Agnes' later addition, but 'John' not erased.
49. Stephen atte Yate . . . Thommen 20d over erasure.
50. 1½ in of membrane left blank after this entry.
51. *Vide* 172.
52. Total over erasure.
53. Untraced.
54. Illegible.
55. *Vide* 223.
56. *Vide* 220.
57. Changed from 2s 9¼d.
58. Glasscock, *Lay Subsidy 1334*, p. 98, identifies this with Coates in Winchcombe parish.
59. Edge of membrane damaged from this point – fractions of pennies lost?
60. Written as local list heading: all vills dealt with below, but not in this order and with others interspersed.
61. *Vide* 241.
62. *Vide* 240.
63. Over erasure.
64. Entry interlined.
65. Edge of membrane damaged from this point – fractions of pennies lost?
66. 'v' legible.
67. 'v' legible.
68. 'ijd' legible.
69. 'vid' legible.
70. Entry interlined.
71. Over erasure.
72. Over erasure.
73. Over erasure.
74. Changed from 7s 7d.
75. '¼d' later addition.
76. '¼d' later addition.
77. Changed from 6s 6¾d.
78. Surely Ashworthy Farm in Cromhall, but there was a tenurial link between Cromhall and Ashleworth: Smith, *Place-Names*, iii, p. 4.
79. Entry interlined.
80. '8s 9d' over erasure.
81. *Vide* 370.
82. Over erasure.
83. Southam heading and Stoke Orchard total interlined, splitting one list into two.
84. Cockbury is the hillfort on Nottingham Hill, O.S. Nat. Grid SO981284, cf. Smith, *Place-Names*, ii, p. 90. Huntelowe is untraced.
85. Entry interlined.
86. Entry interlined.
87. '8½d' struck through.
88. *Vide* 40.
89. Over erasure.
90. '10s' and '1d' over erasures.
91. *Vide* 44.
92. *Vide* 45.
93. Martin, *Record Interpreter*, p. 459, lists Lena as short for Alina or Evelina.

94. *Vide* 42.
95. Changed from 8s.
96. Over erasure.
97. *Vide* 312.
98. *Vide* 310.
99. Over erasure.
100. '1d' over erasure.
101. Changed from 13d.
102. *Vide* 325.
103. *Vide* 324.
104. John struck through.
105. 'swa' over erasure.
106. Over erasure.
107. '£6 19s 6d' over erasure.
108. Changed from 10s.
109. Over erasure.
110. Total over erasure.
111. '£23 18s' over erasure.
112. Written as part of hundred heading, omitting Henbury vill.
113. '½d' erased.
114. '½d' erased.
115. Robert Mattok over erasure.
116. A sixth name erased.
117. '¾d' over erasure.
118. '9d' over erasure.
119. '¾d' over erasure.
120. Over erasure.
121. Over erasure.
122. Omitted.
123. Changed from 7d.
124. *Vide* 387.
125. *Vide* 384.
126. *Vide* 411.
127. Over erasure.
128. Changed from 13s.
129. Changed from 2s 6d.
130. *Vide* 262.
131. *Vide* 378.
132. 'except . . . Tewkesbury' later addition.
133. '8d' later addition.
134. 'with the vill . . . £46 9d' over erasure.
135. Written as part of hundred heading.
136. *Vide* 371.
137. 'Robert' struck through.
138. Changed from 3s.
139. '4s 1d' over erasure.
140. *Vide* 404.
141. *Vide* 391. Woderowa untraced: Forest of Cors was here and Smith, *Place-Names*, iii, p. 146 lists Corse Wood Hill.
142. Entry over erasure.
143. *Vide* 355.
144. Over erasure.

145. *Vide* 354.
146. '11d' over erasure.
147. *Vide* 383 and its note.
148. Written as part of hundred heading.
149. Untraced.
150. *Vide* 382.
151. Entry interlined.
152. *Vide* 361.
153. Sum over erasure.
154. 's 5½d' over erasure.
155. 's' over erasure.
156. '¼d of total' later addition.
157. Local list over erasure.
158. Not given in Smith, *Place-Names*.
159. Changed from 23d.
160. '2d' over erasure.
161. Entry interlined.
162. Changed from 7½d.
163. Changed from 9¾d.
164. Over erasure.
165. 'John de Longe' over erasure.
166. 'es' over erasure.
167. Form of Knud/Canute, *vide* Withycombe, *Dictionary*, p. 189.
168. Changed from 8s 2¼d.
169. Changed from 11s 6¼d.
170. Edge of membrane damaged down to 'John Wynebek', fractions of pennies lost?
171. '11d' over erasure.
172. Omitted.
173. Sum over erasure.
174. Changed from 7s.
175. Error for Fromshawe or similar: Smith, *Place-Names*, iii, p. 123.
176. Local list over erasure.
177. '½d' later addition.
178. Changed from 8½d.
179. Omitted.
180. Changed from 4¼d.
181. '7d' changed from 8d.
182. Total later addition.
183. Membrane damaged, number of whole pennies uncertain.
184. Total later addition.
185. Total later addition.
186. Membrane repaired, pence missing?
187. Total later addition.
188. Total later addition.
189. Total later addition.
190. Total later addition.
191. Total later addition.
192. Total later addition.
193. '& Selwode' later addition.
194. 'Selewode' inserted as heading, but struck through.
195. Later addition.
196. Total interlined.

197. Total later addition.
198. Total later addition.
199. Total later addition.
200. Total later addition.
201. Total later addition.
202. Total later addition.
203. 'Total . . . 8¼d' later addition, and '8d' changed from 1d.
204. Local list over erasure.
205. '7¼d' struck through.
206. Entry interlined.
207. Repeated.
208. Omitted.
209. Over erasure.
210. Total later addition.
211. 's' over erasure.
212. '8s 11¼d' over erasure.
213. 'Total' over erasure.
214. *Vide* 37.
215. '½d' over erasure.
216. Over erasure.
217. Over erasure.
218. Total over erasure.
219. Rubbed. Willard, 'Taxes . . . Edward III', p. 72, has '£1000 17s 4¼d'.

Bibliography

Place of publication is London, unless otherwise stated.

1. Primary Sources

a) Manuscript sources

Public Record Office

C134/42. Inquisition post mortem of Gilbert Clare V, 1314
C135/87. Inquisition post mortem of Hugh Audley II, 1347
E142/24. Contrariants' Survey, 1322
E179/113/4. Lay Subsidy Rolls, 1313
E179/113/5. Gloucestershire Lay Subsidy Roll, 1327

Staffordshire County Record Office

D641/1/2/116–32. Thornbury manorial account rolls, 1327–50
D641/1/4C/1(i)–2. Thornbury manorial court rolls, 1328–52

b) Printed sources

Brown, W., ed., *Yorkshire Lay Subsidy, being a Ninth collected in 25 Edward I (1297)*, Yorks. Arch. Soc. Rec. Ser., xvi (1984).
Browne, A.L., 'Wick Rissington Transcripts'. *Trans. Bristol & Glos. Arch. Soc.*, lix (1937), pp. 211–19.
Calendar of Close Rolls, 1327–1330 (1912).
Calendar of Patent Rolls, 1216–1225 (1891).
Crowley, D.A., ed., *The Wiltshire Tax List of 1332*, Wilts. Rec. Soc., xlv (Trowbridge, 1989).
Fry, E.A., ed., *Abstracts of Inquisitiones post mortem for Gloucestershire. Part V. 30 Edw. I to 32 Edw. III. 1302–1358* (1910).
Fuller, E.A., 'The Tallage of 6 Edward II. (Dec. 16, 1312) and the Bristol Rebellion', *Trans. Bristol & Glos. Arch. Soc.*, xix (1894–5), pp. 171–278.
Gaydon, A.T., *The Taxation of 1297*, Beds. Hist. Rec. Soc., xxxix (Streatley, 1959).
Glasscock, R.E., ed., *The Lay Subsidy of 1334* (1975).
Madge, S.J., ed., *Abstracts of Inquisitiones post mortem for Gloucestershire. Part IV. 20 Hen. III to 29 Edw. I. 1236–1300* (1903).
Phillipps, Sir T., *Gloucestershire Subsidy Roll, 1 Edward III. A.D. 1327* (Middle Hill Press, n.d.).
Powell, E., *A Suffolk Hundred in the Year 1283* (Cambridge, 1910).
Raftis, J.A., and Hogan, M.P., *Early Huntingdonshire Lay Subsidy Rolls* (Toronto, 1976).
Rotuli Parliamentorum, ed. J. Strachey (6 vols., 1767–83).
Stokes, E., ed., *Abstracts of Inquisitiones post mortem for Gloucestershire. Part VI. 33 Edw. III to 14 Hen. IV. 1359–1413* (1914).
Swynnerton, C., 'Some Early Court Rolls of the Manors of Stonehouse, King's Stanley, Woodchester, and Achards', *Trans. Bristol & Glos. Arch. Soc.*, xlv (1923), pp. 203–52.
Williams-Jones, K., ed., *The Merioneth Lay Subsidy Roll 1292–3*, Board of Celtic Studs., Hist. and Law Ser. No. 29 (Cardiff, 1976).

2. Secondary Sources

Atkyns, Sir R., *The Ancient and Present State of Glostershire* (1712, 2nd edn. 1768; reprinted Gloucester, 1974).

Beresford, M.W., *The Lay Subsidies and Poll Taxes* (Canterbury, 1963).

Britton, E., *The Community of the Vill* (Toronto, 1977).

Campbell, B.M.S., ed., *Before the Black Death. Studies in the 'crisis' of the early fourteenth century* (Manchester, 1991).

Franklin, P., 'Politics in Manorial Court Rolls. The Thornbury Peasant Movement, 1328–1352', in Smith and Razi, op. cit..

Franklin, P., 'Thornbury woodlands and deer parks, part 1: the earls of Gloucester's deer parks', *Trans. Bristol & Glos. Arch. Soc.,* cvii (1989), pp. 149–69.

Hadwin, J.F., 'The Medieval Lay Subsidies and Economic History', *Econ. Hist. Rev.,* 2nd ser. xxxvi (1983), pp. 200–17.

Harvey, P.D.A., *Manorial records* (1984).

Harvey, P.D.A. *Medieval Oxfordshire Village, Cuxham 1240 to 1400* (Oxford, 1965).

Hourwich, I.A., *The Economics of the Russian Village* (New York, 1892).

Hunnisett, R.F., *Editing Records for Publication* (1977).

Hunnisett, R.F., *Indexing for Editors* (1972).

Kershaw, I., 'The Great Famine and Agrarian Crisis in England 1315–22', *Past and Present,* No. 59 (1973), pp. 3–50.

Lenin, V.I., *The Development of Capitalism in Russia* (2nd edn., Moscow, 1964).

Lucas, H.S., 'The Great European Famine of 1315, 1316 and 1317', *Speculum,* v (1930), pp. 343–77.

Maddicott, J.R., *The English Peasantry and the Demands of the Crown, 1294–1341* (Past and Present Supplement I, 1975).

Mitchell, S.K., *Taxation in Medieval England* (ed. S. Painter; New Haven, Conn., 1951).

Munby, A.N.L., *Phillipps Studies* (5 vols., Cambridge, 1952–6).

Munby, A.N.L., *Portrait of an Obsession. The Life of Sir Thomas Phillipps, the world's greatest book collector* (1967).

Page, W., ed., *The Victoria History of the Counties of England. A History of Gloucestershire, II* (1907).

Prestwich, M.C., 'Edward I's Monetary Policies and their Consequences', *Econ. Hist. Rev.,* 2nd ser., xxii (1969), pp. 406–16.

Prestwich, M., *War, Politics and Finance under Edward I* (1972).

Ramsay, Sir J.H., 'Statistics from Subsidy Rolls of Edward II', *Eng. Hist. Rev.,* xxiv (1909), pp. 317–19.

Razi, Z., *Life, Marriage and Death in a Medieval Parish* (Cambridge, 1980).

Reaney, P.H., *A Dictionary of British Surnames* (1958).

Rudder, S., *A New History of Gloucestershire* (Cirencester, 1779; new edn. Gloucester, 1976).

Saul, N., *Knights and Esquires: The Gloucestershire Gentry in the Fourteenth Century* (Oxford, 1981).

Smith, A.H., *The Place-Names of Gloucestershire* (Eng. Place-Name Soc., vols. xxxviii–xli, Cambridge, 1964–5).

Smith, R.M., and Razi, Z., eds., *The Manor Court and English Society. Studies of the Evidence* (Oxford, forthcoming).

Taylor, C.S., 'The Northern Boundary of Gloucestershire', *Trans. Bristol & Glos. Arch. Soc.,* xxxii (1909), pp. 109–39.

Willard, J.F., 'The Assessment of Lay Subsidies, 1290–1332', *Annual Report of the American Historical Assoc.* (1917), pp. 281–92.

Willard, J.F., 'A Brief Guide to the Records dealing with the Taxes upon Movables 1290–1350', *Bull. Inst. Hist. Res.,* iii (1925), pp. 27–37.

Willard, J.F., *Parliamentary Taxes on Personal Property, 1290–1334. A Study in Mediaeval English Financial Administration* (Cambridge, Mass., 1934).

Willard, J.F., 'Side-lights upon the Assessment and Collection of the Mediaeval Subsidies', *Trans. Roy. Hist. Soc.,* 3rd ser., vii (1913), pp. 167–89.

Willard, J.F., 'The Taxes upon Movables of the Reign of Edward I', *Eng. Hist. Rev.,* xxviii (1913), pp. 517–21.

Willard, J.F., 'The Taxes upon Movables of the Reign of Edward II', *Eng. Hist. Rev.,* xxix (1914), pp. 317–21.

Willard, J.F., 'The Taxes upon Movables of the reign of Edward III', *Eng. Hist. Rev.,* xxx (1915), pp. 69–74.

Withycombe, E.G., *The Oxford Dictionary of English Christian Names* (3rd edn, Oxford, 1977).

Index of Surnames

All references are to entry numbers, i.e. to the numbers of local lists, and not to page numbers.

Hert (Heort), 52 (*bis*), 113, 122, 124, 130, 171, 311, 343, 402, 404, 446

Hertelaunde, 336 (*bis*), 341

Hertes, 210

Herteshorn, 61

Hertesleye, 336

Hertforde, 3

Hervy, 15, 233, 400

Heryng, *see* Hering

Hesel, *see* Hasele

Heth (Hethe), cf. Inthehethe, 208, 339, 343, 443

Heved, *see* Hed

Hevene, 491

Hewe, 26, 336 (*ter*), 340

Hewekin, 501

Hewergh, 286

Hewet, 177, 304

Hey, *see* Hay

Heybone, 14

Heydon (Heidon), 22 (*bis*), 377, 443

Heyforde, 195, 198, 443

Heyhome, 14

Heylin, 209

Heyne (Heghnes, Heynes) 6, 47, 154 (*bis*), 201, 221, 226, 235, 241, 253, 255 (*bis*), 343, 437

Heysogge, 241

Heyward, *see* Hayward

Hichecokes (Hichekokes), 188, 353

Hicheman, 151

Hickeman (Hikeman, Hikemones, Hykeman), 110, 151, 223, 311, 372, 480

Hicken (Hycon, Hycoun), 194, 406, 412

Hickes (Hikkes, Hykes), 60, 111, 119, 126, 233, 299, 313, 351, 411, 488

Hickumbe, 99

Hide (Hyde), 62, 110, 123 (*bis*), 142 (*bis*), 215 (*bis*), 276, 415

Hideman, 181 (*bis*), 185

Hikedon (Hykedon), 111, 345

Hikedys, 61

Hikeman, Hikemones, *see* Hickeman

Hikkes, *see* Hickes

Hildesleye, 476

Hill (Hull, Hulle, Hulles, *Monte*), cf. Inthehulle, Ofthehulle, 1

(*bis*), 5, 6, 18, 26, 37, 73, 83, 84, 103, 142, 158 (*bis*), 176, 197, 199, 200 (*bis*), 241, 245, 247, 253, 254, 263 (*bis*), 268, 278, 281, 282 (*bis*), 284 (*bis*), 291, 301, 303, 317, 330, 336 (*ter*), 337, 338, 340, 343, 372, 373, 402, 407, 410, 414, 415, 417, 447, 448, 489, 491, 498, 501, 506, 513

Hill, Lady of, 246

Hirdman (Hirdeman), 4, 22, 431

Hobbekines, *see* Hobekines

Hobben, 188, 197, 200

Hobbes, 111, 113 (*bis*), 117, 169, 231, 235, 252, 253, 268, 352, 437, 467

Hobekines (Hobbekines, Hobekin, Hobekynes), 106, 149, 186, 187, 208, 218, 227 (*ter*), 243, 410, 438

Hobelonde, 436

Hobyes, 336, 421

Hockenhale, 268

Hocwelle, 109

Hod. . ., 18

Hod (Hodde, Hodes), 104, 208, 209

Hodde, *see* Hod

Hodeknasshe (Hodeknas, Hodokenassh), 3, 71, 170

Hodes, *see* Hod

Hodinton (Hodynton), 202, 204

Hodokenassh, *see* Hodeknasshe

Hodynton, *see* Hodinton

Hoede, 350

Hog, 322

Hoggeshale, 110

Hogh'de, 184

Hognes, 392

Hogyn, 448

Hok (Hoke), 22, 110, 336 (*bis*), 373 (*bis*), 423 (*ter*), 430, 514

Hokar, 342

Hoke, *see* Hok

Hokelot, 3

Hokesforde, 240

Hokewon, 371

Hokkeleye, 23, 414, 416

Hokstar, 283

Holbrond, 493

Holchip, 3

Holdeborowȝ, 293

Holdelond, *see* Oldelonde

Holder (Holdar, Holdare, Holdere, *Tenatore*), 94, 157, 241, 254, 255, 291, 336, 343, 352, 354, 371, 512

Holdernesse, 366

Holdewold, 144

Hole, 465

Holebrok, 495

Holewey (Holeweye), 132, 244 (*bis*), 377, 379, 447

Holewow, 83

Holkeleye, 22 (*bis*)

Holle, 67, 422 (*bis*)

Holt (Holte), 16, 22, 414

Holteleye, 4, 291 (*ter*)

Holtome, 194

Holurst, 448

Hombrid, 28

Home, 2, 23, 212 (*bis*), 262, 283, 284, 336, 458

Hompton, 68

Hompyn, 449

Honde (Hondes, Hondies, Hondy, Hondys), 208 (*bis*), 281, 416 bis), 425

Hone, 259

Honibourn, 58, 181

Honicombe, 278

Honiton, 3

Honsom (Honsum, Hunsom), 2 (*bis*), 4, 305

Hontar, 416 (*bis*)

Honyma', 416

Honypyn, 34, 449

Hope, 179, 429

Hopere, 2, 3 (*bis*), 8, 16, 18, 128, 136 (*bis*), 142, 157, 252, 253, 291, 294, 302, 446, 473, 475, 491

Horcote, 110

Hore, 45, 54, 82, 240, 294

Horhust, 8

Horleport, 442

Horlere, 169

Hornar (Hornare), 311, 415 (*ter*)

Horncastel, 8

Horne, 479

Hornewy, 204

Horry, 388 (*bis*)

Hors, 494

Horsforde, 328

Machen, Machoun, *see* Mason
Macy, 437
Magdalen, Mary, Prioress of, 345
Maggen, 185, 204
Mahutild, 127
Maiel, *see* Mayel
Maister (Mayster), 342, 350, 359, 385
Malden (Malleden), 6, 515
Malemo, 18
Malemort, 28 (*ter*)
Maliar, 430
Malicorn, 111 (*bis*)
Maline (Malines, Mallyn), 111, 170, 251
Malle, 101
Malleden, *see* Malden
Mallesone, 84
Mallun, 155
Mallyn, *see* Maline
Malot, 246
Maltman, 19
Malvarn (Malvarne), 239, 445
Mammcliue, 336
Man, 447, 487
Manning (Mannyng), 110, 122
Mansshupe, 443
Manstild (Maunstild), 176 (*bis*)
Manygforde, 349
Mapele (Maple), 142, 368
Marcer, 370
Marchal, Marchald, Marchale, *see* Mareschal
Marche, 346
Marcle, 3, 4, 300
Mare, 26, 72, 95
Marech', *see* Mareschal
Mareis, *see* Marsh
Mareny, 259
Mareschal (Marchal, Marchald, Marchale, Marech'), 3, 4, 6, 14, 25, 50, 76, 106, 122, 125, 177 (*ter*), 188, 190, 238, 250, 259, 263, 283, 337, 338, 348, 353, 364, 390, 392, 423, 428, 447
Maresco, see Marsh, Saltmarsh
Mareys, *see* Marsh
Margan, 440
Marges, 443
Margrete, 181
Mariesone, 471
Mariner, 3, 10, 292, 383

Marioten, 180
Markete, 14
Marky, 427
Marleputte, 247
Marmyoun (Marmioun), 27, 195, 445, 446, 486
Mars, 471
Marsfeld, 6
Marsh (Mareis, *Maresco*, Mareys, Mershe, Merssh), cf. Saltmarsh, 6, 117, 122, 159, 171 (*bis*), 246, 253, 423, 433, 459
Martel, 246 (*bis*)
Martin (Marten, Martyn), 22, 54, 110, 133, 150, 188, 204 (*bis*), 284, 294 (*ter*), 316, 344, 366, 392, 498, 512
Marton, 68
Martyn, *see* Martin
Marwent, 302 (*bis*)
Maryman, 3
Masoun (Machen, Machoun), 14, 20, 60, 125, 142 (*bis*), 147, 177, 193, 241, 245, 282, 312, 345, 356, 360, 362 (*bis*), 444, 473
Masud. . ., 2
Mathemo, 366
Matheus, 180
Mathiue, 3, 4 (*bis*)
Mathon, 10
Mattare, 434, 440 (*bis*)
Mattesden (Mattesdon), 24, 43, 245, 250, 289
Matteshale, 3, 16 (*bis*)
Mattok, 342 (*bis*), 347, 439
Mauduyt, 6
Mauger, 262
Maunch, 126
Maundeville (Maundevill, Maundvill), 41, 132, 133, 414 (*ter*)
Maunsel, 252, 272 (*bis*), 274 (*bis*), 384, 429
Maunstild, *see* Manstild
Mautravers, 134, 311
May (Mey), 22, 33, 58 (*bis*), 186, 251, 305, 360, 383
Mayde, 63, 86
Maydegod, 173, 254
Maydenes, 358
Mayel (Maiel), 36, 50 (*bis*), 254
Mayew (Mayou), 99, 223 (*bis*), 263, 294

Mayflin, 308
Maynard, 3, 116, 139, 298, 300, 336, 410, 507, 509
Mayne (Maynes), 110, 457
Mayou, *see* Mayew
Maysaunt, 416
Mayster, *see* Maister
Mede, 97, 368, 402
Medecroft, 152
Medewell, 12
Megre, 3, 39
Meneman, 87 (*bis*)
Menske, 284
Meosyhampton, 232
Mercer (*Mercatore*), 4, 336, 398
Merch, 431
Mercombe, 278
Mere, 135, 336
Meregure, 255
Merewy, 222
Merheye, 298
Meriet (Meriot), 286 (*bis*), 510, 513
Mering, 74
Meriot, *see* Meriet
Mershc, *see* Marsh
Mersman, 514
Merssh, *see* Marsh
Mersshton, 16, 24, 406
Mess', 443
Messager (Messeger), 1, 121 (*bis*), 210, 259, 513
Messer, see Hayward
Methelan (Meth', Methilan), 6, 8, 10, 350
Mewode, 23
Mey, *see* May
Meysy, 115 (*bis*)
Mich, 278
Michel, 29, 154 (*bis*), 225, 274, 291, 330
Michelton, 175
Mickeleie, 317
Middelton, 251 (*bis*), 477
Midewynter (Mydewynter), 173, 369
Midwey, 284
Mildemay, 431, 435
Miles (Mile, Myle), 20, 64, 139, 142, 268, 295, 336
Milkesham, 247
Mill (Mille, *Molendino*, Mulle, Mulne), cf. Buedelesmull,

Riueray, 36

River (Rivere), 449, 465, 467

Robad (Robat), 106 (*bis*)

Robard, Robardes, *see* Robert

Robat, *see* Robad

Robert (Robard, Robardes, Roberd,
   Roberdes), 29, 104, 118, 166,
   180, 181, 183, 201, 268, 313,
   351, 356, 359, 369, 386, 402,
   417, 452, 502

Robert, son of, 244

Robin (Robines, Robyn, Robynes),
   68, 89, 122, 123, 155, 158, 176,
   182, 190, 199, 389

Robus, 16

Robyles 92

Robyn, Robynes, *see* Robin

Roche, 264, 379

Rocleye, 110

Rodbergh (Rodberwe), 99, 143
   (*bis*)

Roddok, 281

Rode, 254, 490, 495

Rodemerton, 126

Rodleye, 22, 23, 301

Rodmarleye, 2

Roger (Rog', Rogere, Rogers,
   Rogger, Roggers), 16, 33, 58,
   59, 64, 68, 69, 99, 104, 110,
   123, 151, 173, 176, 185, 208,
   261, 268 (*bis*), 269, 279
   twice, 292 (*bis*), 358, 379,
   382, 412, 427, 440, 442, 484,
   491

Rok, 26, 54, 179 (*bis*), 330

Rokwode, 268 (*bis*)

Rolf (Rolph, Rolves), 29, 61, 64,
   89, 115, 173 (*bis*), 204, 208,
   211, 253 (*bis*), 278, 312, 315,
   358, 366, 369, 370 (*bis*), 375,
   442, 453, 506, 513

Roluepe, 50

Rolves, *see* Rolf

Rome, 142

Romeneye, 10

Romeseye, 8, 12

Ronde (Rond), 195 *passim*

Rondulf, Rondulph, *see* Randolph

Roo. . ., 2

Roo, 106 (*bis*)

Rook, 132

Ropere, 8 (*ter*), 10

Ros', son of, 336

Rose (Roys), 54, 168, 204

Rosen, 180, 425

Rosselyn, 14

Rosteleie, 96

Rothewell, 16

Rotor, 416

Roubergh, 10, 12

Rouge, 58 (*bis*), 59

Rous, 66

Routare, 261

Roys, *see* Rose

Rudar, 281

Rugge (Rugg), 426, 494

Ruggeweye, 83

Rugwode, 133

Rundulph, *see* Randolph

Russel, 8 (*bis*), 20, 94, 180, 186
   (*bis*), 208, 254, 301, 304, 318,
   343, 344, 348, 383, 412 (*bis*),
   461, 470, 492

Russhel, 339

Rusteshale, 177

Ruyleye, 340

Ruys, 40

Ruyssheleye, 45

Ruyton, 306

Rycheman, Rychemanes, *see*
   Richeman

Rye, 144

Rynde, 293

Ryndecombe (Ryndecombes), 58,
   348

Ryngwode, 16

Ryouns, *see* Rioun

Rysindon, 86

Ryson, 126

Ryvet, *see* Rivet 346

Saad, 186 (*bis*), 196

Sabine, 410, 416 (*bis*)

Sacerdote, *see* Priest

Sachen, 433

Sage, 319, 365, 397

St Albans, 494

St Amand (*Sancto Amando*), 61,
   261

St Augustine's, Abbot of, 241, 244

St Bartholomew's, Master of, 32

St Lawrence's, Master of, 33

St Lawrence's, Warden of, 16

St Lo, 34

St Maur (*Sancto Mauro*), 60

St Philibert (*Sancto Philiberto*),
   106, 117

Sake, 241, 452

Salaman (Saleman, Saloman,
   Saumoun), 200, 233, 248 (*bis*),
   268, 392, 396, 457, 477

Salbrok, 340

Salcombe (Salecombe), 279 (*ter*),
   316

Saleman, *see* Salaman

Salesbury, 109

Salle, 505

Saloman, *see* Salaman

Salop, 14

Salperton, 101

Salso Maresco, *see* Saltmarsh

Saltere, 18

Saltforde, 152, 443

Saltmarsh (*Salso Maresco*,
   Sautemareys), cf. Marsh, 245,
   342, 436, 447

Saltmere, 190

Sampson, 132, 208, 267, 282

Samuel, 462 (*bis*)

Sancto Amando, *see* St Amand

Sancto Mauro, *see* St Maur

Sancto Philiberto, *see* St Philibert

Sanekyn, 8

Sapi (Sapy), 271, 333

Sapiens, *see* Wise

Sapy, *see* Sapi

Sare, 104, 111

Saren, 173

Saumoun, *see* Salaman

Saundres, 86, 99, 143, 159, 233,
   241, 251, 262, 304, 332, 395,
   414, 433

Sautemareys, *see* Saltmarsh

Savage, 111, 382 (*bis*)

Savernag', 350

Sawyar (Sawiare, Sawyare), 14, 62,
   470

Scag, 154

Scalewarde, 147

Schaldem'e, 439

Schursteyn, 204

Schym, *see* Shym

Scir, 6

Scitur, 298

Sclattar (Sclatter, Sclattere), 104,
   160, 215, 318

Index of Place-names

All references are to entry numbers, i.e. to the numbers of local lists, and not to page numbers. All places are in the modern counties of Gloucestershire or Avon, unless otherwise stated. Names which are not those of parishes have been located in their early nineteenth-century parishes, or within Bristol or Gloucester. Untraced place-names are given in italics. 'H' stands for 'Hundred'.